The Persistence
of Cambodian Poverty

I0025627

The Persistence of Cambodian Poverty

From the Killing Fields to Today

Harold R. Kerbo

McFarland & Company, Inc., Publishers

Jefferson, North Carolina, and London

LIBRARY OF CONGRESS CATALOGUING-IN-PUBLICATION DATA

Kerbo, Harold R.
    The persistence of Cambodian poverty : from the killing fields
to today / Harold R. Kerbo.
        p.   cm.
    Includes bibliographical references and index.

    ISBN 978-0-7864-6408-1
    softcover : 50# alkaline paper ∞

    1. Poverty — Cambodia.   2. Cambodia — Economic
conditions.   I. Title.
    HC442.Z9P617   2011
    339.4'609596 — dc22   2011004331

BRITISH LIBRARY CATALOGUING DATA ARE AVAILABLE

© 2011 Harold R. Kerbo. All rights reserved

*No part of this book may be reproduced or transmitted in any form
or by any means, electronic or mechanical, including photocopying
or recording, or by any information storage and retrieval system,
without permission in writing from the publisher.*

On the cover: Village families in Central Cambodia work
together during rice planting season (photograph by the author);
map © 2011 Shutterstock

Manufactured in the United States of America

*McFarland & Company, Inc., Publishers
    Box 611, Jefferson, North Carolina 28640
    www.mcfarlandpub.com*

Table of Contents

Preface

My interest in Southeast Asia started with a 1990 Fulbright award to study at Chulalongkorn University in Bangkok. I have since spent time in Southeast Asia part of almost every year as a visiting academic or researcher. Most of my focused interviews and observations for this book between June 2006 and June 2008 were funded by a generous fellowship from the Abe Foundation, a division of the Japan Foundation in Tokyo. This support allowed me to travel throughout the countryside in all of the Buddhist countries of Southeast Asia (except Burma) for almost two years. I spent time in several dozen villages and many small towns throughout the region during this period (see Appendix). Between 2008 and January 2010, I visited Cambodia several times for followup interviews and observations in the major slums of Phnom Penh (some now totally cleared) and "relocation camps" not far from Phnom Penh, as well as with key Cambodian informants and Western NGO (non-government organization) personnel based in Phnom Penh.

The main sources of my information for this book are interviews with more than two hundred poor families in 20 villages in all regions of Cambodia (again, see Appendix), as well as slum areas in the capital and provincial cities. In Vietnam I interviewed dozens of families in 10 villages in central and southern Vietnam, as well as in urban slum areas. Having spent much more time over the years in Thailand, I focused only upon northeastern Thailand, Issan, the poorest region of the country, where I interviewed dozens of families in eight villages. In Laos I first had trouble obtaining government permission and local academic support to conduct my interviews, but finally was able to do so by the spring of 2008. I conducted interviews in Laos with several families in only three villages, but traveled through villages in three major areas of Laos up and down the Mekong River to assess economic conditions and infrastructure development. In all four countries I had dozens of interviews with government and foreign NGO personnel, as well as academics who had

1

knowledge of poverty conditions in these countries. I was able to obtain additional reports and data from government agencies and/or NGOs about poverty in each country.

Finally I should note that my interviews and observations were focused on "lowland" people who are the majority in these countries (though only a slight majority in Laos) rather than hill tribe peoples. These hill tribe peoples are much more recent immigrants from China and are similar to American Indians in many ways. In every Southeast Asia country they experience more poverty and are certainly worthy of much more attention. But because of many different issues relating to their poverty compared to lowland people, I have focused my observations primarily on the majority lowland people in these countries.

Acknowledgments

I want to first thank the Japan Foundation, who through an Abe Fellowship, supported most of the fieldwork upon which this book is based. In addition to this funding, a sabbatical from California Polytechnic State University, San Luis Obispo, supported research in Cambodia, Vietnam, Thailand, and Laos for almost two years during 2006 and 2007. Other smaller grants and travel funding from my university allow for several followup interviews up to January 2010. From the Western side of the world, though often in Southeast Asia, I have learned much from Professor Robert Slagter based at first in Alabama but now in Chiang Mai, and Patrick Ziltener at the University of Zurich and in Thailand. My fellowship from the Abe Foundation, administered through the Japan Foundation, stipulated that American scholars should be affiliated with a Japanese university. The logical place, and, as it turned out, an excellent location, was the Center for the Study of Social Stratification and Inequality at Tohoku University, in Sendai, Japan. Professor Yoshimichi Sato in Sendai was an excellent host.

Several academics, NGO officials, and government officials in Cambodia gave generously of their time to provide me with insights, data, and inside information about conditions of poverty, prospects for economic development (or the lack thereof), and corruption in the country. I especially want to thank my primary translator/research assistant who was with me for almost every interview between 2006 and 2010. And I want to thank another translator who helped me navigate the slums of Phnom Penh to understand what is happening in the country. But it was my primary translator/ research assistant who helped with his extensive knowledge of political and economic situations in Cambodia, along with his translating, that has most contributed to the information in the coming pages of this book. Finally, I want to thank many dozens of relative poor and very poor village and slum people in Cambodia for the time they took to tell me about their lives, problems, fears, and hopes, for themselves and their children. Unfortunately, for reasons that will be more clear throughout the pages of this book, I cannot thank any of these people in Cambodia by name. Especially in the case of Cambodian academics and government officials because I fear for their safety if they are identified.

In Vietnam I want to first thank President Bui Van Ga of the University of Danang for his assistance over the years. It was two of his young faculty members, Theary Ngoun Ngo and Le Van Chon, who served as my research assistants and translators, both with degrees in economics, and who helped me understand the political and economic situations in Vietnam over a two-year period. In addition to other academics, NGO officials, and government officials in Vietnam who generously provided me with information, I want to thank Hanna Bui-Eve, a Vietnamese-American who heads the San Francisco Bay–area Co-Vietnam, an NGO established to help with various kinds of aid to poor Vietnamese and especially young women at risk of falling into the sex industry. Hanna spent considerable time taking me around the central coast of Vietnam and the Mekong Delta area to talk with many village people, government officials, and NGO officials involved with projects to improve the lives of poor Vietnamese. And again, I want to thank many village and poor slum people in Vietnam who welcomed us into their homes to share their stories of tragedy, hard work, and now more prospects for improvement in their life conditions.

In Thailand I first want to thank my old friend Uthai Dulyakasem, now president of Silpakorn University in Bangkok. For the past 20 years he has been teaching me about the complexities of Thai culture and politics. Also, Pramote Nakornthab, a sometimes advisor to Thai prime ministers and a professor for several decades, has also helped me better understand the complexities of Thai culture and politics. I also want to thank Supaap Budsritud, the administrator of Pramote's small college for those with fewer opportunities in the northeast of Thailand, has helped with accommodations and arrangements for interviews in Nong Khai province. Nantakan Songsuman helped translate and taught me about the Northeast of Thailand in the early stages of this fieldwork. Pam Pamja was my excellent translator and guide in the Northeast of Thailand during the last months of my fieldwork.

In Laos, Dr. Pramote Nakornthab helped make initial contacts from his sometime base in Nong Khai, across the Mekong from Vientiane. David Wharton, a former Buddhist monk in the UK and later Cambodia, now working for an NGO in Laos, was very helpful in providing contacts in the country. James Chamberlain, an American anthropologist living for many years in SE Asia, now doing research for the Asian Development Bank in Laos, provided me with valuable research data and contacts for my interviews in Laos. Nee Fasai from Vientiane proved to be an excellent translator and guide, as did Onuma Sirachai, from the northeast of Thailand who, as most there, could also translate from Lao.

I would also like to thank Professor Martin Piotrowski at Oklahoma University for directing me to villages in the Northeast of Thailand where his colleagues from the University of North Carolina have ongoing research projects on population changes. My old friend, Professor John McKinstry here at Cal Poly provided important comments after reading the first rough draft of the manuscript. Also at Cal Poly, I want to thank my colleague Professor Greg Bohr who custom made all of the maps in this book showing provinces in each country where I conducted fieldwork. Several of my California students helped firm up my ideas during seminars and observing some of my fieldwork in Southeast Asia over the years. Also to be thanked is Hanna Bui-Eve, Director of Co-Vietnam in the San Francisco Bay Area, who helped translate and show me around some of her NGO sponsored projects in Vietnam. Finally, I would like to thank my wife and daughters, Kathy, Nicole, and Emily, for being patient during all my time away from home with fieldwork and all of the hours over the years working alone in my study.

CHAPTER 1

Cambodia Today
An Introduction

Cambodia has become a metaphor for "tragic nation." The Khmer Rouge have become synonymous with genocide. But since UN–sponsored elections in 1993 and the final surrender of the remaining Khmer Rouge by the end of the 1990s, Cambodia has dropped off the world's radar screen. Compared to earlier decades, the first years of the 21st century have been much better for a few Cambodians. Until 2008, annual GNP growth hovered around the 8 to 10 percent range. Every year there were more and more new condos, hotels, casinos, and shopping malls in the capital, Phnom Penh. In Siem Reap, gateway city to the amazing Angkor Wat, there has been a massive building boom now that it is safe for tourists.

For most Cambodians, however, the tragedy continues. While Cambodia is now (basically) at peace, the economic development of recent years has left 90 percent of the people untouched, or in many cases worse off. The global economic recession from 2008 has made poverty worse (for the obvious reasons outlined in this book). The vast majority of Cambodians continue to live in villages with no clean water or electricity (90 percent), and insufficient land to adequately feed their families. The 2008 World Bank Development Report estimated that 66 percent of Cambodians lived on less than $1 per day, and that income inequality is growing rapidly. The 2010 World Bank Development Report estimated that just over 40 percent of Cambodians live on less $1.25 a day, the World Bank's new extreme poverty measure. Historians tell us the vast majority of Cambodians today live pretty much as they did 1,000 years ago.[1]

More recently, however, conditions for tens of thousands of poor Cambodians have grown worse. In almost every village I visited all over Cambodia at least one family (and often more than one family) had been forced to sell

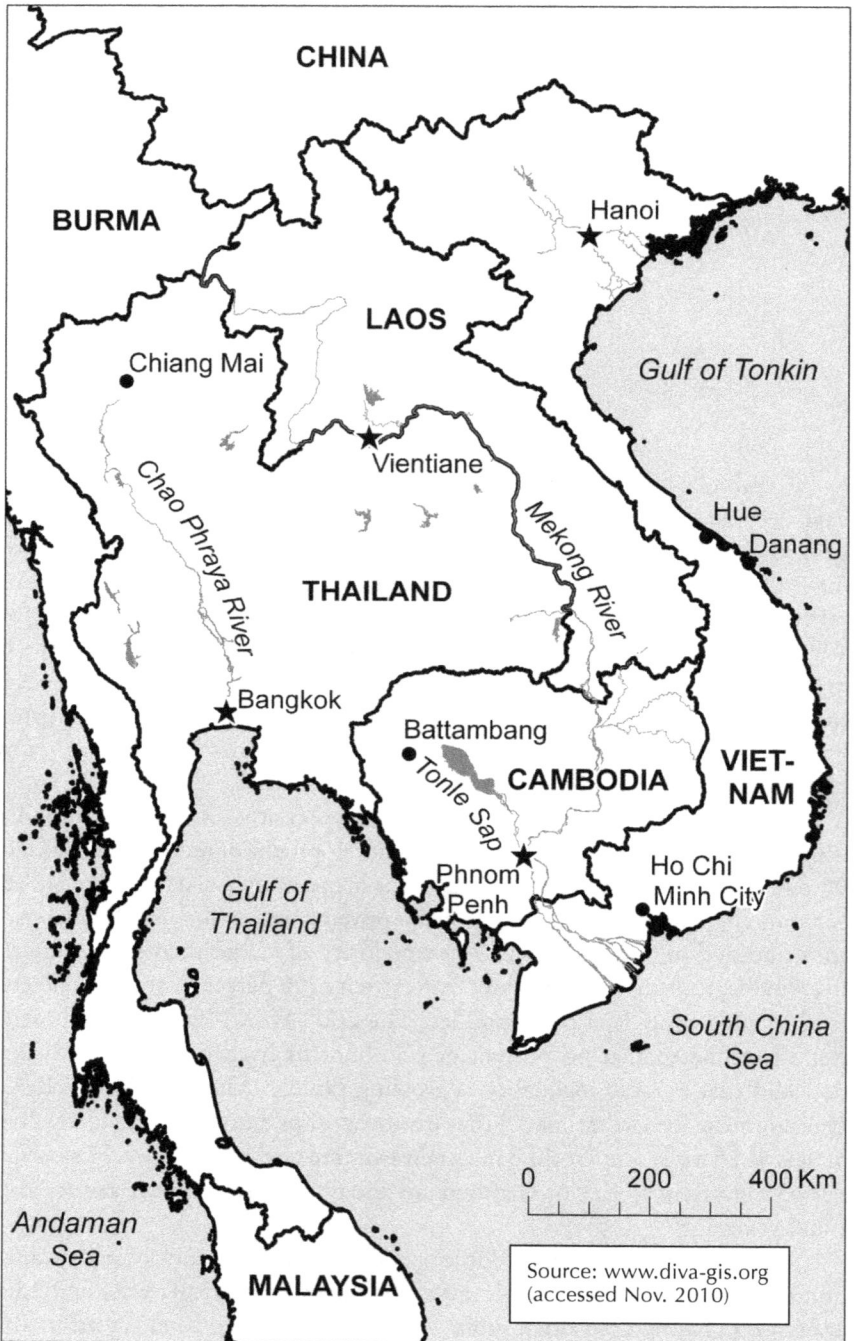

CHINA

BURMA

LAOS

Chiang Mai

Hanoi

Gulf of Tonkin

Vientiane

Hue
Danang

Chao Phraya River

Mekong River

THAILAND

Bangkok

Battambang

CAMBODIA

VIET-
NAM

Tonle Sap

Phnom
Penh

Ho Chi
Minh City

Gulf of
Thailand

South China
Sea

Andaman
Sea

MALAYSIA

0   200   400 Km

Source: www.diva-gis.org
(accessed Nov. 2010)

Map of Southeast Asia.

their land to pay hospital bills to save the lives of their children.[2] Many more poor Cambodians are losing their homes and land because of the economic boom since 2001. A building boom in Phnom Penh has resulted in "land grabs" by rich Cambodians and foreign construction companies (mostly South Korean and Chinese). Land is also being stolen from small farmers so that rich Cambodians and foreign agribusiness firms can create huge plantation-type farms to grow agricultural products for export. These poor rural and urban people have been rounded up like prisoners in the middle of the night and dumped into resettlement camps in the countryside where they most often have no homes, no jobs, nor agricultural land. A kind of Khmer Rouge revisited, but with no irrational communist idealism: Simple inhuman greed.

Such conditions are in stark contrast to almost all other countries in the region where economic development is making many people rich, but also reducing poverty. In all of East and Southeast Asia only the people of North Korea and Burma (Myanmar) have an immediate future which appears more grim.[3] Even the poverty figures for Afghanistan look somewhat better than those for Cambodia. After years of war, a lull in the violence after the Taliban was temporarily subdued by 2004, the UN was able to estimate poverty conditions in Afghanistan for the first time in decades. Some 70 percent of the Afghan population lives on less than $2 per day. This $2-per-day figure for Cambodia is almost 90 percent (89.9 percent). We hear little about poor Cambodia because they have no international terrorists who threaten Western countries, no major earthquakes, no tsunamis, nor as yet significant oil. There is no question that people in many sub–Saharan African countries live in worse conditions than most people in Cambodia. But I will document in the pages which follow how a majority of Cambodians are not far ahead of the people in most sub–Saharan African countries.

Much, but not all, of the continuing tragedy for Cambodians is related to the government in place since the mid–1980s. The 2006 annual corruption report from Transparency International included Cambodia for the first time. Cambodia was ranked among the most corrupt countries in the world. I will explain throughout this book why Cambodian elites should be charged with criminal neglect for their inattention to the needs of their citizens. For their treatment of many people in the country the charge should be grand theft, and in a few cases even murder. These corrupt elites can also be charged with selling their country's resources for short-term personal gains that are destroying the country's future.

Cambodia's government is on paper a democracy. With UN–sponsored government re-organization, Cambodia had a national election in 1993. But Cambodia is far from a democracy. The current political party and prime minister have been in power since the mid–1980s, and as the EU oversight commission reported, national elections in July 2008 were not free.[4] Hundreds of thousands of people discovered at the polling booth that their names had been taken off voter registration lists, opposition party leaders were jailed from time to time during the run up to elections, and opposition journalists have been gunned down in the streets of Phnom Penh. As I will explain in a chapter below, people in formally communist countries in the region, such as Vietnam and Laos, are faced with less corruption and fear from their government than people in Cambodia. I have no reservations about naming my sources for information from my fieldwork for this book in Vietnam, Laos, and Thailand. I will *not* name my sources in Cambodia; in fact, I will give misleading clues about whom they might be because I fear for their safety.

Having made the above charges, I know that blaming only individuals is simplistic. Current political and economic elites in Cambodia should stand accountable. But there are historical influences which allow these elites to remain in power and lead most Cambodians to assume a corrupt government serving only elite interests is inevitable. While I will not dwell upon Cambodian history in extensive detail, we must briefly consider how Cambodian history from more than 1,000 years ago differs in some important respects from other countries in the region. In recent history one must acknowledge how French colonialism has been responsible for much of Cambodia's current problems. But along with the French, the United States bears much responsibility for the mess Cambodia finds itself in today. Cambodia struggled to remain neutral during the American part of the Vietnam War. This struggle was destroyed by a CIA–supported military coup in 1970 that brought in a government ready to fight on the side of the Americans. In the eastern half of Cambodia, American war planes dropped more bombs than were dropped on Japan during all of World War II. No one knows exactly how many Cambodians were killed by these bombs, but estimates are in the tens of thousands. Perhaps even worse, after the United States was defeated in Vietnam by 1975, the U.S. government–supported the Khmer Rouge, *even after* the genocide was well known. We now know that during the 1980s the United States secretly gave the Khmer Rouge leadership at least $150 million simply because they were opposed to the new Vietnamese communist government. In addition to this, the United States blocked most international aid to Cambodia in the 1980s because their old enemy, the Vietnamese, had moved into Cambodia and pushed the Khmer Rouge out of most of Cambodia, despite the fact that Vietnam had stopped the "killing fields."

Even today the United States and the Western world continue to ignore the tragedy in Cambodia. Conditions for the Cambodian poor and tens of thousands forcefully evicted from their homes in recent years forced the U.S. Congress to take notice with a hearing in September 2009. This House committee heard a few stories like the many which follow in this book. But very few Americans outside of this hearing learned anything about it. I could find no major American or Western newspaper which carried the story. My sources of information about this hearing were from the *Phnom Penh Post* (which at the time was published only in English) and one of my key informants who attended the Congressional hearing.

Whatever the combination of causes for the mess Cambodia finds itself in today, unless more sustainable economic development policies are in place quickly, the future for most Cambodians looks dim. Current economic policies which have brought economic growth to Cambodia's capital city cannot bring continued economic growth for the country as a whole. The rich are getting richer with very little "trickle down" to the rest of the population. Tourists arrive with money. Multinational companies from Western countries, China, South Korea, and Japan have come in with textile sweatshops, infrastructure building for the tourist industry, and industries extracting natural resources. But while the tourists may keep coming as long as the country remains relatively safe, the sweatshops will eventually leave as global economic conditions shift. The foreign companies sucking out natural resources will eventually leave as well, enriching only Cambodian elites. Currently there is comparatively little physical and human infrastructure development (things like better roads, electric power, better education) that can help generate domestically driven economic development or more value-added foreign direct investment (FDI) for a brighter economic future in Cambodia. I was told again and again by informants that the little money that is generated from tourism and multinational corporate investment largely disappears.

There is a coming "oil boom" in Cambodia. The amount of oil now known to exist off the Cambodian coast will probably bring in about $1 billion per year by 2011.[5] I met with two Western-based NGOs assigned the daunting task of encouraging the Cambodian government to improve its transparency of natural resource revenues coming into the country from foreign corporations so these funds are not stolen. The staff at both NGOs told me the situation is hopeless. Like oil-rich African countries, the money will be stolen; "It will end up in the pockets of Cambodian politicians and government officials." By June 2010 there were already charges that millions will go missing because $28 million in oil exploration fees paid by foreign companies have been deposited in a bank account with no oversight and accessed only by top Cambodian government officials. There is very little chance this money will be

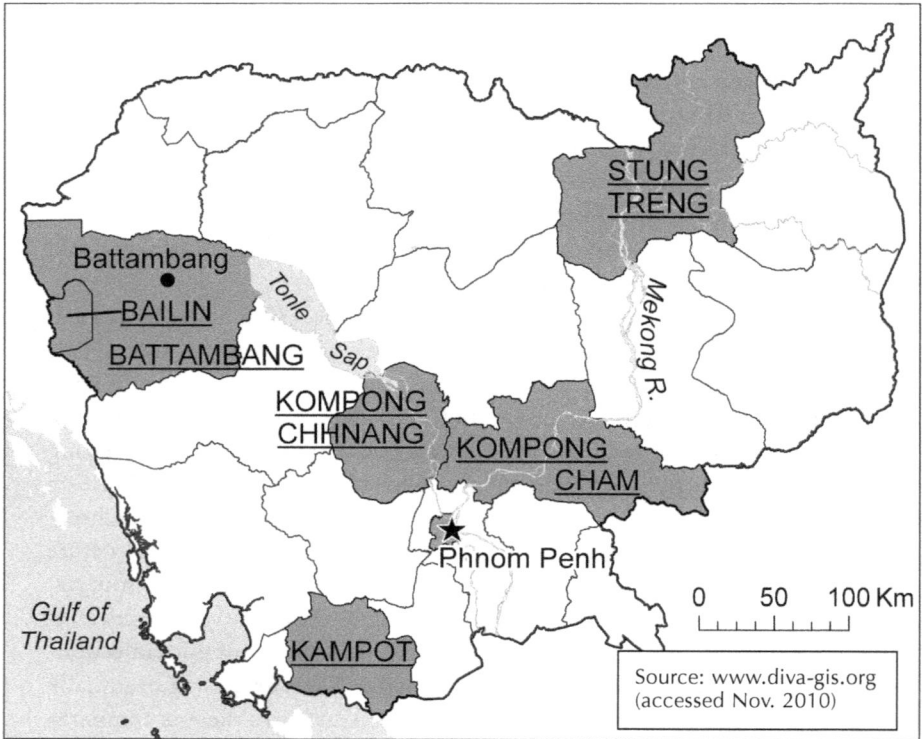

Map of Cambodia.

used to provide fresh water, electricity, better education, or better medical care for the masses of poor Cambodians.

What Follows

This first chapter provides an overview of Cambodia's problems today, then introduces the stories of a few people currently living in extreme poverty today. The second chapter contains a brief history of the country that helps us understand why Cambodians face more desperate circumstances compared to most of their neighbors. The third presents more details about the levels and trends of poverty in Cambodia.

The next four chapters describe the lives and sorrows of poor Cambodians from all over the country, along with what I learned from government officials, NGO personal, and academics. Two of these chapters also focus upon contrasting stories from people in Thailand, Vietnam, and Laos. In large part these chapters summarize the sorrows of Cambodians I observed during my two years of travel through slums and villages in every region of Cambodia. I had the usual World Bank, UN, and Asian Development Bank data available on the web, of course. But I wanted to see for myself what conditions were like, what the poor themselves thought about these conditions, their sorrows and fears, and what they were getting from their government and/or charities, or in most cases in Cambodia, what they *are not* getting. To put it all in perspective, I did much the same in Vietnam, Thailand, and Laos. (I knew from previous experience there was no hope of free travel and open personal interviews with people all over Burma.)

My selection of these four countries was not only because they are Cambodian neighbors but also because they are all Buddhist countries (though Vietnam's Buddhism is of a different verity). It has become common in recent years to assume that cultural values are key reasons for more economic development in Asia compared to other world regions. As will be demonstrated below, this cultural explanation is quite lacking when one considers the contrasting levels of economic development in these Buddhist countries, with Burma, Laos, and Cambodia remaining among the world's poorest, while Thailand is the richest in Southeast Asia, and Vietnam is achieving rapid economic development and poverty reduction.[6]

My original intent was to devote equal attention to these four countries in the region. But a couple of months into my travels I shifted more attention to Cambodia as it became clear that the poor of Cambodia are much worse off. While not perfect, the governments in Vietnam and even Laos are less corrupt and doing many of the right things to help bring their people out of poverty. Despite the political conflict in recent years, Thailand has been doing so for a much longer time.

The final three chapters of this book review some of the most recent social science research on economic development and poverty reduction. They then offer explanations for why Cambodian poverty is getting worse, and why current trends in the country will not lead to sustained economic development or poverty reduction. A corrupt government in place since the 1980s is a large part of the problem. But also missing is "good governance," government efficiency, "institutional capacity," and "human capital," all popular concepts used by development agencies to describe conditions needed for sustained economic development and poverty reduction.

Before turning to all of these subjects, though, the remainder of this first chapter will introduce some of the human reality, some of the stories told to me by a variety of Cambodia's rural and urban poor today. Impersonal statistics can help us understand much about the situations of people in a country such as Cambodia. But a deeper understanding also requires knowledge of the personal realities, the everyday lives and troubles of actual human beings.

The Vanishing Slums of Phnom Penh

Until 2009 Dey Krahorm was one of the last remaining slums in the center of Phnom Penh. At the beginning of this fieldwork in the summer of 2006 the slum consisted mostly of squatters' shacks of plywood and scrap metal scattered around an old, crumbling concrete apartment complex covered with mold. Inside the concrete complex were small individual apartments, each packed with several family members, and more mold and filth. Outside, among the plywood and scrap metal shacks, were piles of trash, green slimy water, and dozens of children playing various games among it all. Razor wire had been strung around trash piles covering spaces newly cleared of concrete or plywood structures. It was quite clear someone didn't want anyone coming back to these cleared plots. A few of the vacant areas showed signs of being destroyed by fire. By the spring of 2008 there were fewer people in Dey Krahorm slum. In 2006 the slum was home for a few thousand people. In the spring of 2008 it was down to about 400 people, then down to about 100 in December 2008.

Among the remaining people in Dey Krahorm in 2008 was the leader of a small resistance movement fighting the ongoing evictions. She told her story as we sat on little plastic chairs in front of her small wooden shack with an earthen floor. There was a small living area inside, plus a bedroom. Her kitchen was an open area in back of the small "house." Other than a few old chairs, some clothing, and a few pots and pans, there was very little else in her home. We can call her Tima, a remarkably handsome lady, especially given what she has been through in her five decades. On this day Tima wore a clean striped blouse and bright yellow sarong wrapped around her slim body, her long black hair pulled back in something like a ponytail. She fanned herself and offered her visitors a glass of water on that mid–April day, the hottest month in this part of Southeast Asia. After Tima began to trust her visitors she described her life as a teenager when the Khmer Rouge took over the country in 1975. She had just finishing eight years of schooling. Like everyone else in Phnom Penh at the time, Tima and her family were rounded up by Khmer Rouge soldiers and marched to distant flat plains where they lived for almost four years as forced laborers growing rice under the AK-47s held by peasant boys wearing black "pajamas." Like many people in Cambodia at the

Dey Krahorm Slum.

time, she lost several family members, including her parents. Soon after the Vietnamese invasion which pushed the Khmer Rouge out of most parts of Cambodia in 1979, she was back in Phnom Penh, looking for odd jobs to keep her from starvation. Outsiders may find it remarkable, she said, but she ended up being an elementary school teacher for a few years. Her eight years of education put her far ahead of the vast majority of Cambodians still alive and still in the country. By the mid–1980s when land was privatized by the Vietnamese-backed government, Tima was given what she thought was "title" to her little plot of urban land where she had scraped together some money to buy plywood and tin for her current "house." More recently, though, she could only find unskilled labor jobs like others in the slum. Again explaining that outsiders will find it hard to believe, these unskilled labor jobs can bring in more money than being a schoolteacher, which is why even today teachers must take bribes just to feed their families. In terms of real purchasing power compared to what a U.S. dollar will buy in the United States, on a good day Tima made about $2.50 in 2008.

After about thirty minutes Tima offered more details about her life. She told of the days she was tortured by the Khmer Rouge for resisting their commands, raising her arms behind her neck to describe how she was tied to a wooden pole as they beat her. Several more minutes into her story, Tima became more agitated, showing anger in her voice and defiance in her eyes as she told how she had been beaten again in recent weeks, this time by Cambodian police trying to make her stop the resistance movement and leave the slum. She showed the bruises around her neck and the side of her face. She gave more details about the human rights NGO trying to help people in this slum, stepping inside her hut for a few minutes, then returning with a legal petition to the Phnom Penh courts the NGO had filed on her behalf. (An American lawyer working for a human rights NGO in Phnom Penh some months later examined a copy of the land "title" Tima has, saying it would not hold up in a Cambodian court. Prime Minister Hun Sen had issued bogus documents to appease protestors a few years ago.)

After describing the beating Tima and others had received, she pointed around to the shacks around hers, saying that though this was one of the most important holidays in Cambodia, her neighbors had not gone back to their relatives' villages like most other people in Phnom Penh: If they leave their slum houses the police or agents hired by the South Korean company trying to evict them would burn their shacks. Tima then pointed to nearby vacant spaces, obviously blackened by fire, where this had already happened.

A couple of young Mormon boys wearing the usual black slacks, white shirts and ties, on their mandatory duty of saving some souls for a few months, were walking through Dey Krahorm slum that day. They talked about how bad it all was in this slum and how these people should move out to cleaner surroundings in the countryside. As will be described later, most foreigners have no clue as to what worse fate these people face when evicted from their smelly, foul, crumbling structures in the heart of Phnom Penh.

In mid–January 2009, the inevitable finally occurred. A human rights NGO in Phnom Penh sent out photographs through email, a few other photographs were in the *Phnom Penh Post* on line. One photograph showed what looked like Tima being dragged away by police and paramilitary guys with big guns, what one American in Phnom Penh described as a sort of "Black Water" private army working for foreign construction companies. Other photos showed more slum people being dragged away and bulldozers smashing the remaining shacks in the slum area.[7] What use to be a vibrant community, Dey Krahorm is now a construction site for the South Korean construction company called 7NG. The slum's former residents of many, many years are now scattered around "relocation camps" in the countryside, and a few in jail. The director of the human rights NGO Licadho was quoted as being shocked in June 2010 when learning that what was part of Dey Krahorm slum is now a construction site for a company fitness center for employees of the big South Korean company, 7NG, which took over the land.

> 7NG violently evicted more than 400 families ... to build an employee gym?... 7NG acquired the Dey Krahorm land illegally, and to this day 7NG has not delivered what it promised, including compensation to the rightful owners of Dey Krahorm and basic infrastructure and services to Dey Krahorm people dumped in resettlement sites.[8]

In 2008 Amnesty International estimated that as many as 150,000 more poor Cambodians could lose their homes in the future because of new building plans in the cities and new large-scale farms being established by rich Cambodians and foreign corporations.

While talking with many people in Dey Krahorm and other Phnom Penh slums still resisting eviction, visits to four "relocation camps" several miles outside of Phnom Penh were recommended. Dozens of families in these "relocation camps," who continue to have no jobs or farm land more than two years after being forced out of their homes, later told us their stories. In one of the worst "relocation camps" a man described how he and his family were pushed into a truck with electric "cattle prods" one morning at 2:00 A.M. as corporate security forces, assisted by the police, burned their home in another Phnom Penh slum. Along with other people in the truck that night, they were dumped in a field about 20 miles outside of Phnom Penh where they remain today, over two years since they were evicted.

To survive in these "relocation camps" many people described how family members sleep in the streets of Phnom Penh where they can work during the day as unskilled laborers making about $2 per day, then return to the "relocation camps" every other week or so, bringing money and food to their families. A round trip from Phnom Penh to the "relocation camps" costs about $2.50, so they obviously cannot come "home" often. In addition to money brought back by "homeless" relatives in Phnom Penh, other families in these "relocation camps" told us they mostly exist on food provided by foreign charities. In two of the "relocation camps" families said they largely subsist on food aid from South Korean Christian missions, ironic given that South Korean construction companies are among those destroying the homes and livelihood of these Cambodian people now in "relocation camps."

No one visiting Cambodia can forget the street children, thousands of them in Phnom Penh. Westerners will be out of their apartments or hotels less than a few minutes before confronted by groups of small children as young as four and five years old, begging, selling postcards, old books, chewing gum, or begging to shine their shoes. During interviews with various agencies, journalist Karen Coates found estimates of 10,000 to 20,000 children working the streets of Phnom Penh.[9] Perhaps 1,500 of these kids live on the streets with a parent, some 1,200 probably live alone on the streets, and the rest have something that might be called "homes" in Phnom Penh but must daily hit the streets to hustle for money. Their average daily take is about $1. Many of these children are in danger of being swept up in the sex industry as Western pedophiles have discovered Cambodia. Western NGOs estimated in 2003 that 4,000 young boys and more young girls had been taken into the sex industry all over Cambodia. To the Cambodian government's credit, a campaign against the child sex industry has shown some success. Almost every hotel in Phnom Penh has signs warning of the penalties for having sex with children, and billboards around town advertise "make sex tourists ex-tourists."

To the discredit of the government, however, in July 2008 another foreign NGO broke the story of people being rounded up on the streets of Phnom Penh in the middle of the night and taken to old Khmer Rouge prisons.[10] These people included prostitutes, the mentally ill, drug addicts, and simply homeless people who had nowhere else to live but the streets of Phnom Penh. The people found in one old prison used by the Khmer Rouge over 30 years ago included children as young as eight years old. After the United Nations Commission for Human Rights investigated, this particular prison was finally closed, though there are rumors of other such prisons holding similar people today.

Cambodians who challenge the government on these atrocities risk imprisonment or death. In 2006 a leading union official was gunned down on a street in Phnom Penh. In June 2008 a journalist writing about government corruption and massive evictions of slum people was also gunned down in a "drive-by shooting." Between these two killings there have been others, especially among people resisting eviction from their land. Since 1993, when first national elections were held in Cambodia, 12 journalists who have written articles critical of the government have been killed, more imprisoned, others threatened with violence. A few men have been arrested for a couple of these murders, but union leaders and foreign NGO people interviewed believe these are bogus charges to cover up for the real killers.[11]

Poverty in the Countryside

It is perhaps useful to begin with a family of women in a central Cambodian village, in Kompong Chnnang Province, about two hours' drive from Phnom Penh. After the Khmer Rouge "killing fields" and the continuing war with the Khmer Rouge throughout the 1980s, a family without male adults is not uncommon in rural Cambodia today.

There were only some 40 families in this village, much smaller than average in Cambodia. The appearance of the village, however, is typical; crude, wooden one-room huts on stilts about five feet off the earthen floor below, a rice straw roof, a little "sitting platform" about five or six feet square with a top of loosely placed bamboo under the hut, usually two feet above the ground. This is the coolest place to be and where families spend most of their time during the day, when not working in the fields. There is usually a "kitchen" with a charcoal firepit toward the back of this living space under the hut. The weathered wooden walls inside the upper room are usually covered with pictures of movie stars, cars, or motorbikes — pictures torn from the pages of old magazines. Hammocks swing from palm trees next to the house. Anorexic chickens peck at the dirt under the house and around the yard; a couple of dogs are usually laying about looking out of place in the high heat and humidity. An old water buffalo cart is often sitting in front of the house, and of course water buffalo are tied to trees throughout the village, though not all families can own a water buffalo themselves. Unlike Thailand, and even Vietnam and Laos, which have "iron buffalos" (small gasoline tractors), buffalos still pull the plows and wagons throughout rural Cambodia. If the family is not so poor, a couple of pigs or even a couple of cows will be just a few feet from the hut. The bright green tropical foliage around the huts, always various kinds of palm trees, coconut trees, and fruit trees, sometimes water lilies covering a small pond, are pleasant to see; that is, if it is not the dry season and close to a dirt road, in which case most plants are covered with dust. Like most village people in Cambodia, this family of women in central Cambodia had some farmland (though the percentage which do is dropping fast in Cambodia), but not quite enough to feed themselves (usually a hectare or less).

The grandmother, her sister, daughters and granddaughters gathered around as we sat on their bamboo table in the "cool" shade under their small wood and straw house. As is typical in the Cambodian countryside, the women wore light cotton blouses and either cotton pants or sarongs around their waists, and plastic sandals on their feet. Two daughters sat in hammocks tied to a tree and posts supporting the house, while granddaughters played in the dirt beside the bamboo table. It is common in this part of Southeast Asia for fathers of young children to be absent. As we will see in more detail in a later chapter, much of mainland Southeast Asia has had a matrilocal family tradition, which means that for centuries women inherited the farmland from their parents, while husbands moved in with wives and helped work this

Typical village scene in central Cambodia.

land. Women have therefore been the more responsible party in taking care of parents and children, with men often absent from the household.

The two older women had been working this land since the Khmer Rouge were pushed out of the area, but not before the husbands of both old ladies had been killed by the Khmer Rouge. As usual the family received no form of aid from the Cambodian government. The response was also negative when asked if there was any kind of aid from an NGO, foreign or domestic. They hire village men to plow their rice fields with water buffalo, they cook their meals over an open fire outside of their wood and straw hut, have no electricity, no fresh water, no motor vehicles, no irrigation or anything to prevent the floods which too often destroy their rice crops, and nothing to control mosquitoes, which bring death to many people across Cambodia today.

Compared to this family of women, however, a growing percentage of people in the countryside today are worse off because they have no land at all despite the fact that land was redistributed to virtually all families after the Khmer Rouge were pushed out of most areas in Cambodia by the mid–1980s.

In most villages at least one family (and usually more) have recently become landless, often because of illegal land grabs by the rich, but also because they had to sell their little plot of land to pay hospital bills to save the lives of their children. One family in this village was reduced to traveling far from home as often as they could to buy fresh vegetables to resell to others in the village. The landless situation of this particular family, we were told, was due to a cute little girl about six years old; her little skirt was low around her waist, showing the appendectomy scare her parents' land had paid for.

Like a small percentage of village families in Cambodia today (though even less since the global economic downturn hit in 2008), this family of women said they are able to buy a few things, and add some meat to their diet, because two daughters (in their late 20s) had textile factory jobs in Phnom Penh. During weekdays they worked in these "sweatshops," leaving their children at home with grandmothers, then coming home on weekends with a few dollars left over after paying for transportation and a safe place to live in Phnom Penh. As we will see in more detail later, however, such jobs are much more limited in Cambodia than in Thailand and now Vietnam, with no higher-value jobs on the horizon in Cambodia, also in contrast to Thailand and Vietnam. And given that these jobs are almost exclusively in Phnom Penh, they are primarily restricted to village young people in central Cambodia. As we will also see later, there is a more dangerous increase in job opportunities for young Cambodian women in the regional and global sex industry. Village people in Cambodia always say their absent daughters are away working in textile jobs, but statistics suggest many are in fact working in this other growing industry.

The "Killing Fields"

The most disturbing images of Cambodia, of course, are from the recent past. Between 1975 and 1979 in Khmer Rouge–dominated Cambodia, almost 2 million people died, approximately 20 percent of the Cambodian population at the time. The most accessible of these "killing fields" today is Choeung Ek, the one that Kaing Guek Eav (or Duch) was in charge of; he was finally convicted by the UN war crimes tribunal in July 2010. No one who has seen it will ever forget it. Today there are several partially excavated pits where the dead were dumped, still half full of earth. Just inside the entrance is a pagoda about five stories tall and perhaps ten yards wide on each of the four sides at the base. Some 17,000 men, women, and children were slaughtered here between 1975 and 1978. The bones of about 9,000 of these people have been dug up. The rest are in the ground somewhere under the feet of people who visit the grounds today. The five-story pagoda memorial to these people which faces the visitor upon entering the Choeung Ek killing field has glass on all four sides to the top. Inside the pagoda, piled completely to the top, are the skulls of these 9,000 people who have been excavated from the pits in this less-than-one-square-mile area.

Just a few miles from the Choeung Ek killing field, on the outskirts of Phnom Penh, is the old high school, now the Tuol Sleng Museum, where these people had been tortured and kept chained for months before taken to the killing fields of Choeung Ek — that is, if they did not die from torture first. Khmer Rouge officials kept detailed records of the people they killed, much like the Nazis during the Holocaust. Pol Pot's officials, however, added an innovation to the record keeping; they took photos of their victims before and after they were tortured. Now on the walls of the old Tuol Sleng High School turned into Pol Pot's torture chamber, one can see hundreds of the photos, many of the people whose skulls now look out to visitors from the glass pagoda at the Choeung Ek killing field.

The impact of those terrifying years will last for many years to come. Visitors can ask almost any Cambodian today and they will tell you, "Yes, I lost close relatives to Pol Pot's mass murder." A taxi driver on my first time visiting the killing fields years ago said he had lost two uncles. The next day a couple of Buddhist monks from the countryside who were in Phnom Penh to see the main temples for the first time said, yes, they had lost three close relatives to Pol Pot's killing machine. The European-funded Transcultural Psychological Organization operates several clinics in provincial cities throughout Cambodia, providing therapy to people who were alive during the Khmer Rouge years. They told us their estimate is that some 50 to 60 percent of people alive during the Khmer Rouge years have lingering mental problems caused by what they experienced. Studies of Cambodian refugees in North America support these estimates and suggest the posttraumatic stress symptoms lead to various forms of mental illness and withdrawal from social activities, conditions we will consider below as possibly related to Cambodian poverty today.[12]

It is not only the victims of the Khmer Rouge who suffer, however; it is also the common soldiers and lesser officials of the Khmer Rouge who saw and even participated in the horror. Most were made to think they were fighting a terrible evil that had brought starvation and violent death to Cambodian people. As noted above, the violent death came largely from intense bombing from U.S. warplanes during the Vietnam War. The evil, in the minds of many rural Cambodians of the time, came also from the government in Phnom Penh which sided with the United States from 1970.

Choeung Ek killing field.

Outside the provincial city of Pailin in the far western part of Cambodia, one day we happened upon a ceremony on the grounds of the governor's offices. Hundreds of people had gathered to hear speeches and receive gifts. After observations and questions, we found it was a ceremony organized by Hun Sen's ruling Cambodian People's Party to offer propaganda and gifts to disabled people. A large percentage of these people were missing limbs, usually legs.

About an hour later, we arrived at the village selected for interviews that day. The first stop was at a small wooden house on stilts which had a bag of rice on the front steps, a bag stamped with the Cambodian People's Party emblem. The family was sitting on their low wooden table in the shade under the house as is common throughout this part of Southeast Asia. It was a Sunday morning so the children, cute as they usually seem to be in Cambodia, were hanging around with Mom and Dad, playing with some handmade wooden toys. After a couple of hours asking this family about their economic status and future prospects in Cambodia, talking mainly to the father with a quiet manner and sad eyes, the bag of rice on the front steps of the house came up, with more questions about the ceremony earlier that day. Yes, he had been there, and pointed to his half-missing left leg. The next question was "Land mine?" He responded, "Yes." The first assumption was he had stepped on a land mine while working in his fields, tragically common, especially in this part of Cambodia which was the last stronghold of the Khmer Rouge.

The UN estimates that several million land mines were planted during the Cambodian civil war fight against the Vietnamese. Some 40,000 people have lost limbs to these land mines since the mid–1970s. During the 1990s about 2,000 people a year were killed working in their fields, though with brave work by de-miners this number was down to about 500 a year by 2006. The day before starting interviews in this particular village, the head man in a village nearby said three people were killed working in his field the previous year. A few days before this interview, in the area of Pailin, seven de-miners were killed in one blast. It was a strange combination of several mines designed by the Khmer Rouge to blow up tanks.

The assumption about the small farmer with the mangled leg and new bag of rice on his porch, however, was incorrect. Thinking of all this, the next question for this man was "When?" The quiet, kind-looking man in his early 50s responded, "During the war." Another question: "On which side?" His answer, "Khmer Rouge." This humble, polite, but cheerless man had been a soldier with Pol Pot's murderous Khmer Rouge. He explained that during the early 1990s many Khmer Rouge soldiers and officials in this part of Cambodia were given land in exchange for putting down their guns.

A deal to stop the fighting, one should think, seems a fair trade for all sides involved. But such is not so much the case for some people in the poorest of poor villages in this region. One is a "village" of about 200 families along the banks of a small river not far from the Thai border. These people are squatters living between villages where former Khmer Rouge are now the small landowners. These poorest of the poor, however, are landless. The children in this village show more signs of malnutrition than most other villages in Cambodia. Their houses are not even up to the standards of the usual wooden and rice straw houses on stilts seen in villages all over Cambodia. Rather, they were more like little straw boxes, maybe five to eight square meters. Except for their cheap modern clothing, mostly T-shirts and sarongs (the traditional cotton wraparound skirts both men and women wear), these people could have come out of the Stone Age. They were refugees in Thailand during the Khmer Rouge terror, forced by the Thai military to return in the early 1990s. Unfortunately, they were pushed out of Thailand a few years after the privatization and redistribution of land occurred in Cambodia. With no land or other livelihood they now work as very low-wage farm laborers on land now owned by former Khmer Rouge.

The Economic Boom

Not everything about Cambodia today is so grim. Surprisingly, given what one sees in the slums and the countryside, the Cambodian economy grew by 8 percent or higher between 2000 and 2007. Almost all economic growth and job production, however, has been in Phnom Penh and Siem Reap, the city adjacent to the famous Angkor Wat. And the global economic crisis from 2008 brought these high rates of GNP growth to a halt, with a slightly negative figure for 2009, and a projected growth for 2010 under 3 percent.[13] The three biggest growth sectors up to 2008 were textile production, the extraction of natural resources, and tourism. The reopening of Angkor Wat since the Khmer Rouge gave up the fight in the 1990s, and the clearing of land mines in the area, caused the tourism boom. Siem Reap has changed rapidly in recent years: At first there were a few hotels and guesthouses, most run down during the long years Angkor Wat was closed and occupied by the Khmer Rouge. There now seem to be hundreds of hotels, large and small, five star to zero star, serving the estimated 2.3 million tourists visiting Cambodia and spending about $1.6 billion annually by 2008.

Sadly, research by the Cambodian Development Resource Institute (a private, independent research institute in Phnom Penh funded by the EU) shows only a few poor families have benefitted from this tourist boom.[14] During interviews in villages around Angkor Wat we found a few families had children working in some aspect of this tourism industry, but very few. It is telling that the province around Siem Reap remains one of the poorest in Cambodia. Most of the new hotels were built by South Korean construction companies, and the company collecting entrance fees and running concessions inside the grounds of Angkor Wat is mostly Vietnamese owned. Foreign corporations and a few urban young Cambodians with English language skills are the primary beneficiaries of this tourist boom.

In the textile growth sector, mostly Asian corporations have been building what are generally referred to as "sweatshops." On the outskirts of Phnom Penh in the evening when the young girls are leaving work, one sees hundreds of the girls along the streets. One would think the area had a massive concentration of girls' high schools as these teenagers pour out of the factories to board funny-looking trailers with benches, pulled by something like a motorcycle, taking them to their dormitories or homes for the night. Interviewees claim that these textile factories almost exclusively employ only girls in their late teens and up to 21 or 22 years of age. Sadly for these girls and their families, though, the textile sector has been hardest hit by the global economic crisis from 2008. Before 2008 some 350,000, mostly young girls worked in the textile industry in Phnom Penh. Research shows that these jobs, while paying only $60 or so per month, did have a small reduction in Cambodia's poverty rate.[15] But before the end of 2008 already more than 60,000 of these girls lost their jobs. Thousands more have lost their jobs since the end of 2008 and had to return to villages, or even worse.

The label "sweatshops" is in quotes because one must be careful not to convey the totally negative connotation the word has in Western countries. Many poor rural families throughout Cambodia proudly talk of a daughter working in a textile factory in Phnom Penh and sending money back home. Other families tell of the money their sons were sending home from unskilled construction jobs in cities like Phnom Penh and Siem Reap. A "sweatshop" job is better than no job when living on less than $1 per day, as are 66 percent of people in Cambodia. A "sweatshop" job can also help keep these girls out of the sex industry, though the big city is still a dangerous place. One young girl back in her village for a holiday said she worked in a textile factory making $50 per month, a little less than she could make in another textile factory. Her selection of the lower-paying factory was based on safety issues: Without a guarded dormitory in the higher-paying factory, she explained that girls are in danger of being kidnapped and sold into the sex industry.

There is also that massive building boom in Phnom Penh mentioned above. All over the city there are new homes and condos going up, new tourist hotels, and massive casino hotels catering mostly to Chinese, Koreans, and especially tourists from Thailand where gambling casinos are illegal. In June 2008 Cambodian officials proudly participated in the ground breaking for Phnom Penh's second and tallest "skyscraper." The 52-story building will mostly house various service and financial offices. Soon after this ground breaking another company unveiled plans to build five towers of condos across the Mekong River from the center of Phnom Penh. Each tower will be 25 stories with condos selling for $300,000 to $350,000 in a country where 66 percent of the population lives on less than $1 per day!

Most of this building boom is funded by, constructed by, and owned by foreign construction companies, primarily South Korean and Chinese. The Cambodian rich and government elite will get their cut, and very little will trickle down to the Cambodian poor. Extensive research by social scientists has shown that economic growth fueled mainly by foreign investment usually leads to unsustainable development and a huge gap between the rich and poor.[16] This is especially the case when the country has a highly corrupt government unable or unwilling to put conditions on foreign corporate investment. Conditions such as demanding investors team up with domestic companies, and pay reasonable taxes and wages to domestic workers, have been placed on this outside investment coming into China, Vietnam, Malaysia, Thailand and the other rapidly growing Asian economies to better insure long-term benefits to the country. The conclusions from this research suggest Cambodia's future will be far different from that of these "Asian tigers."

The building boom in Phnom Penh and Siem Reap, of course, does result in some low-paying construction jobs for Cambodians. But there are many downsides. One is the rising cost of living as the rich get richer and the poor get further behind. The 2008 World Bank report doubled the percentage of people in Cambodia living on less than the equivalent of $1 per day compared to a few years ago because of this rising cost of living. In July 2010 the *Phnom Penh Post* reported that hundreds of these construction workers are going back to their villages or seeking work in countries like Thailand because the average $2.50 per day working on constructions sites in Phnom Penh isn't enough to buy basic necessities there.

Government Corruption and Inefficiency

According to reports by the World Bank and Transparency International, Cambodia has a government among the ten most corrupt in the world. One well-educated lady who, as a young girl, survived the Khmer Rouge period by pretending to be an ignorant peasant, described what she saw as a government official today. Talking in her government office in Phnom Penh that day she brought out a copy of development plans she and her staff had produced, plans that appeared quite reasonable. She then admitted the plans were seldom implemented, and when they were, the money was mostly stolen before it reached the grassroots level where it was to aid poor village people.

This government ineptness and corruption are especially killing Cambodia's future because of an insufficient infrastructure. Some 90 percent of rural people have no electricity or fresh water. Only a small fraction of farmers have irrigation for their corps compared to Thailand and Vietnam. And the roads are terrible. There are many "roads from hell," as Cambodians called them. One is a dirt road connecting the capital cities of two neighboring provinces in west central Cambodia. The road has holes big enough to submerge a little Toyota. The distance is less than 40 miles but takes over five hours by car. And one can get to the next provincial town at all only during the dry season; during the rainy season the road is impassable to all but off-road vehicles.

A few months later we planned another round of fieldwork in the northeast of Cambodia. We couldn't get there; it was the rainy season and roads were impassable, with no alternate transportation. There are only two airports still functioning in the whole country, and only one rail line still in operation between the two largest cities in Cambodia. On another road from Phnom Penh to the Lao border in the north, a road only one year old and paved, the few cars on the road have to slow every mile or so to avoid huge potholes that have already formed. As a courtesy to travelers, village people along the way stick fresh tree limbs into the holes with the leafy end in the air acting as warning flags. This road, like others, was built with money donated by Japanese and Western governments. Informants explained that many roads all over the country are falling apart because corruption takes so much money from the project that they can only be built with half the thickness required. This particular road and a bridge across the Mekong River to open later in 2008 were meant to allow commerce to move in and out through Laos, connecting to other new roads linking Laos to China, Thailand, and Vietnam. These other roads are nowhere near as bad as those in Cambodia. As of now, it looks like Cambodia will miss out on much of this coordinated regional development because corruption has sapped away the needed infrastructure development.

A Summation

One must acknowledge the good about Cambodia along with the bad. Among other things, the extent to which Cambodia's poor take care of each other despite their desperation is impressive. It is much like what happened in Burma during the spring of 2008 when a massive cyclone killed some 130,000 people. The Burmese government did almost nothing to help their people, and even prevented most countries from sending in aid and aid workers for months. After several weeks, when a few outsiders were able to get into the devastated parts of Burma, they were surprised how Buddhist monks and other poor villagers were able to help their neighbors and prevent more starvation and disease in the weeks after the disaster.

Temples are not far from any village in Buddhist Southeast Asia today. The Theravada Buddhist temples of Cambodia, Laos, Thailand, and Burma are much the same — steep tiled roofs of brilliant greens, oranges, and reds, a large golden Buddha image always inside. Cambodia, of course, has some of the oldest temples in Southeast Asia, the massive Angkor Wat being the most impressive of them all. This massive complex of carved stone is the largest religious structure in the world, built almost 1,000 years ago. Next door to Angkor Wat is the even more mysterious-looking Bayon, a temple complex with many carved faces, smiling serenely, much like a Mona Lisa. Next door again is another ancient temple complex, gargantuan tree roots wound around most walls like huge octopuses, left as it was "rediscovered" about 150 years ago.[17] In the south of Cambodia are beautiful beaches hugging dense jungle hills, looking something like California's Big Sur with a tropical jungle twist, and lush green rice fields not far away. There are big hopes for thousands of tourists in new resort hotels now being built. But while beautiful sights such as these stick in the mind of first-time visitors, the troubling, disturbing images always intrude.

Cambodian people 30 years and older have been through some of the worst horrors of the 20th century. In terms of genocide as a percent of population, the Khmer Rouge beat Hitler.[18] But while they are no longer under threat of death from the Khmer Rouge or massive American bombing, their lives are unlikely to improve beyond a meager subsistence level, and can easily become worse as they lose their land because of illegal land grabs or having to sell their land to pay for their children's hospital bills.

One can only describe the current Cambodian government as guilty of criminal neglect with respect to most of its citizens, especially the vast majority of people in the countryside. With respect to the thousands of mostly urban people who have been forced out their homes, beaten, dumped into relocation camps, and in some cases killed, Cambodian elites can be charged with grand theft and in some cases murder. One can only assume their mentality differs slightly from that of the Khmer Rouge. The Khmer Rouge went on their killing spree between 1975 and 1979 with the absurd idea of creating a new society from their "year one" by erasing all material and mental traces of Western, modern influence. This meant getting rid of anyone who resisted, mostly the middle class and educated who were guilty because of Western "thoughts" that would prevent a new Khmer "classless society" from emerging. Current political and economic elites seem almost equally ready to sacrifice any Cambodian who gets in their way. This time, though, it is because of a race to get rich and push the country into an extreme form of capitalism where the less rich are not only left behind but left poorer and cleared from the sight of rich Cambodians and foreigners into old Khmer Rouge prisons or relocation camps.

When contemplating the continuing tragedy, some are tempted to assume that Cambodia's fate has been only self-inflicted. It is true that Cambodians were killing Cambodians during the Khmer Rouge years, with rich and powerful Cambodians now stealing from the poor to give to the rich. But it is far more complicated than this. We must understand how Cambodia's geographical and historical location in the 20th century, and even earlier during the spread of Western colonialism, set the stage for the Cambodian tragedy. This understanding requires at least a brief chapter on Cambodian history before we move to other issues of poverty and lack of economic development in Cambodia today.

CHAPTER 2

How Did It Get This Way?
A Little History

A European friend married to a lady of Cambodian ancestry once held up their infant son saying, "In his veins runs the blood of Europeans who built the grand cathedrals of Europe as well as the blood of Cambodians who built Angkor Wat." The statement was of course true. The problem for Cambodia today is that the high point of that mighty civilization was long ago and has since been in a steep decline for over 600 years.

The Early Angkor Civilization

Archeological evidence shows there were rice farmers on the Southeast Asian mainland at least 4,300 years ago. Some 3,500 years ago these people were already into the Bronze Age. In an old village from that date in Thailand, close to both the Laotian and Cambodian borders, there is evidence that the Bronze Age may have appeared there before anywhere else in the world. To the south, on the island of Java in what is now Indonesia, the people who built the temples of Borobudor some 1,500 years ago were far ahead of Europeans, Arabs, and the Chinese with respect to shipbuilding and traversing the seas from Africa and the Middle East to East Asia. The first great civilization in Southeast Asia, however, in terms of population size, territory occupied, and advanced technology (especially in construction), started coming together around 2,000 years ago.[1] This was the Angkor civilization of the Khmer which forms a rather straight historical line to present-day Cambodia. What can be called a government with a king firmly in power dates to about 1,200 years ago in this emerging Angkor civilization. It was King Jayavarman II who laid the foundation for the strong state which led to Khmer domination of the

Angkor Wat.

region, then King Jayavarman VII who led the Khmer to its apex of domination a little less than 1,000 years ago. Some 100 years later it was King Suryavarman II who was responsible for building the massive Angkor Wat stone complex, usually included today as one of "seven wonders of the world," and still the largest religious structure in history. Not only was the massive Angkor Wat constructed from huge stones that had to be transported more than 20 miles from their source, it took only 40 years to complete. King Suryavarman II commissioned the construction of several other massive stone temples nearby, such as Angkor Thom, finished around A.D. 1200 under King Jayavarman VII with 3.5 square miles within its walls (the giant temple still covered with jungle trees as it was upon its "rediscovery" by the French explorer Henri Mauhot in 1859), and the Bayon Temple, not as massive as Angkor Wat but artistically more impressive. More impressive than their size, these massive temples are almost totally covered with stone carvings depicting scenes of daily life, 1,700 apsara goddesses, and 1,300 other inscriptions.

As with most of mainland Southeast Asia, the Angkor/Khmer culture was highly influenced by India from 2,000 years ago. The dominant religion was at first Hindu, but by the time Angkor Wat was completed, Theravada

Buddhism was gaining influence among the ruling Angkor/Khmer elite. The temples around Angkor Wat first contained statues of Hindu gods, then Buddhist, then back and forth for a number of years until Theravada Buddhism gained the dominance that continues today. Theravada Buddhism came from India as well, via Sri Lanka, first reportedly showing up in western Thailand about A.D. 700. This form of Buddhism spread slowly east, then came to dominate most of the Southeast Asian mainland during the 13th century. It came to shape a relatively common culture in what is now Burma, Thailand, Laos, and Cambodia, with only Vietnam's culture dominated by China and Mahayana Buddhism.[2] Traveling through these four countries today, one sees the same religious practices among the common people and the elites, with only minor architectural style differences in the temples. And it is important to note that the people in these four countries remain highly religious today, unlike people in most advanced industrial societies. After communism took over Cambodia, Laos, and Vietnam, religion was at first banned. The Khmer Rouge controlled most of Cambodia for less than five years, of course, and Buddhism made a quick comeback compared to Laos and Vietnam. Traveling through the cities and villages of Cambodia, Laos, and Thailand, one finds more Buddhist temples (wats) per capita than Christian churches in Texas or Oklahoma. These colorful wats, each with numerous Buddha images and saffron-robed monks, are the heart of community life, where the people come together for all festivals and other community events, and rituals associated with personal rites of passage (births, marriages, and funerals). The communist parties in Laos and Vietnam attempted to suppress religion and Buddhism at first after 1975 but eventually gave up. In Laos the communist party ended up embracing Buddhism, putting the most revered temple, Pha That Luang, back on the country's currency and holding major political ceremonies in Wat Pha That Luang.[3] The communist party of Vietnam gave into Buddhism more slowly, but by the 1990s one could see their Buddhist temples being repaired and full of people as well.

An important point is that a rather common culture shaped by Hinduism and then Theravada Buddhism has existed in Burma, Thailand, Laos, and Cambodia for centuries, with only Vietnam sharing stronger cultural ties with China. While religious principles and values do not solely shape a people's culture, we will see in later chapters that it is difficult to argue that the different levels of economic development and poverty in Burma, Thailand, Laos and Cambodia are related to major cultural differences.

At its high point, the Angkor Kingdom stretched to the far west through Thailand and almost to what is now Burma, as well as north and east through what are now Laos and southern Vietnam. Even today one can see the ruins of Khmer temples in these countries with a design similar to those in the Angkor Wat area. Archaeologists estimate that the area around Angkor Wat was the largest city in the world some 1,000 years ago.[4] It was hundreds of years before its approximately one-million-person population was attained anywhere else in the world. This grandeur, however, survived for less than 400 years. By the 1400s the civilization was in steep decline, with the capital of the kingdom moved southeast, closer to where Phnom Penh is today on the Mekong River. Internal disputes and power struggles turned the Khmer civilization into the weak man of Southeast Asia.

Recent evidence shows ecological disaster was a partial cause of the Angkor demise. A city of one million people was only possible because of the massive water infusion annually from the Mekong River, up through the Tonle Sap River into the Tonle Sap Lake, where Angkor Wat is located. In a rare geological event, Tonle Sap Lake drains into the Mekong River to the southeast and then into the Pacific Ocean through the Mekong Delta in what is now southern Vietnam. But toward the end of the annual rainy season in the region, the flow of water from further north is so great in the Mekong River that the flow of the Tonle Sap River actually reverses, bringing abundant water with rich nutrients from as far away as China. This allowed the Angkor civilization one thousand years ago to grow enough rice to sustain a population of one million people. Angkor kings had to oversee the construction of many canals to get the water to the right places for rice paddies, but such a task was much less complicated than constructing something like Angkor Wat. In their engineering brilliance, however, they created an ecological collapse. The massive stone temples and palaces remain for tourists today. But the vast majority of that one million population 1,000 years ago had to live in wooden structures. In the process of housing a million people, they depleted wood lands around them. During the rainy season, more and more silt and mud flowed down the hills and mountains around Angkor Wat, eventually clogging the canals bringing water to the rice fields.

It was in this weakened state that the Khmer/Angkor civilization was further doomed by the rise of Thais and Vietnamese, especially the Thais. From 1431 to 1432 the Thai army attacked Angkor Wat, destroying most of the non-stone structures. The Thais were to take other parts of the old Angkor/Khmer civilization again and again over the next few hundred years. Angkor kings quickly figured out they must get out of that part of Southeast Asia, with the capital eventually ending up in Udong much further south, and then Phnom Penh where the Tonle Sap and Mekong rivers merge on the urging of the French colonials in 1866.[5] With their move to Udong the Khmer rulers were hoping that new maritime trade coming up the Mekong from

China and other countries in the region would reinvigorate their civilization. But it was not to be. The main ports for this trade were in Vietnam (in the central port of Hoi An and then Saigon) and the new Thai capital close to Bangkok. The Khmer kingdom simply continued to weaken internally. It was in this weakened state with Thailand taking parts of Cambodia from the west and Vietnam taking parts of Cambodia from the east that the next stage bringing further decline in Cambodian began — European colonialism.

The Impact of Colonialism

To understand the fate of Cambodia compared to the other Buddhist countries of Southeast Asia at the beginning of the European colonial period it is important to recognize that Thailand and Vietnam were the ascending powers in the region, while Cambodia and Burma were both in steep decent. Burma also had a relatively strong kingdom in the region some 1,000 years ago called Pagan, though with more ethnic divisions which remain to this day. Burma was never able to spread its dominance as widely as Cambodia's Angkor kingdom. But as the Thai kingdom was in its infancy in the 1200s the Burmese were continually attacking and taking parts of Thai territory (including the older capitals), and continued to do so for three centuries. By the 1600s, however, the Thais were successfully attacking the Burmese, taking more and more Burmese territory to create national borders roughly corresponding to what is now Thailand.[6]

Going back two thousand years, what is now northern Vietnam was mostly occupied by China. In the south the ancient Champa empire remained dominant, attacking and taking parts of the Angkor kingdom. But the last 1,000 years have been a millennium of slow expansion and independence from China for Vietnam, and finally consolidation of northern and southern territories of present-day Vietnam as the old Champa civilization was conquered.

This was the regional situation as the Portuguese and Spanish begin moving into Southeast Asia from the 1500s. But neither country was as good as the British, Dutch, and French at *profitable* colonial exploitation.[7] Territory first settled by the Portugese and Spanish was eventually taken by these other European powers. The Spanish were eventually left with only the Philippines while the Portugese were left with Macau, the small island off the China coast.

From the 1700s the British, French, and Dutch were gradually moving into Southeast Asia. At first it was primarily merchant-driven expansion.[8] Merchants from these European countries first established small protected areas to carry out trade, mainly the spice trade. At the time these Europeans were sailing ships from Europe to Southeast Asia and back bringing cargos giving them 1,000 percent profits on their investments. As they expanded their trade, these British, French, and Dutch merchants pleaded with their governments to add to their "protectorate" territory in parts of Southeast Asia, with the full advent of colonialism coming by the mid– to late 1800s.

The British, of course, already had India and were moving into what is now Malaysia to the south of these Buddhist mainland countries. As in other places in Southeast Asia, there were many setbacks because of Europeans of questionable character seeking their fortunes in Southeast Asia. The British first sent their man to set up what was to be something like Singapore in the far east of what is now Malaysia, close to the Philippines. But his British funding was spent on "wine, women, and song," which later resulted in Mr. Raffles being sent several years later to establish what is now Singapore.[9] The Dutch focused on what is now Indonesia after the British pushed them out of mainland Southeast Asia. (Earlier the Dutch had taken parts of what is now Malaysia from the Portugese, only to be kicked out themselves by the British.) At the same time, of course, the French were moving into Vietnam. Remarkably, the Thais, using shrewd diplomacy, were the only ones to keep their independence. Astute Thai kings in the second half of the 1800s made the French, coming in from the east, and the British, coming in from the west and south, concerned about potential conflict over Thai territory. Consequently, in the second half of the 19th century, King Monkut and King Chulalongkorn were able to keep their county the only one in all of Asia except Japan from being colonized by these European powers, though British influence was significant in Thailand.[10]

The Burmese were not so lucky. British merchants were increasingly eyeing potential resources in Burma, and an arrogant Burmese king at the time played into their hands, believing he should be ruler of the world, repeatedly attacking the British across the border into India. The British were finally fed up and moved their army to take all of Burma. Though European merchants did have economic plans for Burma, in the end the British had little interest in exploiting the country.[11] Nor were the Vietnamese as lucky as the Thais. No matter what it took, and how many were killed, the French were determined to take Vietnam and its riches.

Among the Buddhist countries of Southeast Asia, this leaves Cambodia and what is now Laos, which at the time was actually not Laos but rather several little kingdoms.[12] In a strange event in world history, Cambodia was so weakened by the 1800s, and so much in fear of being gobbled into extinction by Thailand and Vietnam, that the king actually agreed that the French should take the country as a "protectorate" in 1863.[13] Without much enthusiasm the

French did so. About the same time the French also created what is now Laos by moving west from their colonial borders in Vietnam to combine three small kingdoms into the country which now separates Thailand from Vietnam.

A key point of the above for our understanding of Cambodia is that the British and French were not really much interested in Burma, Laos, or Cambodia at the time. All three countries were taken more as an afterthought. And, most importantly, the British and French did little to help develop these countries, unlike what they did in India, Malaysia, and Vietnam. In Vietnam the French wanted rubber and other resources, and they considered the Vietnamese to be relatively cultured people, a people the French could better relate to. The French built grand cathedrals and opera houses in Saigon and Hanoi, beautiful cream-colored French villas, and much more. A few of these old French villas can be seen today in Phnom Penh and Battambang in Cambodia, and Luang Prabang, Vientiane, Pakse, and Tha Khaek in Laos, but very few compared to those throughout Vietnam. In an analysis of the impact of colonialism in almost 100 countries in Asia and Africa, two sociologists at the University of Zurich found that Cambodia had one of the lowest levels of trade and development from their French colonial masters compared to most of these other countries. But Cambodia was one of the most changed and disrupted countries during and in the aftermath of colonialism.[14]

European colonials, however, were eventually shown to be as arrogant as the Burmese king who believed he was the rightful ruler of the world, only to be put in his place by the irritated Brits in India. There had been resistance movements in Southeast Asia against the British, French and Dutch for decades (though relatively few in Cambodia), all put down with more or less violence. Weakened by self-mutilation during World War II, the Europeans could no longer hold on to their empires. The Japanese moved into East and Southeast Asia temporarily, at first welcomed as liberators in much of Southeast Asia. But it didn't last. The Southeast Asians, along with the Chinese, soon realized the Japanese were worse occupiers than the Europeans. As the United States began trying to protect European (and American) interests in Asia, threatening to blockade Japanese oil supplies if Japan took any more Asian territories, the Japanese attacked Pearl Harbor, only temporarily forestalling America's attempts to stop the Japanese. The Thais were again among the few not to be dominated by a foreign power when they decided to "declare war" on the British and Americans as Japanese troops crossed the Mekong River from Laos into Thailand.[15] The Thai government, however, never officially served the U.S. and Britain with their declaration of war, with some of the Thai political elite actually setting up a "government in exile" in Washington,

D.C. The results were that the Japanese did not brutalize Thailand as they did China, Vietnam, Burma, and the rest of Southeast Asia. At the end of World War II Thailand could tell the U.S. and Great Britain they "didn't really mean" a declaration of war against the Allies, and that it was only under duress, thus suffering no negative consequences from the Allies.

After the end of World War II the British took their exit somewhat gracefully in India, though they hung around Malaysia for several years helping Malays prepare for government and economic stability after independence. Great Britain, however, is responsible for much of the political turmoil in Burma today: The British pretty much said, "Here is your country and the boundaries we created for you — goodbye." These national boundaries were not what smaller ancient kingdoms and hill tribe people had in mind. A harsh military dictatorship using extreme repression to hold it together has been the result.[16] In southern Southeast Asia, the Dutch took steps to regain their old colony but were stopped by the Americans. Taking "the moral high ground," the United States declared colonialism inhuman and unfair. The Dutch were told they must get out or lose Marshall Fund money; Holland pulled out. The Americans, of course, could take the moral high ground because their only colony was the Philippines, and keeping the rest of Asia open would benefit U.S. commercial interests in the region.

The Indo-China Wars

With the French, however, it was a very different story. France was also told by the United States that colonialism is no longer acceptable and there would be penalties for any French movement back into its old Indochina territories. A difference was that the French had remained in Vietnam throughout World War II because Germany occupied France early on in World War II and Germany's ally, Japan, agreed to let the French stay in Vietnam to help run the country. With Germany defeated and Japan still at war in mid–1945, hostilities broke out between the French and Japanese in Vietnam. With Japan's defeat, France had the pretext to go back into Vietnam to protect French subjects, defying American complaints.

All of this changed before 1950. East Europe was occupied by the Soviets, and China had suddenly gone communist. The Cold War had begun. The Americans now not only agreed the French should stay in Indochina, they offered to pay for much of the French effort to fight communism there. Thus began the Indochina Wars, which set the stage for further devastation of Vietnam, and then Laos and Cambodia.

Renewed French domination, of course, didn't last long. By 1953 the French were soundly defeated by Ho Chi Minh's Viet Minh around the mountains of northern Vietnam in Den Ben Phu. Colonial arrogance again. The French figured they would take a stand in a flat plane with some high mountains protecting their rear. They would lure the Vietnamese communists into the flat plain in front of the French and then destroy them. It didn't happen as planned. First of all, the Vietnamese dug many tunnels up to the French lines in the flat plain, then secondly took apart artillery pieces so hundreds of Vietnamese young people could pull them up the steep mountain slops on bicycle frames. The French woke up one morning to find artillery pointing down from above, and Vietnamese soldiers popping out of tunnels in front of them.[17]

What followed were the Geneva Accords which gave North Vietnam to Ho Chi Minh's forces, while South Vietnam would remain non-communist, though both North and South were to have elections to determine "the will of the people." When it was clear the southern Vietnamese would not favor the corrupt government put in place after 1953, the election idea was conveniently forgotten by the Americans. Slowly but surely the United States entered the next stage of the Vietnam War, losing over 58,000 Americans with an additional million or so Vietnamese killed.

It actually started with a secret war in Laos organized by the CIA, using mostly Hmong hill tribe people as their army. These hill tribe people initially held their own against the Viet Cong in eastern Laos, but by 1965 the North Vietnamese had the strength to increasingly attack South Vietnam, at which point the Americans finally invaded in full force in central Vietnam on the beaches of Danang. Soon after this, the CIA agent now famous for the Iran-Contra scandal during the 1980s, Richard Secord, was sent to Laos and Northeastern Thailand to take charge of this secret war, changing policies so that Hmong anti–Vietnamese fighters were simply thrown at the communist Vietnamese as cannon fodder to keep them from killing American soldiers in South Vietnam.[18]

Back to Cambodia and the relevance of all this for our country of focus. The Geneva Peace Accords of 1953 also gave independence to Cambodia and Laos. There were communist movements in both countries as the American part of the Vietnam War escalated in the late 1950s and through the 1960s. But despite the CIA secret war in Laos and the ever-growing "Ho Chi Minh Trail" running through eastern Laos and Cambodia, both countries were able to more or less keep out of the war for several years. Cambodia's ever politically agile King Sihanouk, put on the throne by the French before World War II, played a balancing act between Vietnam and the Americans to keep Cambodia out of the war.[19] But it all fell apart when the Americans could no longer tolerate Cambodian neutrality and backed a military coup displacing Sihanouk in 1970.[20]

The highly incompetent Lon Nol took control in Cambodia and the situation quickly deteriorated.[21] The Americans invaded eastern Cambodia in 1970 in a failed attempt to block supplies coming down the Ho Chi Minh Trail into South Vietnam, which prompted all-out war between the Cambodian allies of the U.S. and the communist Khmer Rouge supported by North Vietnam. As the Americans were finally defeated in Vietnam and were completely pushed out in 1975, the communist Pathet Lao in Laos and the Khmer Rouge in Cambodia took control of their respective countries.

Things were certainly not pleasant for communist opponents in Laos and South Vietnam. It is claimed that the "political reeducation camps" in Laos were worse than those in Vietnam.[22] People in southern Vietnam continue to complain about discrimination because they or their parents were somehow connected to the Americans or the South Vietnamese government during the war. There is a rickshaw driver in Danang, for example, a young guy obviously bright, speaking English well, who couldn't go to higher education because his father was in the South Vietnamese Army. Or in another case, there is a very old lady who is completely destitute in a central Vietnam village. She has absolutely nothing but a rickety shack to live in. Others in the village give her food and take care of her in other ways. There are five official-looking certificates in frames hanging on her wall. They were given by the South Vietnamese government for her husband and each of her four sons who died fighting with the Americans in the Central Highlands. Had her husband and sons been fighting for the North, her picture would be in the special room at the Army Museum in Hanoi devoted to "multiple star" mothers, and she would be living on a substantial pension instead of destitute and ignored in a poor village in central Vietnam.

The Killing Fields

The plight of these people in Laos and Vietnam, however, pales to those caught up in the prisons and "killing fields" of Cambodia from 1975 to 1979. There has never really been anything like it in history. Pol Pot and the Khmer Rouge (Red Khmer) believed the only way they could build a true communist society was to destroy all Western influence, along with most of Cambodia's Buddhist past, thus developing a new society from "year one," 1975. Phnom Penh was cleared of all people and they were forced to march into the countryside and dig new rice paddies. Most Cambodians over 30 years old have horror stories of being marched out of the city at gunpoint and made to work in these new rice fields for four years. They tell of seeing others killed because they were not working hard enough to please their Khmer Rouge guards. They were reduced to surviving on muddy water in puddles beside the road and a small amount of rice handed out by Khmer Rouge guards, which they augmented with bugs, mice, and lizards they could catch when the Khmer Rouge boys with big guns had their eyes turned away. This treatment was in part to punish and control those who were most Westernized and assumed to be former allies of the United States, but also because after so much war devastation, the country was starving. As depicted in the famous movie *The Killing Fields*, a result was the deaths of almost 2 million Cambodians, about 20 percent of the total population at the time. What devastated the country's future even more was that educated Cambodians were targeted by the Khmer Rouge. The peasant boy soldiers recruited by the Khmer Rouge leadership before 1975 were easy candidates for mental manipulation. Their villages and families had been decimated by more bombs dropped upon them than all of Japan in World War II, and they hated the relatively rich and educated in Phnom Penh who were seen as supporting the Americans before 1975. One estimate is only some 300 university-educated Cambodians were left in the country by 1979. Two of these surviving Cambodians with a college education at the time, for example, are now government officials in Phnom Penh who hid their educated backgrounds while captives of the Khmer Rouge.[23] They have stories about how Khmer Rouge guards would sneak up behind them and speak in French and English to see if there was a flicker of response. Had there been they would have been dead.

Vietnamese Defeat of the Khmer Rouge

While the communist Vietnamese had given material support to the Khmer Rouge when fighting the Americans, the Khmer Rouge had always hated the Vietnamese, both North and South. Remember that for the past few hundred years the Vietnamese had been on the rise and dominating Cambodia, which is why the Cambodian king invited the French into the country in the mid–1800s. Thus, as soon as the communists in Laos, Cambodia, and Vietnam took over their respective countries in 1975, conflicts broke out between Cambodia and Vietnam. At first it was the killing or deporting of all people of Vietnamese ancestry living in Cambodia. Then it was Khmer Rouge attacks into Vietnamese territory. By 1979 the Vietnamese had enough;

they organized a massive invasion of Cambodia, quickly pushing all Khmer Rouge forces to the far west along the Thai border and the far north. And, of course, something the Vietnamese have never been given enough credit for, the killing fields were stopped.

For the next 10 years the Vietnamese occupied Cambodia and helped reorganize the government.[24] Throughout this ten-year period the United States continued to support the Khmer Rouge, even after the killing fields were well known. The Khmer Rouge hated the Vietnamese, so the Americans went for the philosophy "an enemy of my enemy is my friend." The United States blocked any attempt in the United Nations to remove Khmer Rouge officials from their seat in the United Nations, prevented aid agencies from helping the Cambodian people, and secretly gave the Khmer Rouge at least $150 million to keep up the fight against the Vietnamese after 1979.

Before the Khmer Rouge were kicked out of most of Cambodia by the Vietnamese in 1979, many lower-ranking Khmer Rouge figured out it was all insane. Their main goal was to not end up in the Tuol Sleng torture chamber and then underground in the killing fields themselves. Many were unsuccessful. But a few lower-ranking Khmer Rouge in the eastern part of the country who had seen the light figured their only chance was to get out by defecting into Vietnam. One of these people was Hun Sen, the current prime minister (or one should say, "dictator") on top of the Cambodian government since 1985. Hun Sen and his colleagues were recognized as a potential resource by the Vietnamese government and given training and support. Soon after the 1979 invasion, they were given leadership positions by the Vietnamese.

Back in Vietnam, by the mid–1980s (as we will see in a later chapter), it was becoming ever clearer that the old communist economic policies "perfected" by Stalin were failing badly. There was growing starvation, especially due to farm collectivization. Thus, even though the Vietnamese were behind the scenes of the new Cambodian government throughout the 1980s, they had lost their taste for communist economic policies. Hun Sen was encouraged by the Vietnamese to follow more open market economic policies as was starting to be done by the Vietnamese themselves after *doi moi* in the late 1980s. One of the first results for Cambodia in the mid–1980s was privatization of land, rural and urban. With great benefit to the Cambodian people (though in a manner causing future problems we have already seen), all families in rural Cambodia were given an equal plot of land for cultivation, and people in the urban areas were given some legal rights to the housing where they lived.

Cambodia Since 1990

The next crucial periods for Cambodians came when the Vietnamese decided they were ready to leave in 1989, and then when most Khmer Rouge, though not all, decided it was time to give up the fight in the early 1990s. What followed was a massive outpouring of foreign aid, along with a United Nations program to rebuild Cambodian government institutions laid to waste during the Indochina Wars and the Khmer Rouge horror, primarily funded by the Japanese. Much has since been written about the success or lack of success by this UN effort. As usual with such controversy, one can conclude the results were in fact mixed. Peace did basically return to Cambodia, and there were democratic elections. But the problem was that the country wasn't really ready. There was so much fear, mistrust, anger, and divisions remaining within the country that political stability was still quite tenuous. The first election results were so evenly split between two parties, one led by Hun Sen's Cambodian People's Party, that the UN agreed to a co–prime minister deal. This shaky situation lasted until 1997 when most of the remaining Khmer Rouge leadership decided to give up. The new problem was that most of these defecting Khmer Rouge in 1997 were against Hun Sen and his Cambodian People's Party. Knowing he would most likely lose in a future election, Hun Sen's supporters created situations in which it seemed like violence was directed against Hun Sen (such as a hand grenade thrown into the front yard of his home) so that Hun Sen could plead justification for what was basically a military coup. The army was called in to "restore the peace," and of course arrest Hun Sen's opponents. This is pretty much where Cambodian politics remains today.

One must give some credit to Hun Sen and his government for achieving relative stability in Cambodia after the Indochina Wars, then war against the Khmer Rouge up to the 1990s. The Cambodian army under Hun Sen kept the Khmer Rouge pinned down in two rather isolated regions throughout the 1980s, then made deals with the Khmer Rouge in the 1990s to finally stop all fighting. But as we will see in more detail later, Hun Sen also repressed any political opposition and created more and more loyalty among his political supporters and the rich by allowing corruption to flourish up to the present.

We can take leave of this subject for now, returning in a later chapter to the nature of Cambodia's corrupt and incompetent government which has its roots in this recent history. For now it is time to explore further the focal subject of the book, the precise conditions of poverty in Cambodia today.

CHAPTER 3

Poverty in Cambodia
How Bad Is It?

We live in a world with more global inequality than at any other time in human history. As recently as 1820, World Bank–sponsored research estimates that the annual per capita (average per person) income was not so different around the world. The range in today's dollars was about $500 annual per capita in China and South Asia to between $1,000 and $1,500 in the richest countries of Europe. Today there are some countries actually under $500 annual per capita, with the countries of North American, Europe, Australia and Japan at the upper $30,000 level to over $40,000.[1]

This estimate for 1820 seems quite reasonable when one thinks about it. Most people in rich countries today have grandparents or great-grandparents who lived on farms without electricity or indoor plumbing. Since 1820, of course, some 20 percent of the world's population have had dramatic jumps in their standards of living, leaving most other people far behind.

Today some 1.3 billion of the world's more than six billion people live on less than $1 per day. Approximately 2.8 billion people, almost half of the world's population, live on less than $2 per day. In 2006 the United Nations attempted the first worldwide estimate of wealth inequality (wealth is defined as assets such as land or real estate rather than periodic money income). Their findings were quite shocking. The richest 2 percent of the world's people own over half the world's wealth, while the bottom half of the world's people own less than 1 percent of the wealth. People living in North America, Europe, and the Asian Pacific countries of Japan and Australia own 90 percent of the world's wealth.[2] The United Nation's Food and Agriculture Organization estimated that almost a billion people in the world were chronically undernourished in 2002, with another two billion people experiencing crucial deficiencies of nutrients. UNICEF figured malnutrition was a factor in about 55 percent of

Street children in Phnom Penh.

the 12 million preventable deaths every year among children under five years old.[3] During the global economic crisis by mid–2009 the UN estimated the number of chronically undernourished rose to over one billion.

There is speculation as to whether and by how much these figures have been improving in recent years. Poverty was probably going down before the global recession in 2009, but to the extent it was, the improvement is almost exclusively in Asia. However, the extent of improvement was thrown in doubt again when the World Bank admitted in early 2008 that its $1 a day poverty estimate, first calculated with early 1990s prices around the world, is now incorrect in many countries, and as we will see below, especially Cambodia. Suddenly, average incomes in many countries were much lower than we had thought; they were down by 40 percent in China and India, 17 percent in Indonesia, 41 percent in the Philippines, 32 percent in South Africa, and 24 percent in Argentina.[4]

Before proceeding it must be noted that the $1 per day and $2 per day figures, and the comparisons of average incomes around the world today, are based upon what is called purchasing power parity (PPP) estimates. This means we are *not* looking at what an actual one dollar bill will buy in France, India, China, or Cambodia, but what one dollar will buy in the United States. This PPP estimate then looks at the same package of goods and estimates how many people in other countries have money for the same package of goods. For example, one dollar buys perhaps a cheap sandwich in the U.S., or a cheap loaf of bread. When we say that people in Cambodia live on $1 a day or less it means that they have enough money in whatever currency to buy an equal amount of goods that the $1 would buy in the U.S. The 2008 re-estimate of the PPP was necessary because previous estimates of the cost of basic items in a few of these countries like Cambodia, China, and India are no longer valid today. In other words, the cheap sandwich or loaf of bread, or whatever, now actually costs more than was earlier believed.

Soon after this new estimate by World Bank economists, the world was again getting poorer because of rapidly rising food prices and a global recession. In early 2008 some basic food items such as rice shot up 50 percent, though this price rise slowed with global recession later that year. The shift to "biofuels" is a main cause of rising food prices; quite simply, by shifting a big percentage of corn, or whichever crop, to producing biofuels, there is less corn for people to eat. The costs of all basic food items go up because corn now costs more and other foods become more expensive as more people are buying these other foods instead of the corn. Climate problems, of course, have affected food prices, but the bottom line, according to the global anti-poverty agency Oxfam, is that 30 million more people around the world have been pushed back into poverty because of rising food prices alone.

Statistics, Poverty Estimates, and "Lies"

One point of the above is that statistics on poverty, malnutrition, average incomes and so on are always rough estimates. Sometimes they are off for various reasons, and because agencies like the World Bank, Asian Development Bank, and United Nations must rely on contracts with in-county agencies around the world, some country estimates may be more reliable and accurate than others. There are also different measures of poverty; what do you include as income, where is the line between poverty and non-poverty drawn? But if we understand what differing methods and measures of poverty are being used, this is actually an advantage in painting the most accurate picture about different aspects of poverty in a country.

The old saying "you can lie with statistics" is mostly untrue. You can only lie with statistics when the person you are talking to knows very little about statistics, or the statistics have not been scrutinized by others who are knowledgeable. In Cambodia, for example, there has been some debate in 2007 and 2008 over a new World Bank report suggesting that income inequality is not going up as much as most NGOs and social scientists had thought, and poverty in Cambodia has actually gone down slightly since the early 1990s.[5] One problem is differing estimates of inequality used in the most recent World Bank–sponsored study. There are actual income estimates of inequality vs. inequalities in the consumption of goods, which is what the recent World Bank study measured. For several reasons, for example, a consumption measure can underestimate how much higher income groups have because much of their income can be saved or invested rather than spent to consume for goods and services. This, of course, made inequality look smaller than in previous reports. But this is a useful new estimate as long as we recognize the differing estimates of poverty and inequality.[6] Another problem was that in the early 1990s some parts of Cambodia were still controlled by the Khmer Rouge and unaccessible. To get an overall picture of poverty in Cambodia, the World Bank made an estimate of poverty rates for these Khmer Rouge areas. It now seems that the estimates of poverty in those Khmer Rouge–controlled areas during the early 1990s were too high, thus making it look like poverty for all of Cambodia dropped somewhat between the early 1990s and 2008.[7]

A final point of the above: In part, the fieldwork in all regions of Cambodia, central and southern Vietnam, the northeast of Thailand, and the flat Mekong basin areas of Laos, was conducted to gain more qualitative information about conditions of poverty and standards of living, and to hear what hundreds of people in these villages and slums had to say about their lives and problems. For the most part, this fieldwork confirmed that the statistics about poverty across these countries are pretty accurate. But these qualitative observations and interviews from the fieldwork indicate that poverty and the future for the poor in Cambodia compared to other less developed countries is worse than the broad statistical surveys suggest. In other ways, however, the fieldwork indicated that poverty is not as bad in Cambodia compared to most sub–Saharan African countries. The fieldwork in these Southeast Asian countries also led to a conclusion that will surprise most people: In one respect, poverty can actually be worse in the United States compared to Cambodia. Before we turn to these nuances, however, we need a more detailed examination of the situation in Cambodia and some of the basic poverty figures.

Poverty in Cambodia

It was noted earlier that one historian of Cambodia offered the conclusion that people in rural Cambodia are probably living much like they did 1,000 years ago. This takes us back to the Angkor period. The nobility, of course, lived quite well back then, as nobility have been able to do all over the world. Throughout history the nobility have expropriated the production of the masses and required them to provide all kinds of services, like building temples such as Angkor Wat. Some 1,000 years ago Cambodian peasants worked hard in the fields, plowed with water buffalo, and carried their cargos of whatever kind in water buffalo carts. The archeological record shows their diet was meager and often not enough. Many people died early from diseases borne by mosquitoes. They lived in very small huts of wood and rice straw on stilts providing protection from high water, reptiles, and rodents, and giving them a shaded open area under the hut to cook and relax during the heat of the day.[8]

Traveling from village to village in all regions of Cambodia today, one sees that the above description is pretty much what it is still like. The vast majority of people are still without electricity or fresh water. Most villages have a TV run by a modified car battery, often owned by the local school-teacher who is paid only a little more than village farmers are able to produce. A few villages have wells, usually drilled by an NGO such as World Vision.[9] Most other villages get their water the old-fashioned way — buckets in rivers, mud holes, or streams, and big jars catching rain water. There are a few bicycles and motorbikes in rural Cambodia, but very few compared to neighboring countries. There are almost no cars or trucks, and when they are seen, license plates indicate they are coming from urban areas. Moving through rural Cam-bodia by car means often pulling to the side of the road to get around the traffic of water buffalo carts carrying goods and people from village to village. Cooking utensils are few and primitive (though iron and other metals except bronze were not common 1,000 years ago), and the kitchen is a little hearth where gathered firewood or, if more "affluent," some charcoal is burning. The biggest contrast to 1,000 years ago is cheap textile production the British began with the Industrial Revolution. T-shirts and blue jeans are common, though women are still often seen wearing skirts made locally with weaving technology going back to the Angkor period.

The point again is that there is little reason to question the statement that most of these village people are at a standard of living little higher than people in the area some 1,000 years ago. This is also to say that one is not surprised to read the World Bank figures from around 2004 to 2006 telling

Water buffalo on muddy roads in Cambodia.

us rural poverty in Cambodia (using that consumption measure of poverty) has gone down only very slightly (or not at all as noted above) since the early 1990s. If the World Bank had poverty figures for more years in the past they could have perhaps written something like "Well, it has come down somewhat since A.D. 1000."

The Poverty Data

First the worst news, but with some qualifications below. One of the most useful international poverty comparisons available since the World Bank's calculation of purchasing power parity (PPP) is the percentage of a nation's population living on less than $1 a day and $2 a day.[10] With data from the late 1990s, Cambodia looked bad, with 34 percent of the population living under less that $1 per day and 78 percent living on less than $2 per day. With the more recent recalculation of the World Bank's PPP figures to update price changes since the first calculation in the early 1990s, Cambodia looks much worse. With 2004 data, some 66 percent of the Cambodian population are

Table 3-1:
Gross National Product per Capita, Economic Development, and Poverty Rates*

	Per capita gross national income (PPP, 2008)	Annual % GNP growth (2000–2008)	% At/below poverty level (2003–2005)†	Percent below‡	
				$1 per day	$1.25 per day (2003–2008)
Cambodia	$1,820	9.7	35%	66% (2004)	40%
Thailand	5,990	5.2	12	<2 (2005)	<2
Malaysia	13,740	5.1	---	<2 (2005)	<2
Indonesia	3,830	5.2	16	7.5 (2002)	21
Philippines	3,900	5.1	25	14.8 (2003)	23
Vietnam	2,700	7.7	29	---	22
Laos	2,060	6.9	33	27 (2002)	44
Burma	1,290	---	---	---	---

Gini Coefficients for Inequalities§

	Income inequality	Land inequality
Cambodia	.42	.69
Thailand	.42	.47
Malaysia	.49	—
Indonesia	.34	.46
Philippines	.44	.57
Vietnam	.34	.50
Laos	.35	.41

*Sources: World Bank *World Development Report*, 2008 and 2010, and World Bank *World Development Indicators, Poverty Data Supplement, 2008*; United Nations *Human Development Report, 2008/2009*.

†Includes estimates of value of income from family production such as the family's own agricultural production, which is not the case with the World Bank $1 per day or $1.25 per day estimates.

‡Based on new World Bank PPP calculations from 2005; see World Bank *World Development Indicators, Poverty Data Supplement, 2008*.

§A Gini coefficient is a statistical measure of inequality, which runs from 0.0 when there is perfect equality to 1.0 when one person or family has all of what is being measured such as income, wealth, or land.

estimated to live on less that $1 per day, with 2007 data showing 68 percent live on less than $2 per day. This recalculation of prices by the World Bank did not affect figures for Laos and Thailand a great deal, and sorry to say the World Bank has never published $1- and $2-a-day figures for Vietnam, though we do have their new $1.25-per-day figures which are already about half of those for Cambodia and Laos (see Table 3-1 above). As of 2007 data for Laos, 44 percent of the population lived on less than $1.25 per day and 77 percent on less than $2 per day. Data from 2007 for Thailand show less than 2 percent live on less that $1 per day and 11.5 percent of the population live on less than $2 per day. For all of Southeast Asia, the percentage living on less than $1 per day was almost 40 percent in 1990. As of 2005 that figure was down to 18.9 percent, and would be much lower, of course, if Cambodia and Burma had reduced poverty like the other countries.[11]

Why the big jump in the World Bank's measure of extreme poverty (less that $1 per day) for Cambodia? Most obviously it is the jump in the cost of living that Cambodians are bitching about these days, mostly driven by urban economic growth in recent years. Price changes have been much less in Laos and Thailand. The 2004 international poverty estimates for Cambodia put the county in league with the poorest African countries. For example, the $1- and $2-per-day figures in the 2008 World Bank Development Report for the Central African Republic are 66 percent and 84 percent of the population, 45 and 79 percent for Ghana, 71 and 92 percent for Nigeria, 60 and 88 percent for Rwanda, 58 and 90 percent for Tanzania, and 54 percent and 78 percent for Haiti in the Caribbean.[12] The Cambodian comparison to the poorest countries in Africa, however, can be misleading.

We can consider a typical village in central Cambodia. Like most rural Cambodians, the people in this village are mainly rice farmers. During an interview with one family in this village, for example, there was only the mother (we can call her Sokha) and two-year-old child at home when the interview began. Sokha was in her early 30s. Her rather attractive face was already darkened and a bit rough after years of work in the hot rice fields. She wore a brown print shirt and clashing bright orange and blue skirt of cheap *batik* cotton material of the region that day. Sokha explained that her two-year-old daughter had been ill, so she was not working with the others in the rice fields that day. Around the half-mud, half-grass area where their house stood were the usual scrawny chickens busily pecking at the ground, and one small cow. Their house was about 10 by 20 feet, on the usual stilts, with the four walls and roof made of woven straw. There was no furniture inside or outside of the house. The "kitchen" was a little fireplace on the ground under the house, with a couple of pots. A rusty old bicycle was the only other man-made object to be seen. The most striking scene around this village was the bright green vegetation, mostly from their rice fields and coconut trees, in contrast to the red dirt and mud, much the same color as the soil in Oklahoma and northern Vietnam. As usual in these villages, Sokha and her family had no electricity or running water, and certainly no appliances, no TV or radio in the house. It was the rainy season, thus a small stream was between the dirt road and her house, with only two bamboo poles lying across the stream as a foot bridge. It was difficult to imagine that seven people lived in this hut, and equally hard to believe the house could keep out much rain.

Sokha and her husband have five children, the oldest a 13-year-old girl they are trying to keep in school like two other children of school age. As is common in this village, and most others throughout Cambodia, this family had 1.5 hectares of land, which without fertilizer or irrigation in this part of Southeast Asia is not quite sufficient to grow enough rice to feed the family

Sokha, her house and children.

for a whole year. This family had 2 hectares of land a couple of years ago but had to sell their two water buffalo and a half-hectare of land to pay doctor bills for the young child at home with Sokha that morning. They must now rent a water buffalo from neighbors to plow their rice paddy.

To make ends meet, three months of the year Sokha said they can harvest some sugar palm growing on their land and sell it for about 3,000 riel per day (about $0.75) for those three months. With their usual rice yield per year Sokha can only afford to serve about 3 kilo of rice a day for the whole family in two meals per day. When she can she buys about .5 kilo of fish per day for the family, which costs 2,500 riel a day (or about 50 cents).[13] Sokha also has to pay extra for their three children to go to school; while primary school is supposed to be free, in reality almost all Cambodians are forced to pay for part of their children's schooling because teachers' salaries are so low, in rural areas not much more than the average income of rice farmers. This cost per day for all three of her children is about 100 riel each, for a total of just under $0.10 per day, a sum which adds up quickly for people with as little money as Sokha's family.

Sitting on a crudely made bamboo table in front of the wood and straw hut, talking with Sokha that morning, other village people started coming in from their rice fields for lunch. Her husband arrived with two other young men carrying crude hoes; other villagers were then coming along the muddy, potholed road in front of the house on water buffalo carts, three or four on old bicycles. No motorized vehicles were in sight. Looking down the road at the "traffic" of water buffalo carts and old bicycles, a TV antenna could be seen in the distance. There was an old black and white TV that this family ran off of a modified car battery they could periodically get recharged in the small city about 10 miles away.

Other families in this village reported other ways they make a little money to add to their less than adequate rice yield per year. One family, for example, sells chickens and frogs in the nearest little town to get about 30,000 to 40,000 riel per year (about $10 per year). A few days earlier families in another village about 25 miles from Sokha told similar stories. Over a few months it became apparent that families in most villages in Cambodia could not grow enough rice to feed their families, much less any rice left over to sell on the market. For extra money, because the other village a few miles from Sokha is closer to a river that fills up with water coming from the big Tonle Sap River during the rainy season, they could fish three months of the year and make just under $1 per day for many days of those three months of the rainy season. Other families gather and sell coconuts and firewood they collect in the forest around them.

The first point of the above description of average poor villages all over Cambodia is that the World Bank figure of about 66 percent living on less than $1 per day is certainly believable. Almost 90 percent of Cambodia's population live in rural areas, some in villages poorer than the ones described above, some in villages that are a bit better off and able to sell a little rice on the market every year. But, the second point of the above descriptions is that most of the poor village people in Cambodia (though the percentage is shrinking fast) have some land of their own and are able to grow *almost* enough rice to feed their families. They hustle in any way they can to bring in a little cash to buy a few things like fish to add to their diet and cheap clothing to cover themselves. The same cannot always be said for people in the poorest African countries who periodically die of hunger in the thousands and hundreds of thousands. While a useful tool in comparing poverty around the world, this is where the "less than $1 per day" international poverty measure must be considered in relation to specific situations for people in differing regions of the globe. The $1- or $1.25-a-day per capita income figures, for example, do not consider whether people have their own land which can provide them with some food above what this cash income might buy for them.

Other poverty estimates presented by international agencies such as the World Bank and United Nations are based on local definitions of poverty and consider the value of basic necessities they are able to produce themselves, mostly food, as well as cash income. Two recent Cambodian poverty reports from the World Bank office in Phnom Penh were published in 2006 and 2007.[14] Both reports provide various poverty estimates using different measures. In both reports, poverty is estimated using a food plus non-food consumption poverty line set at about $0.50 per day per person. The first report estimated that poverty came down from 47 percent of the population in 1994 to 35 percent of the population in 2004. However, most of this drop was in urban areas, primarily in Phnom Penh, while some rural areas actually had poverty *increases* during this ten-year period. And as noted above, the 1994 figure is likely misleading because Khmer Rouge–controlled areas (thus, inaccessible to researchers) were assumed poorer than they actually were.

The World Bank staff in Phnom Penh has also calculated what they call a "food poverty line." This poverty line is based on the consumption of 2,100 calories per person a day, or the cost of buying this much nutrition per day if it is not produced by the family. They admit that people in cities who have only enough to buy this much nutrition per day must spend some of this money on non-food items. But this "food poverty line" does give us a rough measure of hunger. The picture presented with this measure of poverty is a little better, but not much. In 1994 the level of food poverty in rural areas of Cambodia was 22 percent of the population, compared to 6 percent in Phnom Penh, and 17 percent for all other urban areas. By 2004 the percentage of people falling below this "food poverty level" had improved slightly — down to 17 percent of the population in rural areas, 3 percent in Phnom Penh, and 13 percent for other cities. (Some local NGO staff and government officials, though, criticize the figures for Phnom Penh, saying the study has missed many of the homeless people not officially registered as living in Phnom Penh.)

The 2008 World Bank *World Development Report* tells us Cambodia has to rely on about 27,000 tons of donated grain per year. But despite this level of "food poverty," while the country imports about $76 million of food per year, the most productive Cambodian farmers are still exporting about $50 million of food per year. Prime Minister Hun Sen was proud to announce recently that Cambodia is among the world's top 10 exporters of rice. But what he didn't say is less than 30 percent of Cambodian farmers have enough rice to export after feeding their families, while the other 70 percent of Cambodian farmers *do not grow enough to feed their families*. In other words, while a significant percent of the population is unable to feed themselves properly the country is exporting food to richer countries. Most of the small drop in poverty in rural Cambodia has come in areas like Battambang province in west central Cambodia where, in 2007, we saw farmers loading tons of rice on trucks for sale on the world market (through Vietnamese merchants).[15] This area is the traditional rice basket of Cambodia which has finally recovered since major fighting between government forces and the Khmer Rouge stopped in the early 1990s.

The bottom 20 percent of people in Cambodia (almost all rural people) had their consumption of food and non-food items increase only 8 percent in this 10-year period, according to a 2006 World Bank report.[16] The top 20 percent of Cambodians had their food and non-food consumption increase by an average of 45 percent, while even the middle 20 percent of Cambodians in terms of consumption had an increase of only 1,696 riel to 2,077 riel per day per person between 1994 and 2004, an increase of about $0.10 per day. Obviously, as these figures suggest, the gap between the higher- and lower-income people in Cambodia is increasing rapidly, and this is largely a rural vs. urban gap. But inequality *within* rural areas is also increasing rapidly. The primary reason is almost certainly due to the growing loss of land by many poor farmers and the growth of big farms owned by elites who have been able to legally or illegally increase their land holdings in the past 10 years. As we will see in a later chapter, many of these rich Cambodians, along with the Cambodian government, are leasing the land to foreign agribusiness corporations after they evict Cambodian peasant families. In 2006, for example, more than 1,000 families were displaced after violent protest over eviction from a 8,000-plus hectare plot that was taken over by a big sugar corporation. In 2010 another 1,000 families were being evicted in the same area while the government was leasing this land to the wife of a leading senator in Prime Minister Hun Sen's Cambodian People's Party for $1 per hectare.[17]

This trend of land loss among Cambodia's small peasant farmers is dangerous because statistical and case studies show that economic development is *very difficult to sustain* with such raising inequality within a country. The World Bank's *World Development Report, 2006* was devoted to the issue of how increasing inequality in less developed countries will make economic development much less sustainable. More recently, the World Bank's *World Development Report, 2008* was devoted to why sustainable economic development is only likely when the development of agriculture for small farmers goes along equally with economic development in urban areas. *Cambodia fails badly on both issues.* As we will consider in more detail below (also see Table 3-1 above), these Cambodian figures are in contrast to only small increases in inequality in Vietnam and Laos, two countries about as poor as or poorer than Cambodia 10 or 15 years ago. In Vietnam the level of poverty in the rural areas has dropped by some 50 percent in the last 15 years compared to a 10 to 15 percent drop in the Cambodian poverty rate, and probably much less of a drop given the questionable poverty figures from the early 1990s.

Other Indicators of Poverty

There are other indicators of poverty conditions worth mentioning before leaving this subject. The United Nation's *Human Development Report, 2009,* for example, lists several troubling statistics for Cambodia. Some 33 percent of Cambodians are estimated to be undernourished, compared to 19 percent in Laos and 16 percent in Vietnam. The International Food Policy Research Institute ranks the world's 88 least developed countries in terms of what it calls a "Global Hunger Index" made up of the overall level of undernourishment in a country, malnutrition among children, and child mortality.[18] In 2008 Cambodia ranked 64th out of 88 countries, with all the countries ranked below Cambodia located in sub–Saharan Africa except India, Haiti, Bangladesh, and Tajikistan. Thailand ranked 23rd on this 2008 "Global Hunger Index," while Vietnam ranked 32nd, and Laos ranked 57th.

As for indicators of poor economic development, only 17 percent of Cambodians have "improved sanitation" (meaning mostly indoor plumbing), compared to 30 percent in Laos, 61 percent in Vietnam, and 99 percent in Thailand. Only 41 percent of Cambodians have access to "improved water sources" compared to 51 percent in Laos, 67 percent in Vietnam, and 99 percent in Thailand. Both recent World Bank poverty reports which were focused on Cambodia (described above) note that one bright spot for Cambodia has been improvements in access to primary school education. As informants liked to point out, now almost every village in Cambodia has a primary school within walking distance. As a consequence, the UN Human Development Report lists primary school attendance at about 99 percent for Cambodia, 84 percent for Laos, and 94 percent for Vietnam. Several village schoolteachers around Cambodia, however, claimed this information is misleading because, while officially enrolled, their pupils miss many days of school every term to help their parents work in the fields.[19] In addition to this, all village people with children who were interviewed complained the extra money demanded by schoolteachers per day meant they couldn't afford to send their children to school every day. Still, the literacy rate for Cambodia has improved, and is now about 74 percent, compared to 69 percent for Laos, and 90 percent for Vietnam.[20]

Indicators of health, however, are dismal in Cambodia. Life expectancy at birth is about 56 years in Cambodia today compared to 62 years in Laos and 73 years in Vietnam. The infant mortality rate is still high at 98 deaths per 1,000 births in Cambodia compared to 62 in Laos, and only 16 in Vietnam. The number of physicians per 100,000 people is only 16 in Cambodia compared to 53 for Vietnam (with no data for Laos). The percentage of births attended by a "health care professional" is about 32 percent for Cambodia compared to 19 percent for Laos, and 85 percent for Vietnam. This 32 percent figure seemed surprisingly high at first, but then thinking back over the two years of fieldwork and interviews in villages in every region of Cambodia, it became obvious the data provided by Cambodia used a rather loose definition of "health care professional."

Indeed, traveling through rural Cambodia shows that healthcare is one of the major shortcomings compared to other countries in the region. In almost every village in Cambodia there are complaints about the lack of medical care and the loss of land or water buffalos to pay for health care. Spending levels on health care by the Cambodian government are clearly misleading. Several studies have shown, and some high government officials have admitted

Rural health clinic.

in confidence that a small percentage of government healthcare dollars actually get to patients. Several government officials admitted that as much as 60 percent of healthcare funding is lost in mismanagement and corruption. The situation is so bad that a European-funded NGO has set up a field experiment in an attempt to overcome these problems. This NGO pays money directly to some government-run healthcare districts in Cambodia, while in other districts the NGO has taken complete control of the clinics and hospitals.[21] The latter have proved much more efficient in providing health care and improving healthcare statistics.

One clinic in the far north of Cambodia, along the Mekong River coming down from Laos, comes to mind as an example. This rather rundown little clinic is almost two hours from the provincial city and, so they claim, serves about 30 villages in the area. Later, however, Cambodian officials with more knowledge about healthcare organization in Cambodia thought the claim must be exaggerated; the reality is more like an average of one small clinic for every 10,000 people in Cambodia. Still, this particular clinic in northern Cambodia was one of the best clinics visited in rural Cambodia, and obviously in one of the districts where the European NGO has funded the operation. Inside the clinic one first sees the usual examining room, then an office for record keeping, a small room with a stainless steel examination table, a room which served as their small pharmacy, and a somewhat larger room with two beds where patients could stay for a few nights if need be. The place was covered with government health education posters about not smoking, drinking too much, the danger of mosquitoes, and the need to use condoms to prevent HIV infection. Despite looking rather dingy and very run down, they had made attempts to keep the place rather clean.

Arriving at the clinic one Sunday afternoon, no one seemed to be around except a couple of young boys scraping the old wooden building in preparation for a new coat of paint. After asking to speak with some medical personnel, the boys pointed to a small wooden building in back, from which three young girls soon emerged. They explained they were "midwives" at the clinic, living in this small house in back. After introductions these girls seemed excited and ran back into their lodging, emerging a few minutes later wearing their more official-looking pink smocks. There were no patients that afternoon, so these "midwives" could sit and talk for a while. The closest doctor lived in the provincial city about two hours away. There were four other midwives attached to this clinic in addition to themselves, with four nurses in this part of the province on call. These midwives had not finished high school, though had taken a several-month course to become midwives.

These girls in their late teens and early 20s are the frontline "medical professionals," assisting child births, stitching up severe cuts, mending broken bones, and tending to all more serious emergencies until an ambulance can arrive from the provincial city hospital. One should not take away from the dedication of these young girls or their courage in performing such a life-and-death job. It was only two years ago that medical care at their clinic became free to village people in the area, but they didn't know why. They knew nothing of the NGO now funding health care in the area. Drugs, however, were not free but at a lower cost than elsewhere in Cambodia. These girls showed real concern about the desperate poverty of people in the area, saying with sad looks that they sometimes paid for drugs out of their own pockets rather than make their patients do without. Interviews with people in several villages in this area indicated that these village people had no idea how lucky they were compared to most other rural people in Cambodia who have nothing like this clinic with free health care.

But They Look So Happy?

During slide-show presentations to make certain points about conditions in Cambodia, a common reaction is "But they look so happy?" The question is actually an excellent one. First of all, like Thailand with its slogan "the land of smiles," Cambodians are extremely polite people, almost always greeting others with smiles. Most foreigners, however, don't realize there are many subtle differences among smiles in this part of the world, some conveying dislike, even mild anger, or embarrassment, as well as a friendly greeting. Secondly, in many remote Cambodian villages they have never seen a white guy, so in some ways it was quite a spectacle to see a visiting American researcher, with many families coming out of their homes to see what was going on.

But are they really happy? A beginning answer might be, if they have enough food for their families, if their children are healthy and can get good medical care if not healthy, and if their lives are not in danger from political repression, then, yes, we can say they can be relatively happy. But unfortunately in Cambodia today these conditions are not in abundance.

Some anthropologists a few years ago compared the lifestyle of Native Americans living on what is now Manhattan Island several hundred years ago with New York City residents today. The Native Americans, they believed, come out ahead; with a low population density, these early Americans had abundant food which took only part of their day to gather, had no pollution, lived fairly long lives before the Europeans brought all kinds of germs, and had none of the stress Americans usually experience today. More recently a

Scandinavian sociologist designed a questionnaire to measure "happiness" in rich nations around the world. Scandinavian countries came out on top, with Americans pretty far down the ranking. When asked why Scandinavians ranked so high, he responded that his questions indicated Scandinavians learned to expect and want less.

The French sociological master, Emile Durkheim, back in the 19th century explained much the same thing. An American sociological master, Robert Merton, in the mid–20th century expanded upon these ideas. If a person's means and goals are in sync, that is, if people have come to aspire to things that are quite attainable, then their means and goals are relatively in line, and the attained goals make people happy. People with goals way beyond their means to attain are usually the most unhappy. Americans are taught to "reach for the sky," "anyone growing up in a log cabin can still become a CEO," etc., etc. Visiting Buddhist monks from Thailand have told of their surprise at how unhappy and depressed many Californians seem to be given their standards of living and secure environment.

Back to remote Cambodian village people: One must admit it is refreshing to be with people who for the most part seem less stressed compared to Americans whose pursuit of more and more material possession pushes them to work longer and longer hours, often neglecting their children who can end up with many emotional problems because of it. Few people realize the U.S. teenage suicide rate has been going up dramatically and is among the highest in the industrial world. For the typical Cambodian peasant family in remote parts of the country, *if* they have enough to feed their families, *if* their children are not sick, *if* they have a secure environment, then, yes, they can be comparatively happy. Sadly, these are not conditions many Cambodian villagers experience to a high degree today. And there are the estimates that 50 to 60 percent of Cambodians over 30 years of age have mental problems because of what they experienced during the Khmer Rouge period.

Added to all of this is the spread of television. Most remote Cambodian villages have at least one television run from a modified car battery. The village young people are now growing up with the images of rich Phnom Penh people they see on TV, and even more glittering scenes if they pick up channels showing Thai soap operas. These TV programs jack up the goals of village teenagers in Cambodia way beyond their means. These poor teenagers are willing to leave their villages and work in some of the worst sweatshops in Phnom Penh to pursue their dreams. It can be much worse in the case of many pretty young girls who become tricked into, or seduced into, the sex industry in Cambodia, Thailand, or beyond. An old Thai friend, now a university president, use to work with several different NGOs to keep such things from happening in

Thai villages. One of their techniques was to bring village headmen to the slums of Bangkok and the worst brothels so they could go back to their villages and describe to their young people how they might end up. He admitted this technique didn't work very well, which is confirmed when walking though any of the brothel areas in Bangkok teeming with young girls from the countryside.

"But they look so happy?" In one fundamental way, *compared to many of the poor in richer countries, especially the United States*, yes, many of these poor Cambodian village people are happier or, perhaps one should say, at least more secure. In terms of their actual material existence, unless they are among the one million or so homeless poor in the United States, the Cambodian poor are at a much lower standard of living. As noted above, the Cambodian national poverty line is set at around 50 cents per day per person, though we must recognize the cost of living is much lower than in advanced industrial nations. But even more importantly, the Cambodian poor often have one major advantage: They have a strong extended family system where even quite distant relatives feel a strong obligation to take care of family. This is one aspect of what social scientists call "social capital" in contrast to material capital such as property and money.

A few years ago, after Hurricane Katrina blew away parts of New Orleans, the whole world was amazed that the mighty and rich U.S. government did an extremely poor job handling the disaster. Several years later, many of New Orleans' poor are still homeless and jobless, without much hope of picking up their old lives. The BP Gulf oil blowout in 2010 is expanding the damage to many of these people's lives. Considering some of the major contrasts between the American and Thai societies, one can speculate about what would happen if Bangkok had been hit like New Orleans. The answer is quite clear; people made homeless and jobless in Bangkok would simply filter back into ancestral villages to be given a place to stay, a place to work in the fields, and the food they need for themselves and their families as long as it was needed. Many other examples come to mind. When a women and her child is left alone because her husband has died or abandon them, they are taken in by village relatives in Southeast Asian countries. A retired sociologist from Chulalongkorn University heading an NGO serving people in the biggest slum in Bangkok, Klong Toey, a slum with over 100,000 people living in a southern port area of the city, once explained how it works. The 1997 Asian economic crisis was well underway when he was asked what was happening in Klong Toey; "Is the number of homeless and jobless people growing in Klong Toey because of massive job losses in Bangkok?" He seemed rather surprised by the question: "Oh no, the number stays about the same. Many people filter back into their home villages as others come into Klong Toey still hoping they might eventually find another job, only to filter back into the villages with relatives like the others if they can't find a job in Bangkok."

The point is that the Cambodian poor often have an advantage over many of the American poor because of a stronger family system. This, however, is one of the few advantages the Cambodian poor have over some people in rich Western countries. The Cambodian poor live in a country with growing inequality, with their children increasingly ill and no way to pay for hospital care except to sell their land and/or water buffalo. Future prospects for jobs and poverty reduction are being destroyed by an inapt and corrupt government. For many years foreign aid has equaled about one-half of the total GNP of the country each year, much of which has gone missing. There is a big increase in the percentage of Cambodians who are now landless. Some 150,000 people in rural and urban Cambodia have had their homes stolen and have been forcefully moved to areas where they have no agricultural land or jobs. People are losing life and limb to land mines while working in their fields. A majority of Cambodians over 30 years of age today, alive during the long civil war with the Khmer Rouge, suffer from various mental problems.

Putting to rest this question of whether they are happy, we can conclude on an ironic note: The rural Cambodian poor are currently less angry about the rising cost of food and energy than most poor people around the world. The rural poor of Cambodia mostly grow their own food, export very little, and while they must buy a little extra food, it is often from neighbors who also have been little affected by the rising food prices. Rising gasoline prices are hurting small farmers in Thailand and elsewhere in the region. Oil and gasoline costs much the same no matter what country one lives in. Rural Cambodians have far fewer motor vehicles than rural people in other countries around them. They plow their fields with water buffalo, they transport goods and themselves in water buffalo carts. Most Cambodian small farmers could never afford fertilizer or other chemicals for their crops, so the rising prices of these things impact them only slightly, if at all. But as we will see in more detail below, such primitive conditions are a very small compensation for the other problems the Cambodian poor face to a greater extent than others in the region, and compared to most of the world's poor.

To better understand the poverty and related problems of most people in Cambodia today, the next few chapters will take the reader on a mental journey through all regions of Cambodia, as well as some of the areas in Thailand, Vietnam, and Laos where, by their country's standards, they are also considered among the poorest. Through these people's stories, one can obtain a better sense of why, besides Burma and North Korea, and despite the rapid economic growth in the capital city, Cambodia remains one of the most troubled countries in Asia today. The final chapters of this book will attempt to explain why Cambodia has a future less bright than her neighbors, again with the exception of Burma today.

CHAPTER 4

Cambodia's Poor,
The Villages

Cambodia is primarily a county of small farmers on the mostly flat plains between Thailand, Vietnam, and mountainous Laos to the north. With only two small mountain ranges in the northeast and south-southwest, Cambodia is host to mighty rivers snaking their way through the country's heartland seeking an outlet to the sea. It was the Mekong River flowing down from Tibet, China, Thailand and Laos, and the wide Tonle Sap Lake and Tonle Sap River in the west central part of the country which kept some one million people fed during the Angkor civilization some one thousand years ago.

With a similar environment, approximately half Thailand's territory, but only 14 million Cambodians compared to 65 million in Thailand, one would think Cambodia has the capacity to close in on Thailand's position as the world's number one rice exporter. Poor Cambodia, however, cannot even feed itself. It is actually Vietnam with much less agricultural land and 84 million people that is closing in on Thailand's position as champion rice exporter. Anyone spending much time in Cambodia's rural areas would agree these peasant farmers are extremely hardworking people. The problem is mostly a lack of infrastructure (see Table 4-1 on page 63). Over 90 percent of Cambodians are without electricity, almost as many without safe drinking water, and the rural roads are often impassable. While 45 percent of Vietnam's arable crop land is under irrigation, the figure for Cambodia is only 7 percent. Even poor Laos has more than twice the percent of irrigated arable land compared to Cambodia. A sad conclusion one gets from traveling through the country is not just how much poverty there is in Cambodia, but how easily one could remedy the situation. A little medical care and clean drinking water so their children don't get sick and die so often, a little water control in their fields, roads to get agricultural products to market, and a little money to buy a $60

Table 4-1
Comparative Conditions for Agriculture
and Rural Infrastructure*

	Health care	*Fresh water* % of pop.	*Improved* *sanitation*	*Irrigation* % Farm land
Cambodia	almost none+	41	17	7
Thailand	basic health care free	99	99	31
Vietnam	basic health care free++	85	61	45
Laos	—	51	30	19

	% Roads *paved*	*Fertilizer* Kg per hectare	*Electric power* Kwh per capita	*Electricity* % of pop. with
Cambodia	6.3	5	15	9
Thailand	98.0	133	1988	99
Vietnam	25	324	573	84
Laos	14.4	—	179	—

*Sources: World Bank, *World Development Report, 2008*; United Nations, *Human Development Report, 2008*; World Bank, *Sustaining Growth in a Challenging Environment, Cambodian Country Economic Memorandum*, 2009.

+ Foreign NGOs have experimental programs for health care in a few regions of Cambodia. They are testing policies of funding local government clinics or funding clinics run completely by the NGO.

++ Outpatient clinic visits for minor injuries or illness costs around $3, though hospital stays can cost around $700. There is low-cost annual health insurance for about $70 per year which cuts hospital costs in half.

bag of fertilizer a year; again and again, all over the country these are the things most village people say what they need. Instead, what more and more Cambodian farm families are facing is the loss of their small amounts of land either to pay medical bills or because of "land grabs." Between 1993 and 2004 the percentage of landless peasants in Cambodia increased from 3 percent to 23 percent, with little doubt the percentage has increased at a higher rate since 2004.[1] The contrast to Vietnam, Laos, and Thailand where land inequality is increasing only slightly, if at all, is striking.

Central Cambodia

Almost all peasant farmers in Cambodia grow rice. While they may grow fruits and vegetables, and raise some farm animals such as pigs, chickens, and water buffalo, they are primarily rice farmers. But the map of annual rice yields by province provided by the World Food Programe report of 2005 shows big variations around Cambodia.[2] The three most productive provinces are Battambang in west central Cambodia, and Kompong Cham and Prey

Veng in the southeast. Five other provinces around these two areas are at the second level of rice yields, with provinces in central Cambodia much further behind. Provinces in the north and northeast are at the bottom, as is Pailin on the Thai border, which has yet to fully recover after being one of the two last Khmer Rouge strongholds until the end of the 1990s.

We will begin our exploration of central Cambodia in Kompong Chhnang province, a province just northwest of Phnom Penh with a medium to low level of rice yield. The provincial city of Kompong Chhnang is rather typical for Cambodia. A few main roads running through the city are paved, while most are not. Motorbikes far outnumber cars and trucks, which are almost completely taken over by water buffalo carts soon after leaving the city for one of the villages. The center of town has the usual dusty Chinese-style shop houses with a store or shop of some kind for the family business on the ground floor and family living quarters on the second story. Toward the center of town, in this case along the Tonle Sap River, is also the usual open-air market where people from villages many miles away come to buy cooking oil, spices, clothing, tools, toiletries, toys, anything they can't make in the village. Venders with French baguettes staked like pyramids throughout these outdoor markets in Cambodia, as in Laos and Vietnam as well, are one of the nice legacies of colonialism.

Kompong Chhnang City.

As one would expect, village farmers also bring their produce into town, giving some indication of agricultural specialization and productivity for the area. Open-air meat markets always catch the eye; slabs of raw meat lay on wooden tables or hang on racks in the hot sun, keeping venders busy swatting at flies. Because Kompong Chhnang City is on the Tonle Sap River, venders also display various kinds of fish swimming in metal buckets waiting to be taken home for dinner. Large piles of rather anemic-looking corn were stacked along the river front, little wooden boats bringing in more all the time, suggesting corn is one of the local agricultural specialties. In the midst of this market bustle was a river boat docked along the muddy shore with a few Western tourists disembarking onto a rickety platform, apparently on their way to or from Angkor Wat, a five- or six-hour trip up the Tonle Sap River from Phnom Penh.

It is obviously impossible to describe every village and every family interviewed during fieldwork throughout Southeast Asia. But we can consider select villages either because they represent rather typical ones for the particular region of Cambodia, or because of something memorable or particular about certain villages and families in different parts of Cambodia.

The first village selected for interviews is not far off a main paved road running about 200 miles from Phnom Penh to Tonle Sap Lake, with Angkor Wat on the other side. There were just over 140 households in the village. The first family we met consisted of a fairly young mother and father, their five-year-old daughter, and an old aunt living with them. We call the mother and father Tevy and Vatana. Tevy was an orphan when first her father died, and then her mother died of illness a few years later. Tevy was raised by her unmarried aunt whom they are now caring for in her old age. Tevy appeared quite cheerful during our visit, while Vatana never smiled, seemingly rather sad and serious. Tevy's aunt never spoke, mostly watching the young daughter playing with her dog in the yard, who gave the visiting foreigner a big smile whenever eyes met.

Their house was smaller than most in this area; just four wooden polls taking it only three or four feet off the ground, with a floor of bamboo and walls and roof of straw. Four people were obviously rather cramped while sleeping on the bamboo floor at night. With no space for the family under the house during the heat of the day, we sat in an area next to the house with a low bamboo sitting table and a straw roof over our heads, which also served as their kitchen. Vatana wore the usual dark cotton pants and old t-shirt men seem to wear in villages throughout Cambodia, while Tevy and her aunt usually wore *sarongs* (traditional wraparound skirts) and t-shirts. There were various types of palm trees around the house, a lush green jungle starting not

Villagers Tevy (right) and Vatana (far left).

far from the white sand around their house where a few chickens pecked at whatever they could find. As is usual in most villages all over Cambodia, there were no motor vehicles round their house, not even a bicycle, though there were a couple of motorbikes further down the dusty road in this village. In line with other family homes in this and most villages in this part of Cambodia, there were wooden carts to be hitched to water buffalos when the people needed transportation. There was of course no electricity and certainly no appliances needing electricity. Their possessions were quite meager — a few articles of clothing, some old cooking pots, with about the only thing of any value the traditional drums described below.

Tevy and Vatana had less than a hectare of land, land Tevy's aunt took over from her parents after they died.[3] As was the case all over Cambodia, the family was given this land a few years after the Vietnamese pushed out the Khmer Rouge. Also as is the case all over Cambodia, this family mainly grows rice, and typical as well, Vatana said one of their biggest problems is water control.[4] Most often these days they don't get enough rain, then other times too much and the Tonle Sap River a few miles away floods, meaning their rice paddy is also flooded, destroying much of their rice crop. At times the

Tonle Sap River is also a blessing; during a normal rainy season the river swells, bringing water, and fish, close to this village. During this time the fish they catch adds to their diet, and they can even sell some of the fish in the provincial capital bringing them about $0.75 to $1 a day during the rainy season. This is almost their only cash each year, which goes to buy their meager amount of clothing, cooking pots and other things they can't make themselves. Vatana could occasionally make a little money with a rather untypical side profession; he has two rather nice old drums inherited from his father which he plays with a small troupe of traditional musicians at the local temple for special festivals, weddings, and funerals.

While we were talking that day Tevy sent her five-year-old daughter off to collect firewood in the jungle for cooking their main meal of the day. Their water comes from a well in front of another village house about 20 yards away. We later went over to inspect it; there was a concrete wall around it, about two feet high, and sure enough, there was water down there. It was rather muddy, but no doubt much cleaner than water most other village people around Cambodia must drink and use for cooking. We later learned this is one of the few villages that had a well in the area, drilled about three years before by a Western NGO. Tevy and Vatana couldn't remember the name of the NGO at first, but after a little conference with neighbors, one remembered it was World Vision. Another family in this village later said that people from World Vision had also come through the village to give immunizations to children.

As in all other villages in Southeast Asia visited over the next two years, Tevy was asked what would happen if they or their daughter became ill. Where would they go for medical care, and could they afford it? She explained there was a small clinic a few miles away for minor medical attention. Given examples of various injuries and asked about the price of medical care for each, Tevy said the most minor treatments would cost two or three dollars (a substantial amount for the usual 50 cents per day in this area); but she had no idea how they could pay for hospitalization which would have to be in the provincial city. Asked if Cambodian government officials ever came to the village with *any kind* of help, all they could remember were some health workers a year ago giving out information about how to avoid the mosquito-borne dengue fever.[5] Two other families in this village the next day said their children had been very sick from dengue fever. Both sold their paddy land to pay for hospital care, which luckily saved their children's lives. Four days later we saw Tevy and her daughter again along a road outside the village collecting money from travelers to donate to the local temple. At this roadside booth were two bigger-than-life papier-mâché human characters wearing pink and green clothing, dancing to attract the attention of travelers.

On the way to the next village a few days later, as usual, the one-lane dirt road was sometimes crowded with water buffalo carts or farmers herding a dozen or so water buffalos down the middle of the road. The next village was much like others in the area, though smaller with 40 or so households. Like in most other villages these people are rice farmers without enough land to grow sufficient rice for their families. A dozen or so people were lined up in their rice fields just outside the village, wading in water and bent over transplanting bright green rice sprigs. A car coming into the village created a bit of excitement, so several of these people took time out from planting rice to smile and wave. One thing different in this next village, much further off the main road than the first one, were a couple of small concrete bridges and water canals directing water to the paddy fields. Stopping for a closer look one could see a German flag stamped on one concrete bridge with an inscription "Federal Republic of Germany, Flood Repair Project, 2001." In all other regions of Cambodia over the next two years there was seldom any indication of such projects constructed by the Cambodian government as there were from NGOs from Europe or Japan.[6]

Most significant about this next village in Kompong Chhnang province was an interview with an elementary schoolteacher living on the edge of the village. One of the few improvements in rural Cambodia in recent years is that most villages now have an elementary school not too far away, many of these schools built with Japanese government donations. It was a Sunday morning and the teacher's family was sitting next to the main house, in a small wooden structure, with one of the four sides open. It was their kitchen area where two women were making lunch. The schoolteacher's main house was unlike all the others. It was somewhat bigger than other houses, with two bedrooms and a living room, made of concrete and tiled walls and floors in white and pink, instead of the usual wood, bamboo and straw. In the living area were a TV and stereo, powered by a modified car battery. As usual the village had no electricity. Two motorbikes were in the yard, another arrived later with the teacher's oldest daughter driving. While the pay of a government teacher is very low, it was obvious he had much more money than any of the rice farmers in the village. He later said his teaching salary is about $40 per month. His wife runs a kind of open-air, dirt-floor 7–11 serving the village, and they make a little more money from fees the villagers pay to use their little rice mill in a shed next to the house. As the car with a foreigner stopped in front of his house, the teacher could be seen going inside to change into proper "teacher's clothing." As we later sat on the porch of his new house talking for three hours, the teacher, about 35 years old, was dressed in a clean white shirt and dark slacks, with a big stack of papers to grade on a desk next to him.

Over the course of the fieldwork it became obvious that village school-teachers in Cambodia are usually the most knowledgeable about problems and conditions in the village. This is generally more so than village headmen in Cambodia, especially compared to village headmen in Vietnam and Thailand, later fieldwork would show, which is a critical difference and problem for local governance in Cambodia. In Thailand and Vietnam the official headmen are more like small-town mayors (now elected in Vietnam as well as Thailand and Cambodia), with much more detailed information about the village, working more directly with higher levels of government for development planning and problem solving. As will be described in the last chapter, after two years of fieldwork it was obvious this is a key problem for Cambodia. Local government officials in Cambodia have little training or influence in higher levels of government, and thus are extremely inefficient as advocates for the people they should be serving.

This village teacher in central Cambodia told us his elementary school is about two miles away (which we had seen on the road to this village) and has six other teachers serving four villages and about 300 children. He and

Schoolteacher's house and family.

his wife have three children, all girls, 17, 10, and 3 years of age. While he talked, his wife was in an old wooden shack next door preparing food, watching and smiling, showing she had few teeth left, and looked much older than she actually was. After a few minutes the teacher's 17-year-old daughter drove up to the porch on a new motor bike. She had the usual long black hair and was wearing a traditional bright green *sarong* and a black cotton turtleneck top. The teacher said this daughter has one more year of high school, a school located several miles away and thus unaccessible to most village young people who can't afford the extra "unofficial" tuition money and the daily trip by motorbike. He added that his daughter dreams of becoming a doctor so she can help people in Cambodia like the ones in this village. She has very good grades and test scores, but sadly, he said she had no real prospects of fulfilling her dream. There is simply no way the family can afford a university education. And there is no likelihood of a government scholarship which is possible for such bright young ladies in Thailand where young nurses from poor villages who finished high school with good grades can apply for government scholarships covering all expenses to at least become nurses. In return these Thai young people serve four years at a government-run village clinic with low pay, but certainly higher pay than the average pay back in their village. After these four years as a village nurse there is the option of another government scholarship if they are accepted into a medical school. Thinking of this, one is reminded that there are only 17 doctors per 10,000 people in Cambodia compared to 50 or more per 10,000 people in neighboring countries in the region such as Thailand.

Toward the end of talking with this teacher that day, the subject turned to problems in this village. The biggest one, he was certain, is that people are losing their land. Most are so much in debt they can't repay small loans taken out to buy such things as fertilizer or pay medical bills for their children. Most villagers must use local loan sharks and then lose their land which was required as collateral for these loans. We learned later that small loans, like micro-loans, are available in Cambodia from a private bank, with a few foreign NGOs now coming into Cambodia to set up micro-loan programs. But unlike Vietnam, Thailand, and even Laos, banks in Cambodia charges a comparatively high interest rate and requires land as collateral; no collateral is required for most government- or NGO-sponsored micro-loan programs in these other countries.

The discussion then turned to his schoolchildren in villages like this in Cambodia; do they have problems related to drugs and crime? His answer was quick and emphatic: "Oh no, all those problems are in Phnom Penh." In these small villages the children have much more parental supervision and no time or money for such trouble. These problems occur when young people go to big cities like Phnom Penh seeking jobs that don't exist in these small villages. The biggest problem in the village, he thought, other than ill health and poverty, is poor school attendance. They miss many days of school each year to help their parents work in the fields.

Several other families in the same village later confirmed all the teacher had said. Again and again there were stories about dengue fever and the medical cost if their children must enter a hospital in the provincial city. Every year three or four children must spend a few days in the hospital to save their lives. This costs the family about $75. One hectare of land in this part of Cambodia sells for about $100. We asked people in this village if Cambodian healthcare workers have been trying to do anything about the dengue fever problem, perhaps giving out mosquito nets or educating people about how to reduce the threat such as minimizing stagnate water. "No, there is no help from the Cambodian government" was the usual reply. Some people, however, remembered that World Vision had recently come through the village with an education campaign about dengue fever.

Finally, in this village and others in the province, another common response to questions about their biggest problems was flooding. They need water control. They either have too much or too little water. The Cambodian government provides no help with this. There are only a few places one sees anything being done, such as the canal and concrete bridge with the little German flag stamped upon it upon entering this village.

West Central Cambodia

Returning to Cambodia for another round of fieldwork after similar work in central Vietnam, first there were interviews with government officials, union leaders, and NGO people in Phnom Penh, interviews that will be detailed in a later chapter. The original plan was to travel by domestic airlines or train to the far provincial cities in the west, from there renting a car or motorbikes to villages. Cambodian assistants laughed at the plan. New maps of Cambodia showed the old provincial airports and rail lines. There was no mention on the maps that these had not been functional for years. We later saw the central railway station in Phnom Penh full of rusting rail cars which hadn't been used in decades. A few months later we saw the provincial airport in Stung Treng Provence, in the far north. It was where the map said it should be, but cows were grazing on the potholed runway, and the little airport terminal had partially collapsed.

So it would all be by private car. To west-central Cambodia it was first to Battambang, then on to Pailin along the Thai border. It was one of the "roads from hell" described earlier. The forty- to fifty-mile route took almost five hours. Considering that Pailin was one of the last strongholds of the Khmer Rouge, with thousands of former Khmer Rouge officials and soldiers still living there, perhaps the government in Phnom Penh is happy to keep this road almost impassable. We soon learned, however, there have been comfortable relations between the current national government in Phnom Penh and these local Khmer Rouge officials for many years.

Pailin, before 2009, was actually not a province but a super-sized independent municipality not far from the Thai border to the west and otherwise surrounded by the province of Battambang. Pailin's unique status is related to peace deals worked out in the 1990s, with most Pailin government officials, including the governor, former Khmer Rouge. Until 2008, Ieng Sary, or Big Brother number 3 in the Khmer Rouge rank order, lived freely in Pailin. Since the fall of 2008, however, he has been in a Phnom Penh jail awaiting his trial for war crimes. After Kaing Guek Eav, or Duch, was the first convicted in late July 2010, Ieng Sary and three other top Khmer Rouge leaders are next in line for trials, but probably the only others to ever come to trial for the mass murders of almost two million people when the Khmer Rouge were in power between 1975 and 1979.

Pailin is the poorest Cambodian town of its size to be found. A World Bank poverty map indicates up to 70 percent of the people in this area are below the national poverty line, which roughly equates to $0.50 per person per day. A couple of city streets are sort of paved; meaning they look as if they had once been paved but are now pretty much falling apart. It was the dry season and dust was everywhere from trucks and other vehicles passing by. The town square covers a two- or three-square block area that is an open-air farmers' market. Around this center are a few old-style concrete Chinese shop houses with a business on the ground floor and family living quarters up stairs. Except for two hotels, most other buildings are old wooden shacks. Dust covered the outside of the main hotel, stray cows roamed the grounds. The hotel was empty except for members of two de-mining teams funded and supervised by the Dutch government. Their big Land Rovers went out early in the morning and returned at sundown, after which the men could be seen drinking their well-deserved beers in the hotel restaurant.[7]

The most profitable economic activity in the area is limited to gemstone mines, which, along with American CIA founding, kept the Khmer Rouge in business for many years. Agriculture production is primarily for local consumption, though some gets across the border into Thailand. With no other

Pailin.

means of transport to the rest of Cambodia except over the "road from hell," farmers in Pailin said they sell almost no agricultural products in Cambodia. Chapter 1 above noted that most small farmers in the area, and a few big ones, are former Khmer Rouge soldiers who were given land for putting down their weapons in the 1990s. The poorest in the area are former refugees who escaped into Thailand, now landless and working the Khmer Rouge farms. Only one other village in this area was significantly different from what has already been described.

Just outside of Pailin there is a village obviously more prosperous than the others. Or, perhaps more accurately, one part of this village appears more prosperous. There are larger wooden houses clumped together in one part of the village, electricity lines coming in, a couple of satellite dishes, new motorbikes, even a couple of trucks still operative. Stopping first at a compound of wooden buildings, there were several young boys seated around a new TV watching Thai kick boxing. It appeared to be a village community center. The "big boss" and head of household soon appeared wearing dark slacks and a white shirt stained with ink. His face showed a combination of kindness and authority, even nobility. Throughout the interview that morning he was, in fact, rather polite and cheerful, showing deference to a professor from California about his own age.

It was a surprise to learn the big house under construction across the street, the trucks, everything in this part of the village was his, including the big house next door which looked like a community center. It was even more surprising to learn he owns over 40 hectares of land. This compares to an average of one hectare owned by the vast majority of rural Cambodians who are not landless. When asked how he acquired so much land the answer seemed evasive: "Oh, I bought a little here and there from other people over time." Asking my translator for clarification, his response was something like, "let's talk later." That night the translator said he wasn't sure what the landowner meant, but something seemed suspicious. It was the next day we discovered most landowners in Pailin are former Khmer Rouge, something even most educated Cambodians are not aware of. This polite, likable man with an ink-stained shirt was almost certainly a high Khmer Rouge official or army general. Over the next few of days we met other ex–Khmer Rouge soldiers, but found none with land holdings that large.

Perhaps not surprisingly, traveling away from this far western part of Cambodia, there was another unique opportunity in this extremely poor area along the Thai border that involved the world sex industry. On one trip to villages south of Pailin we drove by what looked like an empty school in the middle of rice paddy and fruit orchards. Five long, single-story buildings were arranged in a semicircle, a large vacant courtyard in the middle. Nicely painted in the Cambodian version of "institutional yellow," with no tropical mold on the walls and no landscaping, they were obviously very new.

On the closed gate a sign read, in Khmer and English, "Integrated Women's Empowerment Center of Pailin." As we parked the car for a closer look a guard came running up to the gate, and after a request for interviews we were invited inside. Within minutes the staff of this new institution arrived, explaining it was set to open the following week. The proud staff, two middle-aged women and a man, began a tour which lasted about three hours. The principal of this school explained it is one of three new schools for young girls built and funded by the Japanese government, the other two located in the south and northeast of Cambodia. The Cambodian prime minister and Japanese ambassador were arriving for an opening ceremony next week.

The basic idea behind these three new "women's empowerment" schools is to teach job skills to young girls at risk of falling into the sex industry. One of the five new buildings was designed as a dormitory for 125 teenage girls already selected from poor villages in the area, especially from female-headed households. The other large buildings are classrooms for teaching employable skills. In the first we found about 100 new state-of-the-art sewing machines where girls would be taught tailoring skills. About 50 new weaving looms in the traditional style were in another building, obviously for similar training in a newly revived Cambodian art form. Another building contained all sorts of beauty salon equipment where these girls will be taught hair styling, nail painting and such. Once again, one point of describing this "Integrated Women's Empowerment Center" is that only foreign governments and NGOs are the source. We saw nothing like the government- or domestic-sponsored and -funded programs in Cambodia that one can see all over Thailand and Vietnam.

Battambang

Battambang is one of the largest provinces in Cambodia and agriculturally the most productive. With 140,000 people, the capital is the second largest city in Cambodia, and except for Phnom Penh, had the largest French presence during the colonial period. It was also the seat of the biggest rebellion against the French colonials, put down with huge casualties, all on the Cambodian side.[8] As a consequence of this presence one sees many old crumbling French villas along the river running through the city. It was only in 1907, though, that Battambang was returned to Cambodia through a treaty between the French and Thais. Before this time the city had gone back and forth from Thai and Cambodian control for centuries.

Battambang city is more prosperous than other cities in Cambodia except Phnom Penh and perhaps Siem Reap, but certainly not booming. There are no high-rise buildings, no big factories, no huge hotels or condos, and only a few foreign tourists. The town is primarily sustained by the high level of agricultural production in the area.

Leaving town for interviews in villages one can see why UN and World Bank reports describe this province as one of the richest agricultural areas in Cambodia.[9] But it is not that this part of Cambodia has more irrigation, electricity or any other infrastructure development, but because Battambang has better quality soil and higher than average rainfall. There is the same level of neglect by the central government throughout the province. Few people have electricity (13 percent) or fresh water (21 percent), or decent medical care. The infant mortality rate is about average for Cambodia (98 per 1,000 births, the national average) and 36 percent of the children are underweight and moderately malnourished (slightly above the national average) despite having one of the highest levels of rice production in Cambodia.

Because rice farmers in this area have greater yields, they can sell more rice on the market, and because of this income some farmers are able to slowly expand their land holdings when other small landowners, for whatever reason, sell their land.[10] Interviews with government officials and villagers around the province suggested the loss of land is mostly due to the misfortune of illness rather than land grabs by the rich to build large plantations as in other areas of Cambodia. Without a medical safety net in this part of the world, prosperity or poverty in life is largely based upon the luck of family health.

The headman of the first village in this province indicated it was rather large, with about 700 households. The first family interviewed turned out to be one of the poorest in the village, mentioned briefly in the first chapter. They have 10 children, rather unusual by Cambodian standards, and are landless after one of their little girls had an emergency appendectomy. The family now buys vegetables from other villages in the area to resell from a little wooden table in front of their house on the main dirt road through the village.

While we are talking, one of the neighbors buying vegetables invited us to visit her family a couple of houses down the road. Arriving at her little wooden and straw hut, much smaller than the other houses, we found she is alone with a small baby. Her husband had recently left and she could only assume he was in Phnom Penh or Battambang doing construction work. As is typical in villages all over mainland Southeast Asia, however, she is not totally alone. Next door is her mother and father's household so she continues to live in an extended family. After talking with her for a while we learned that her father is a teacher in the village, though not as well off as the teacher described earlier in Kampong Chhnang province.

After a couple of hours we moved next door to her father's household. They have seven children, including the daughter next door. The comparative poverty level of this teacher's family is striking. Their house is of shabby construction, with a corrugated tin roof and dirt floor, not the traditional house on wooden stilts bringing it off the ground. We soon learned the reason for their poverty; this family had recently had two children in the hospital, one with dengue fever and the other with appendicitis. They had to sell their better house and their land to pay the hospital bills.

Help, however, was on the way. A completely different kind of house for Cambodian villages was being built next to their current shack. This almost completed new house is of concrete and tile, in the modern style favored by the middle class in Cambodian cities. Their daughter living next door explained that this new house was paid for by her unmarried sister now living and working in a restaurant in France. For more than a year her sister had been sending monthly payments for the house, and soon the total $13,000 cost of the house will be funded by their daughter. This sight is common in the northeast of Thailand, but not in Cambodia, at least not yet. A recent university study, described in the next chapter, estimated 15,000 Thai girls are married to foreign men, with millions of dollars coming into the northeast of Thailand because of these European marriages. While there are certainly some other cases, on only two other occasions in Cambodia, both in this province, did we see new houses being built with money coming from men, husbands or boyfriends from European countries.

After admiring the new house and listening to their stories, we returned to questions about the village, again finding teachers best able to answer in Cambodia. With some personal bias perhaps, the teacher said the biggest problem in this village is lack of healthcare. Several families have lost their land because of hospital bills, more than any other village we visited.

Something else, though, was different. While driving to this village we saw huge piles of rice bags being sold and loaded onto trucks. Driving through this village before stopping for interviews, there seemed to be a higher level of inequality than we had noticed in any other village. The teacher agreed with these impressions; in his words, "about half the families are in the middle, with the other half either much higher or lower." The more "affluent" in this

The new house in this village.

A wat full of rice bags.

village, though, *were not* the rich city people grabbing land illegally as is happening in other parts of Cambodia these days. Here most of the better off are families who have lived in the village for many years. The more affluent are small farmers who simply have been more successful, successful through a combination of good management, hard work, and probably most important, good luck in having a healthy family. Because rice productivity is higher in this region of Cambodia, almost all families with at least the average one hectare of land can sell some rice on the market to make a little money. But when problems occur, due to illness, bad luck, or poor money management, some people still must sell their land as in other provinces. In this area, though, when a neighbor buys the extra land there is a multiplying effect; the neighbor can then sell much more rice and have even more money to buy more land from other neighbors who get in trouble. A sort of rural "cowboy capitalism" at work.

On the way to this village was a temple with thousands of rice bags being sold and loaded onto trucks headed for Vietnam, and from there, we discovered, to the world market (no doubt part of why Vietnam is now the second largest exporter of rice in the world). The temple serves a district (called a commune in Cambodia) of 10 villages in the area. Along with the Vietnamese merchants, we talked with two farmers from this commune sitting on their bags of rice, looking quite happy, waiting to be paid. The first man, in his 40s, was from a nearby village where he, his wife and three children had lived all their lives. He had 15 hectares of land. Unlike the vast majority of village farmers all over Cambodia, he could also afford fertilizer and had an "iron buffalo" to plow his rice paddy, plus enough money to buy a long pipe device with a pump on one end which works as irrigation equipment for his paddy fields. He is able to sell about 20 tons of rice a year. The second farmer also had three children and eight hectares of land. He can sell about 10 tons of rice a year. These two men were really no different from other village farmers all over Cambodia; quite likable, seemingly good fathers, hard working, with just a few years of elementary school education. They are simply the lucky ones who had healthy families in a region of Cambodia with good soil and a higher average rainfall.

There is one other point of importance that needs further comment. Tons of rice from this area are being exported to Vietnam. This is in a region where malnutrition is still quite high (around the national average). The surplus rice production, in other words, does not feed the hungry in this area but goes to the world market. Cambodia receives about 27,000 tons of cereals in foreign aid a year, yet at the same time exported about $50 million worth in 2005.[11] As will be described in more detail below, this is a typical pattern for poor countries without governments taking steps to protect the needs of their poorer citizens.[12] This is not a pattern one finds in Thailand or Vietnam.

Battambang Slums

One more village in this province is worth description before moving to other areas of Cambodia. This village is only some five miles down river south of Battambang City, in reality a suburb. Less than two miles down river from Battambang City, however, it seems one is back in the jungle. The forest blocks out the sky, and roads are more like dusty pathways in the dry season. The village is large, containing more than 1,000 households, and right away one sees another striking contrast. Most houses resemble those in a city slum, very small in most cases and crudely built of scrap metal and plywood. Though close to the "big city," most houses had no electricity, though some had blue PCP pipes bringing in fresh water, and even more had motorbikes parked in front.

No one in this village/slum owned any farm land, and most were renting their crudely made homes for $2.50 a month. These people are mostly construction workers, vendors, and unskilled laborers in Battambang City. None worked in factories because there are none of any size in the city. (There is nothing in Cambodia like Thailand's CBIRD with factories outside of the major urban areas described in the next chapter.) Most of the people in this village had been pushed back into Cambodia from refugee camps in Thailand in the 1990s. In other words, like the village of landless people in Pailin, they missed out on the land redistribution in the 1980s because they had fled the murderous Khmer Rouge.

In one household was a married couple in their mid–30s with two children, one year old and 14 years old. The father was a "handy man" making about $2 per day, that is, when there is work. The mother explained that while refugees they were mostly separated from extended family and continue to have less of that familial safety net that provides at least some protection for most of Cambodia's poor. While boring, she added that in some ways life in the refugee camp in Thailand was better; they always had food and clean water. Here, back in Cambodia, life is scary; they never know if they will have enough to eat from day to day, and there is no extended family to turn to for help.

Next door was a young woman expecting her first child. She met her husband in this village after both came from refugee camps. They survive, though one could see not well, because they grow some vegetables around the house which her husband sells in the city. Like others he also works as an unskilled laborer when there is work. She smiled as she told of her dream; she must somehow get to Siem Reap, the gateway to Angkor Wat about 120 miles by road, to have her baby in the famous hospital run by a Swiss doctor. The government clinics and hospitals in Battambang, she said, are expensive, understaffed, dirty, and crowded, so she fears for the health of her new baby.

There were similar stories until finding two new large houses being built in another part of this village. Next door to these, in a shack similar to most others, there was a young woman with a six-year-old son. She had the usual stories, such as returning from the refugee camps and the father working as an unskilled laborer. She was then asked about the new two-story wooden house being built next to hers. This house will be for her sister, about 30 years old, married to a retired teacher from France, able to visit Cambodia only two or three months a year. The other nice house being built nearby belonged to a lady in her late 20s married to a Canadian man.

A few minutes later her sister arrived with a friend, also her late 20s, both dressed in the moderately fashionable clothing one can see on more affluent ladies in Phnom Penh. She claimed she met her French husband "in the Battambang market." Perhaps this was so. One should not pass judgment on these two ladies, and what appears to be a more economically secure life. These ladies and their situation are interesting mainly because they are still so rare in Cambodia compared to northeastern Thailand. As we will see later, there are many European men, and a few Americans in Thailand, who met their wives because they were university colleagues, or nurses in clinics, and in a few cases because they were both working in Christian charity organizations. But many in Thailand met their "farang" (Western) husbands in the "go-go bars" of Bangkok. One wonders if such cases will increase as Cambodia attracts more Western tourists.

East-Central Cambodia

We will consider east-central Cambodia only briefly, and only one village. But it is important to understand a different pattern in this rural region of Kampong Cham Province which borders Vietnam. The province as a whole has a level of rice production almost on par with that of the traditional rice basket around Battambang Province in west-central Cambodia. The countryside and villages look similar, though the provincial city is much smaller than Battambang City. A few dozen miles from the Vietnamese border, though, one can find a striking difference.

The small town of Memot, just a few miles from the Vietnamese border, is pretty much like all the other little towns with muddy streets in the rainy season, the Chinese-style shop houses of concrete, though a few more houses are of brick as one gets closer to the famous red clay found in much of Vietnam. While obviously poor, and with no new buildings, the town seemed to be doing okay with electricity, a few cars and motorbikes, and outdoor markets full of fruit, vegetables, and meat.

As we left the town on the main highway heading east and then north up to Laos, at first going closer to the Vietnamese border, things quickly looked different. Instead of the usual lush green rice paddy, the fields first changed into vast rubber plantations. Few villages could be seen, but there were many laborers walking through the rubber plantations tapping the trees and collecting sap in the traditional manner. There are some factories nearby where the latex is collected and processed. Further up the road there were large fields of sugar cane. Certainly fewer small farmers with roughly equal (one hectare) land holdings existed in this region of Cambodia.

After another dozen or so miles driving northeast, there was an extremely rare sight for Cambodia, or Laos, Vietnam, and Thailand for that matter. To the right of the road in a huge freshly plowed field of red soil like one sees in north Vietnam and Oklahoma were four big American-style tractors plowing the land. To be more precise, they weren't those big rigs seen in Nebraska, Kansas, and Oklahoma that have air conditioning and CD players, and can pull a plow that looks to be almost 20 meters wide, but they *were* big tractors. In southern Cambodia we had seen some plantations for fruit and nut trees on the way to the coast from Phnom Penh. Those plantations, we learned, were recently put together by rich friends of the long-standing prime minister, Hun Sen. Now close to the Vietnamese border we stopped at that first village in east-central Cambodia with many questions.

The village is rather small, with some three dozen households. There are few other villages in the area, no doubt because much of the land was taken by these big plantation estates. It is first interesting to note that all the people in this village are Muslim Cham ethnic minorities. The Cham are from the old Champa civilization that existed at the time of Angkor over 1,000 years ago.[13] The center of the civilization was in what is now central and southern Vietnam, but because they were mostly seafaring people, one might say pirates, they were spread throughout Southeast Asia. At first this civilization was Hindu, but later converted to Islam. There are few Cham in Cambodia today, and still fewer since the Khmer Rouge tried to kill them all, but there is a small concentration of Cham villages along the Tonle Sap River moving up from Phnom Penh to Siem Reap, where they are fishing people.

There were three families in this first compound, two have three children each, the other two children. All adults wore a red checkered cloth which symbolized their Islamic group, women wearing this cloth on their heads much like turbans and men wearing the cloth around their shoulders or waist, with Islamic-style skull caps on their heads. Though they couldn't tell us, it is likely that these Cham at some point in history came into Cambodia from the old Cham lands in Vietnam. Their houses are traditional Cambodian, however — small houses on stilts made of wood and straw. The families in this Cham village were asked the usual questions, but here we will consider answers from more pressing questions.

The freshly plowed fields close by, among the other big plantations for rubber and sugar cane, are for casava (a kind of tuber like potatoes), clearly massive amounts of casava from the size of the fields on a scale big enough for those tractors. These villagers said (and later checking confirmed) that these plantations are owned by Vietnamese corporations, though this was technically inaccurate information given that foreigners cannot legally own land in Cambodia. It was later confirmed there is a deal with Cambodian government elites so in reality the Vietnamese corporations leased this land for an extended period of years, usually for 99 years. Many news articles since 2007 have reported that some Arab countries as well as South Korean and Vietnamese corporations also have been given big land deals, with substantial bribes and benefits for the Cambodian political elite. The families in this Cham village have very little land of their own, less than one hectare, mostly growing casava they sell to the Vietnamese corporation nearby. In addition, they work as laborers in those big Vietnamese-run casava fields. None in this village works in the rubber plantations they believe are also Vietnamese owned, though most people in other villages in the area work as rubber tappers. Once leaving this village we were told to go a few miles further up the road to see a big processing factory where the corporation turns the casava into starch to ship back to Vietnamese markets to make noodles and other things.

A couple of miles up the road, there it was. A massive building with pipes going in and out, and large trucks full of casava lined up at the entrance to dump their loads into the intake bin. Back in Phnom Penh several days later, NGO and academic contacts, one even an agriculture professor, were asked if they knew what was going on. They suspected big plantations were being formed from land stolen form Cambodian peasants, but they were yet to learn many details. This was before news articles started reporting Prime Minister Hun Sen had plans to give huge agricultural leases to Arab countries.

In this rather remote part of Cambodia one can see some of the land inequality World Bank figures indicate is rising sharply. A *Phnom Penh Post* article in September 2008 began a series of many articles explaining that Prime Minister Hun Sen was on his way to visit some oil-rich Middle Eastern countries. As we will see in more detail below, with newly discovered oil off the coast of Cambodia, the prime minister figured it was good to get better relations with these oil-rich countries. But a key reason stated for his first visit was that while Middle Eastern countries are rich because of oil, they can't grow enough food in the desert. Cambodia, he told his citizens, can grow plenty of food which they can sell to these Middle Eastern countries. Considering Hun Sen's other "deals," one can fully expect that more huge plantations will appear if these new food deals bear any fruit. And that is almost certain to mean more peasants will lose their land to new agribusiness firms owned by Hun Sen's rich friends and foreign corporations.

The Far North

We will mostly neglect the far south in this description of rural Cambodia, the coastal area south of Phnom Penh. Driving south from Phnom

Penh there are more rice fields and some new plantations, and a few small cities infamous as the birth places of some Khmer Rouge leaders. As one gets to the coast, of course, there are many fishing villages that look as if they are doing relatively well economically. The biggest change in the coastal south is the development of Sihanoukville with its nice beaches. Sihanoukville is far from obtaining the status of a major tourist area, though the big developers are trying. The biggest issue around Sihanoukville for now are the land grabs and forced resettlement of people from poor villages to make room for new resort hotels. This subject will be covered extensively in Chapter 6 below.

Toward the end of fieldwork in Cambodia we headed north to the Lao border for Stung Treng Province. The province is dominated by the Mekong River coming down from Laos and down to Phnom Penh before flowing into the South China Sea through Vietnam's Mekong Delta. Stung Treng Province is listed as one of the poorest, with the lowest rice yield, though there is some potential for economic development. Regional development plans in this part of Southeast Asia, however, will likely have less success in Cambodia. One reason for this becomes evident driving to the provincial capital.

Governments along what is called the Lower Mekong River Basin have coordinated projects for economic development centered upon a new system of roads and rail lines connecting these countries and several bridges spanning the Mekong River. One of the first bridges in this development scheme was finished about 12 years ago, crossing the Mekong River to connect Nong Khai in Thailand with the Lao capital. In 2008 a rail line across this bridge connected Thailand with Laos for the first time. Most of these new roads and bridges have been paid for by various country donors and grants from the Asian Development Bank, a large percentage coming from the Japanese and Australian governments. One of these new bridges in Cambodia crosses the Mekong just outside of Stung Treng, capital city of the province just a few miles south of Laos. Set to open in late 2007, the bridge looked substantial enough, but the new road going south toward Phnom Penh is a disaster. This is one of the roads mentioned earlier; only a year old in 2007 it already had big potholes, flagged every few meters, by tree branches. These new roads built to stimulate regional development in Thailand, Laos, and Vietnam are nothing what one sees in Cambodia. The problem, informants say, is substandard construction. Originally enough money to build sound roads in Cambodia was allocated, but bribes and simple corruption reduced the amount by almost half. The result was a much thinner highway than required for any level of traffic. One can only imagine the disaster if significant traffic within the region actually occurs in this part of Cambodia once the bridge over the Mekong opens.

The provincial town of Stung Treng looks like most others, except for nice views across the Mekong River. The town is far enough north on the Mekong to see rock formations sticking out of the river, the beginning of rapids. Only a bit further upriver is the famous area where the Mekong turns into serious rapids, making shipping impossible. The French colonials tried to channel around them, then laid track for a small train to transfer goods around the rapids, but neither worked well and the Mekong is still blocked to shipping further north at that point.[14] An Asian Development Bank project somehow allowing ships around this point would probably do more for economic development in the region above than entrusting money to the Cambodian government to build roads.

Until the new bridge is open in Stung Treng, the only way of crossing the Mekong for many miles up- and downriver is a ferry which leaves from the middle of the town, running only a few times a day. With almost no commerce or tourism in the town, of course, there is still little traffic to warrant more ferry crossings. The town has made an attempt to spruce up their river front with a walkway and landscaping, but it remains rather unattractive. The biggest attraction is simply the wide, mighty Mekong flowing by. The *Lonely Planet* advises "visitor attractions are extremely limited," but a half-dozen Western backpackers made it to this remote provincial capital, along with a couple of social scientists.

There are only narrow dirt roads leading out to villages in this province; many are muddy and full of big holes, sometimes impassable during the rainy season. Most dangerous, however, are the many old wooden bridges over streams and rivers many yards below. These old bridges were always considerably bowed in the middle and creak loudly as anything larger than a motorbike crosses them. In places there are holes between the wooden planks big enough to easily see the river 30 or 40 feet below.

After the long and sometimes dangerous journey one is pleasantly surprised at conditions in some of these small villages. The money income of these people is quite low, probably all below the World Bank $1-a-day measure, and even under the approximately $0.50 national poverty line. But food seems plentiful. As usual, there is no electricity or fresh water in the remote areas, and almost no motor vehicles. The small wooden houses in these villages in the far north are much like the others throughout Cambodia. And there is the same array of material goods such as farm tools, pots and pans, as found in other poor village households around Cambodia.

In the first village the headman and his assistant sat down to answer questions and talk about conditions in the village. Village headmen and -women are now elected by people living in the village, as they are in Vietnam,

Laos, and Thailand. This man was the first to be elected under the new law in Cambodia. Previously they were all appointed by the district or commune council which Hun Sen's Cambodian People's Party (CPP) firmly controls. The headman and assistant in this village were strong CPP members, however, as are most others in nearby villages and the district council. One sees a few signs in Cambodian villages showing support for the main opposition party in Cambodia, but far fewer than signs showing support for the CPP. Many NGO and academic informants told of various forms of bribery and intimidation that continue to keep the CPP firmly in control of these now-elected commune councils and village headmen.

The job of headman or -woman, it should be noted, is to meet with the district commune council once a month to discuss various issues, or more often if problems arise. They are then supposed to somehow deal with problems in their villages. Their last district meeting, the headman of this first village said, was about the potential threat of dengue fever, though he admitted the biggest health threat in this area is malaria, with about 6 percent of the population infected. But it was obvious that they had few resources to deal with any major problems. Nor were their meetings anything like the technical, detailed meetings and many seminars with central government specialists in northeastern Thailand which will be described below. And as will also be described in more detail in a later chapter, this is one of Cambodia's key problems involving a lack of governance.

There were 337 households in this first village. As usual, their main economic activity is growing rice. Few of these families, however, grow enough rice to feed their families, and only 60 households grow enough rice to sell a small amount in a good year. These people add to their diet and income with various kinds of farm animals, vegetables, and a little fishing (which is now very limited for reasons described below). Their biggest need, according to the headman, is electricity. He hopes someday they can get electricity from all the hydroelectric dams being built in Laos. After electricity their greatest need is water control and irrigation. Villages along the Mekong River have fewer of these problems, but villages further away from the river have much greater need for irrigation and water control to stop flooding in the rainy season.

On the next topic the headman was quite happy; this area has free medical care. This area is one of the few in Cambodia where a European-funded NGO had the ongoing experiment providing free medical care. The headman said all basic medical care is free, minor illnesses, cuts, etc., as is hospitalization in the provincial city about one hour away by car. The only cost is a co-payment for drugs. As a consequence, of course, no one in this area had lost their land to pay medical bills. In another village the next day there was more confirmation from several families. They provided specific examples; one man had a serious eye injury and had to go to the provincial hospital for care. It cost him about $7, and though he didn't know it, most likely only for drug co-payments. Another villager had a tooth pulled for $1, and another spent a week in the hospital with a stomach problem at a total cost of $7.

A few days later we visited a small village clinic in the opposite direction from the provincial city to talk with healthcare workers. They confirmed what the headman of the first village in this province had said about healthcare. Like other clinics in remote village areas all over Cambodia, this one was rather shabby. But the basics were there: the examination tables, medical tools for emergencies, and a room where a couple of patients could stay overnight if necessary. There was one nurse on the staff and four young girls trained as midwives. It is obviously very unfortunate that other villages throughout Cambodia where dengue fever was rampant has no such health care, which is also to say that it is unfortunate that the European NGO lacks funds to expand this program all over Cambodia. The results of the experiment where an NGO takes over the healthcare, as will be noted in more detail when we consider corruption and mismanagement in the Cambodian government, show the NGO-run healthcare system does a much better job, and most money coming from the EU actually gets to patients.

Conclusion

It is time to offer a conclusion or summing up after our journey through rural Cambodia. Yes, there is a big percentage of the Cambodian rural population living on less than $1 per day. But there is almost no extreme starvation in these rural areas. Malnutrition is at 30 percent or more in some places, however, and we did see some children who looked malnourished, mostly children of landless people in some areas. Most Cambodians are able to get by, if just barely. The sad part is, a little aid for irrigation, fresh water, electricity and better roads could do wonders for these people, but almost none is forthcoming. These are strong, hardworking people, people who take better care of their extended families more than almost anywhere else in the world. At present they are caught in a cycle where they must use all of their energy and resources just to get by. Only a little help from outside the village would have amazing results in raising their standards of living.

In every village visited around the country one standard question was if there is anything the government was doing to help their plight. The resounding answer was nothing! The government has lots of plans, and hundreds of millions of dollars pour into the county every year (with half of government spending coming from foreign aid) with very few results in the countryside. This is the corruption and neglect by government elites that will be consider in last two chapters.

The future for rural people in Cambodia is looking worse. With no money for medical care in most places, and sick children, their children are dying early, and they are losing their land. Many sub–Saharan African countries have roughly similar percentages of people living on less than $1 per day. The main advantage held by the rural Cambodian poor is their small plots of land with a somewhat favorable climate for agriculture. But as we will see in Chapter 6, in addition to the loss of land to pay for medical care, the legal and illegal "land grabs" in the countryside and cities are becoming so blatant and common that even the relatively timid Cambodian poor are starting some significant protest movements.

For decades sociologists specializing in inequality within societies have conducted research and written books on why some people are able to move up the economic ladder while others do not.[15] All over Cambodia one sees many of the personal and family characteristics, along with strong determination to succeed, that matter in rich countries as well as poor countries. But few of these exceptional personal and family characteristics can pay off in Cambodia, especially in rural Cambodia. Strong determination and character, hard work, and family unity simply cannot get someone out of poverty if the opportunities are not there. There will be a few people like the homeless young man from Phnom Penh who in 2008 was matching world class times in a long distant run. A few Cambodians heard about him and bought him a few things like proper running shoes so he could participate in the 2008 Olympics. But there are only a few extremely gifted people like this in any society. It is the job of governments all over the world to help make these opportunities possible for their people. This does *not* mean governments should always directly make these opportunities with such things as government-funded jobs. Rather, the job of governments is to help with the underlying physical and human infrastructure (roads and schools, as well as a fair economic environment so people's properties are not stolen) so the people can create these opportunities for themselves. The Cambodian government has done a miserable job with all of this compared to other countries in the region (as always, with the exception of Burma).

There are many contrasting cases in Vietnam. For example, there was a 50-something-year-old mother in central Vietnam who lost her husband in the late 1980s. She had secure title to her land that was given back to people when the communist government moved to private property and relatively open-market capitalism from the late 1980s. She also had some government health care protection and the village had government loans for an irrigation project. With this, as well as electricity and good roads to get her farm produce to market, she could make a little extra money each year. She raised her two children alone, worked hard in their rice field, saved and saved, and pushed her kids to do well in school. When talking with this mother in 2007, her two children were home for the weekend. She pushed her son through high school with good grades, then helped pay for a technical junior college in Danang while her son worked part time in Danang to pay for his other expenses. He now has a good job in an electronics store in Danang. Much of his salary now goes for tuition to a business junior college in Danang for his sister. She was there that weekend, too. Neither son or daughter were married yet, but when they start families they will have fully moved into the Vietnamese middle class from their poor peasant origins.

In a small town in the poorest section of northeastern Thailand there was a young lady whose mother pushed her to do well in elementary school, then high school. Her mother was on her own after the young lady's father left home before she was born. Her mother opened a little "store" in a wooden shack in the village where she sold a few things like soap, cooking oil, and cold drinks. This young lady's dream was to become a nurse. In Thailand if you have good grades and test scores, the government will give you complete tuition, room and board in return for four years of low-paid service in a rural clinic after you become an RN. She was about to finish her four years of rural clinic service as an RN where she helped deliver many healthy babies and no doubt saved many lives. She had just landed a new relatively well-paying job with an American-funded NGO in Burmese refugee camps on the Thai border helping educate these people on how to detect possible cases of bird flu and how to prevent HIV infection. One is reminded of this young Thai nurse when talking to someone such as the teacher in a poor village in central Cambodia whose daughter wants to be a doctor. She has no chance compared to this young Thai nurse.

CHAPTER 5

Cambodia Compared with Thailand

In the spring of 2010 "red shirt" protestors from poor rural areas (especially the northeast of Thailand) and working-class areas of Bangkok took over the streets for many weeks, finally burning several large shopping complexes as the Thai army moved in to stop the demonstrations. Some 80 people were killed and hundreds more were injured. Some of the less respected newspapers around the world had headlines such as "Poverty Bomb Explodes in Thailand." Even more respected newspapers and television news programs implied that serious poverty in Thailand was a cause of the bloody demonstrations.

Deprivation and poverty in and of themselves do not make for protest or rebellion. If this were the case Cambodia would be "exploding" much more than Thailand has been. For decades sociological research has shown that much more than deprivation is needed for a social movement or rebellion against the government. "Resource mobilization" theory and research, for example, show that protesters against a repressive government must have some resources such as the ability to organize, meet each other without being imprisoned or killed, and simply feed themselves so they are not so weak.[1]

A case in point; the civil rights movement in the United States did not start when conditions got worse for African Americans in the 1950s. Back in the first half of the 20th century conditions were much worse. But by the 1950s African Americans were more urban people, had big urban churches which helped them organize across the cities and states of the American South, and with more national and world media coverage, it was more difficult to simply kill African Americans who fought back against the white police than before the middle of the 20th century.[2] This is not to say that Martin Luther King Jr. was not an important element for the American civil rights movement.

What it does say is that Martin Luther King Jr. would have probably been killed back in the 1920s even before he could get the civil rights movement off the ground.

It is only when some of these various kinds of resources for protest exist that social movements by the lower classes and poor can occur, and possibly lead to improvements in their lives. We will see that some of these resources have existed for the rural and working-class poor in Thailand for a long time, resources which have helped lower-class Thais to keep some pressure on the government to make slow improvements. And we will see that the Thai government has relatively effective government institutions able to bring about economic development with poverty reduction. Unfortunately, both of these things are sorely lacking in Cambodia today.

A History of Poverty in Thailand*

Year	1962	1975	1981	1988	1990	1992	1994	1998	2006†
Percent below poverty line	57%	33%	24%	22%	18%	13%	9%	13%	13%

*Sources: Data for 1962 to 1988 were compiled from various studies presented in Muscat 1994. *The Fifth Tiger: A Study of Thai Development Policy*. New York: ME Sharpe, p. 243. Poverty estimates for 1990 through 1998 are from World Bank development reports. The 2006 figure is from Thai government estimates published in the *Bangkok Post*.

†One must keep in mind these are estimates of poverty based on the cost of basic necessities in the country, not the World Bank's new estimates of below $1 per day or $2 per day which do not include "income in kind" such as food produced by each family.

A Little Economics 101 for Developing Countries

It is clear that Cambodia is headed in the wrong direction compared to all of her mainland neighbors, except, as usual, Burma. As we saw in Chapter 3, excluding the small country of Singapore, Thailand has the second highest per capita income in Southeast Asia since the World Bank revised its PPP (purchasing power parity) index for 2006 data. Malaysia has a higher per capita income than Thailand; even with this lower per capita income Thailand has less than 2 percent of its people living on less than $1 per day. The Philippines follows Thailand for third in per capita income in Southeast Asia, but with a much higher rate of poverty.

Poverty began dropping fast in Thailand during the 1970s and 1980s, and is today probably lowest in the region.[3] Four decades ago Thailand's rate of poverty (measured with a cost-of-basic-necessities poverty line) was over 50 percent compared to today's 12 to 13 percent. Through the 1980s and 1990s Thailand was considered the "world champion" among developing countries for poverty reduction.[4] Vietnam began reducing poverty even more rapidly through the 1990s and continues to have one of the best rates of poverty reduction in the world.[5] The biggest surprise during fieldwork in the region was in Laos.[6] In Vientiane one sees a little more development in the past 10 years, but nothing compared to the rapid development going on in Phnom Penh. As we will see in more detail in Chapter 7, however, it is clear that small Laotian farmers are substantially ahead of small farmers in Cambodia. Traveling through these countries one sees much hope for the future in Thailand, Vietnam, and even Laos. When visiting poor rural families in these countries there was always the question if economic conditions and opportunities over the last 5 to 10 years have become better. Poor farmers in Thailand, Vietnam, and Laos in almost all cases said, "Yes!" This was almost never the answer received in Cambodia.

The continuing tragedy in Cambodia is not only about the high level of poverty, or how badly most of the poor are being treated. It is also about the trajectory of the country's political and economic system. Cambodia's growth in GNP is almost completely in Phnom Penh and Siem Reap, and benefitting only a small segment of the population.[7] *Without basic changes in Cambodia even this trend in urban development will not be sustainable.* Social science research and country case studies show that sustainable economic development must be accompanied with poverty reduction.[8] Significant poverty reduction will not happen if economic development policies are focused only on tourism and foreign manufacturing industries for low-skilled production in the cities. Such development policies will create a small middle class, make the rich much richer, but do little to help the rest of the population. There is no automatic "trickle down" to the poor. In fact, in most cases these kinds of policies can make the poor poorer as foreign agribusinesses are able to exploit poor farmers in the country, taking their agricultural products on the cheap, usually forcing small farmers out of business in favor of big landowners. These small farmers lose their land and migrate into those poor slums we read about in many countries in Latin America, India, and Africa.

One simple reason economic development policies favoring only low-skilled industries in the cities are less sustainable is that the country is left with only a small consumer class. In this situation, for an economy to grow or even remain stable, the country must focus primarily on exports to rich countries. While a focus on exports can work for a while, without other economic policies the country is left with a growing gap between a small group of rich and a mass of poor, leaving the country more vulnerable to downturns in the global economy and exploitation by rich multinational corporations. This is to say, economic development policies focused on exports to rich countries must be accompanied with other policies to develop the domestic infrastructure and education, along with the nation's own domestic industries creating jobs, profits, and thus, poverty reduction because domestic consumers can help sustain these domestic industries.

Let's consider a simple example of a typical *rich country* that has a natural resource such as copper. A company must get the copper out of the ground, which produces jobs, wages, and profits for the company. All of this goes to stimulate the domestic economy. We can assume the copper is then sold to another domestic company which shapes it into copper tubing, sheets of metal, etc., which other domestic companies need to make kitchen appliances and other consumer goods. Again, jobs, wages, and company profits are made all around. Finally, the company making kitchen appliances has domestic consumers to buy these appliances because that chain of economic activity beginning with copper underground has produced jobs, wages, and profits all along the way.

Now consider a *poor country* that has copper. Most often the copper is taken out of the ground by a foreign corporation with some jobs and wages going to workers in the poor country, but most profits going to the foreign corporation. The copper ore is then put on a ship to the rich country. The remaining economic cycle that began with copper ore goes to companies and workers in the rich nation. The foreign company making kitchen appliances then sends its products to the poor country where only a small middle class and upper class can afford them, who send money back to the rich country to pay for the appliances. Simple Economics 101, but a logic sadly not followed by many poor countries around the world today, especially outside of East and Southeast Asia. Considerable research, in fact, shows that less-developed countries rich in natural resources are most often poorer in the long run because of this situation.[9]

All of this is to say that a more sustainable policy for economic development is one that seeks to create more domestic consumers as GNP expands, with people in the less-developed country able to buy stuff produced domestically. Profits can be generated for reinvestment in the country and more jobs for people in the country, and thus, sustained economic development. In the vast majority of poor countries today, this simply means the less-developed country must also have economic development policies to improve the standard of living for rural people who make up 70 or 80 percent of the population.

As it now stands, this last part is going to kill Cambodia's future. A small elite of wealthy business people and corrupt government officials will do quite well for a while. Along with foreign corporate executives, this small Cambodian elite will be able to buy those $350,000 condos being built in Phnom Penh on land stolen from Cambodia's poor. Poor families like those we've met in central Cambodia may not starve, but they will not see their lives improve.

Before we turn to more specific comparisons with the countries around Cambodia, we can put the above into perspective by considering trends during the 20th century in Latin American countries and East Asia. Most Latin American countries gained independence from European colonial powers in the 1800s. From the beginning of the 20th century, for example, Argentina and Chile were considerably ahead of Japan, Korea, and Taiwan in GDP per capita, with Colombia and Brazil just a little behind Japan. What a difference a century can make; now Japan, South Korea, Taiwan, and Singapore have moved way ahead of these Latin American countries in poverty reduction. Even Thailand and Malaysia, extremely poor countries 100 years ago, have now basically caught up with these Latin American countries in their level of economic development as a percentage of the population. These East Asian countries, and then some Southeast Asian countries, have been pursuing development policies that keep inequality relatively low and reduces poverty among rural people. As they were developing at the beginning of the 20th century, the rich Latin American elites were all of European origin. They had little concern about conditions for the poor American Indians who made up the vast majority of the population and owned very little land if any.[10] In fact, while these indigenous Latin American masses were kept poor, it provided cheap labor for the agricultural products the rich in Latin America were exporting to North America and Europe. Except for a couple of very poor African countries, Brazil now has the highest gap between the rich and poor in the world, with continuing high rates of poverty. This uneven economic development has led most Latin American countries to economic stagnation in the later decades of the 20th century and up to today.[11]

In the last 25 years of the 20th century, economic growth in almost all Latin America countries was either flat or negative, with the exception of Chile. During this same 25 years, most countries in East and Southeast Asia have had growth rates in the range of 4 to 8 percent, with even higher rates throughout the first eight years of the 21st century. In the next 15 years the World Bank projects the percentage of the population living on less than $1 per day in East and Southeast Asian countries will drop by 60 percent. The projection for Latin America is maybe a 5 percent reduction, with an *increase* of about 40 percent for sub–Saharan Africa.

The key point here is that with current policies and the nature of Cambodia's corrupt and dysfunctional government, *Cambodia will at best follow the trajectory of Latin American countries, and quite possibly the trajectory of many African countries*, rather than the trajectory of most of Cambodia's neighbors in Southeast Asia. We will consider the nature of the Cambodian government in much more detail in the last two chapters of this book. We will now turn to the contrast with Thailand, while in Chapter 7 we will consider the same contrasts in Vietnam and Laos, and summarize what these countries have been doing for economic development and poverty reduction compared to Cambodia.

Thailand's History of Economic Development

In one sense this is an unfair comparison: Thailand is way ahead of Cambodia in economic development and poverty reduction. The World Bank's *World Development Report, 2010* lists Thailand's gross national income (GNI) per person at $5,990, with less than 2 percent of the population living on less than $1.25 per day, compared to $1,820 GNI per capita and just over 40 percent below $1.25 per day in Cambodia. The World Bank's *World Development Report, 1990* provided us with poverty estimates for Thailand using the national poverty line estimate for 1962 and 1986. (There were no $1-per-day estimates back then.) As shown above, while the measures may be a little different for these early years, we get a rough idea of the changes: In 1962 Thailand's poverty rate was 57 percent of the population, and by 1988 it had come down to 22 percent of the population. Currently Thailand's poverty rate is about 12 to 13 percent of the population. That is what a few decades of poverty estimates should look like.

The nationally based poverty line for Cambodia is said to be 35 percent of the population, with a rate of 38 percent in rural areas compared to 18 percent in urban areas.[12] Because of civil war during the Khmer Rouge years, no one could obtain accurate poverty rates for all of Cambodia before the early 1990s. By official poverty estimates from the World Bank, there has been only a slight drop in Cambodian poverty for at least the last 10 years. But as we have seen, given what appears to be an overestimate of poverty in Khmer Rouge–held areas of Cambodia in the early 1990s, any poverty reduction in Cambodia since then is more likely close to zero.

Thailand was not even a country when the Angkor civilization was at its high point a bit less than 1,000 years ago. Siam first appeared as a country (renamed Thailand in 1932) in A.D. 1253. The capital was moved to what is now Bangkok in 1782 to get further away from the Burmese who kept attacking and burning the previous two Thai capitals, and to get closer to the Gulf

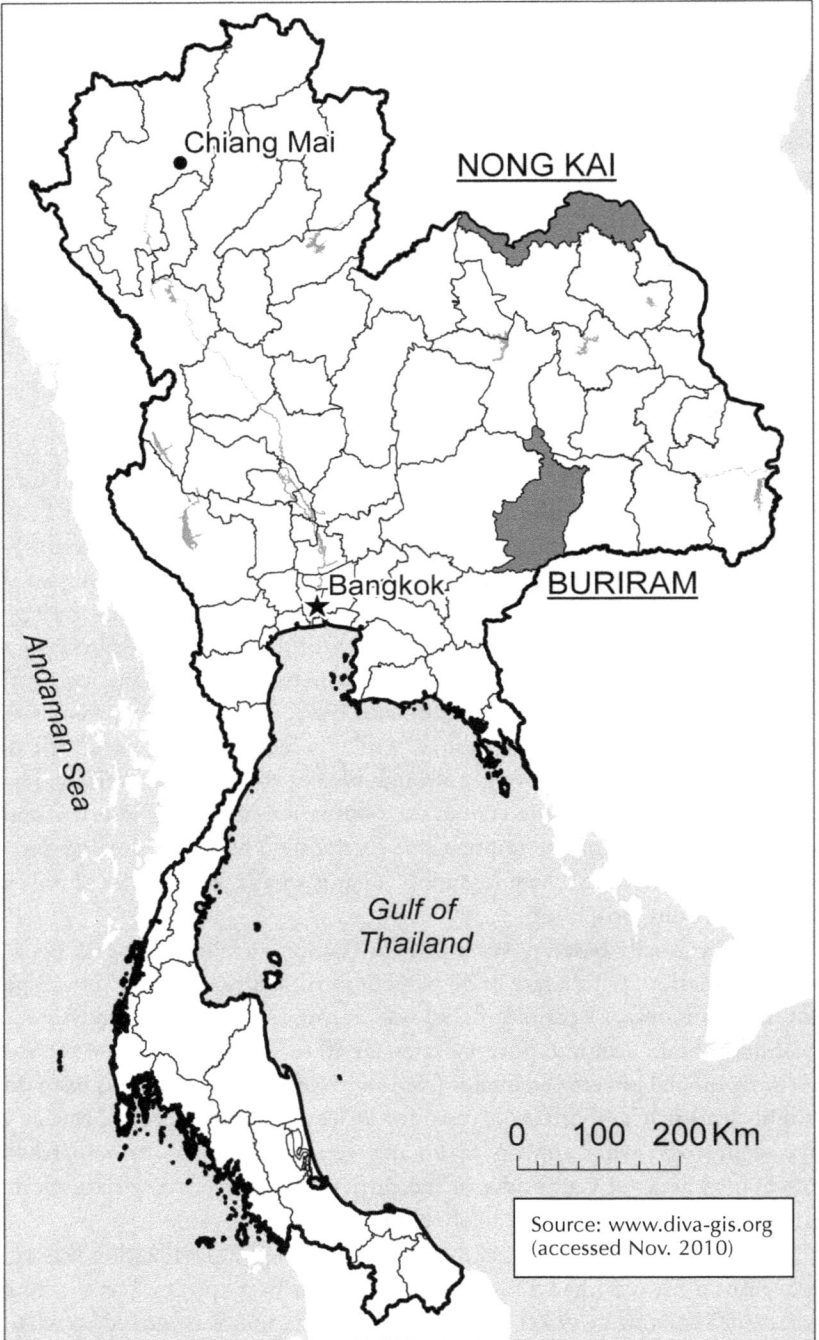

Map of Thailand.

of Thailand where trade and commerce were heating up in the region.[13] Europeans were coming into East and Southeast Asia big time by then. Before the end of the 1800s, all of Southeast Asia except Thailand was a colony of one European power or another. It is here that a Thai advantage first emerged. Thailand was the only country in the region not to fall into the hands of Europeans for as much economic exploitation. Shrewd Thai kings of the late 1800s played off the British, moving in from the west and south, against the French, moving in from the east. In short, the Thais manipulated the situation so the Brits and French became worried of each other's intentions in the region, enough to decide they would allow Thailand to remain relatively free so as not to create conflict between the two European powers. While the British did end up with considerable influence in Thailand, the Thais had nothing like the economic exploitation experienced by Vietnam, Laos, and Cambodia. The second advantage gained by not being colonized is that Thailand escaped the destruction caused by anti-colonial wars and later communist control faced by Cambodia, Vietnam, and Laos. Thus, Thailand had the advantage of an earlier start with economic development compared to Vietnam, Cambodia, and Laos, and less destruction from the Indochina wars.

Thailand began some modernization during the second half of the 1800s. But it was very little compared to what Japan, the only other nation to escape European colonization in Asia, was producing with their Meiji Restoration during the same time period. From 1932 Thailand became "sort of" a democracy when the absolute monarchy was overthrown in a military coup, but with the military more or less in control of the government for the next 40 years. Since the 1970s, Thailand has gone back and forth between civilian and military governments, the last military government lasting from September 2006 to the fall of 2007.

As is the case with most East and Southeast Asian nations, however (though a major exception in Cambodia), whether the nominal head of government is civilian or military, *career bureaucratic civil servants* are usually more important to day-to-day government operations, and quite often more influential in setting long-term policies. (There will be much more on this for Cambodia in the final two chapters.) Elected politicians *do* have influence over policies, but not as much as people are accustomed to in Western countries. This is the primary reason that when there is a military coup in Thailand, or "yellow shirts" take over the main airport, or "red shirts" from the poorer classes of Thailand take over parts of Bangkok, the Thai stock market seems to sort of hiccup, then move on as if nothing happened to the economy. These career civil servants help write legislation for elected politicians to enact in parliament. The legislation is usually written is such a way the bureaucratic ministry officials have considerable leeway in interpreting and enforcing the laws.[14]

It was not until the 1950s that Thai prime ministers, the Thai king, and the powerful Thai bureaucratic ministry elite began to think seriously about economic development, with more development plans coming in the 1960s and 1970s. And they did so with a better understanding of development policies and with a reasonably efficient government better able to carry out those policies than most less developed countries in the later years of the 20th century. In earlier attempts at rapid economic development in places as varied as the Soviet Union in the 1930s, China in the 1960s, and Japan in the early 20th century, economic development policies were largely based on "milking the peasants" by paying low for their agricultural products then selling high in the urban areas, using the extra profits for industrial investment. It never worked very well in the long run, and created rural starvation and political violence when peasants were hurting. One reason Japan achieved much more rapid and sustainable economic development after World War II was due to a radical decrease in the level of inequality in the country.

From the beginning of their economic development push, the Thais put their small farmers on a relatively equal footing with urban industry. Much of this was on the insistence of the currently revered Thai king, Rama IX. There is no question that this king, Bhumibol Adulyadej, pushed these rural development policies to help his people. However, in one of the most informative new books about Thailand in the 20th century, *The King Never Smiles*, extensive inside information describes the conflict between the court, military, and sometimes civilian politicians since the coup which overthrew the absolute Thai monarchy in 1932. It was this conflict which in an important way helped promote these policies of rural economic development from the 1950s.[15] The king and military/civilian governments were in competition for the hearts and minds of the Thai people from the 1950s to the present, and King Bhumibol sought the support of hearts and minds through economic development and charity projects in rural areas where the vast majority of Thais lived.

In a sense, therefore, the Thai poor were lucky to have such a king and the competition their king had with the government and military. Rural development projects helped small Thai farmers with irrigation, electricity, and good roads which increased production and their standards of living.[16] While rural-urban income differences remain in Thailand, and in recent years have increased somewhat, they are fewer than in most developing countries.

With a stronger economic base in the countryside, Thailand could then begin the usual policies of "import substitution." Using high tariffs, import quotes, and other protective measures, the country tried to minimize the amount of manufactured goods they must buy from other countries. When achieved relatively well, this means sending less money to other countries to pay for their imports. The money was then saved for investment in Thailand to produce goods that would otherwise be imported, most importantly, producing jobs and profits for Thai corporations and their employees.

Thailand was highly successful with this kind of policy in the auto industry, for example. The Thai government put tariffs and import duties of up to 400 percent on imported cars and trucks. After doing so, however, the Thai government went to foreign automakers with a deal; if these foreign automakers would come to Thailand and form joint ventures with Thai companies to make cars and trucks in Thailand, the foreign company would get many incentives.[17] Eventually, almost all of the world's automakers took the deal. (U.S. automakers were the last to do so.) Both the Thai economy and foreign automakers made out well as Thais were adding 20,000 cars to the streets of Bangkok by the 1990s, that is, 20,000 every month!

The next step, of course, is developing your own industries to export goods to the rich countries. When done successfully as Japan, then South Korea, Taiwan, and now China have done, the country obtains cash reserves for further capital and reinvestment and domestic economic growth. Thailand is now referred to as the Detroit of Asia (before the U.S. auto industry fell apart in 2008 and 2009, of course) and has been successful in exporting autos throughout the region. Similar economic policies have been pushed with high tech electronic components to rich nations, making Thailand a key global competitor in this industry as well. But we must also remember that before all of this, Thailand started its development drive with infrastructure development in agriculture. Thailand remains the number-one world exporter of rice as well as a top exporter of several other agricultural products.

This "Economics 101" for less-developed countries seems quite logical and simple. But the tricky part is having a government that has the *interest and ability* to make sure their small farmers are productive, then can carry out import substitution and export policies efficiently and consistently. There must be a government willing and able to carry out policies for the long-term interests of the country *as a whole*, and *not just for the short-term interests of the wealthy* within the country, or their foreign corporate friends. The wealthy in a developing country, for example, want their Mercedes without a 400 percent tariff and they want it *now*, not waiting until new auto companies make the Mercedes within the country. In addition to this, the wealthy in a developing country are too often less worried about a higher standard of living for the masses; the short-term interests of the more affluent often favor keeping wages low, which keep labor costs low, and thus keeps the multinational corporations who are enriching the domestic elite from leaving the country. To achieve all of these long-term development goals, a country must have a relatively efficient and strong government able to restrain various interest groups from acting only in their short-term self interests. It is here that we find one of the biggest contrasts between Thailand and Cambodia, as will be presented in more detail in the last two chapters of this book.

Village Thailand

Even by the early 1990s one could see most rural areas of Thailand were far more developed than what is found in Cambodia today. Back then there were some villages with no running water, but very few without electricity. Most villages already had good roads to take their produce to market, and government projects to aid the expansion of water control and irrigation, as well as schools and clinics near every village.[18] And since 1990 one could see the slow transition of a key indicator of rural economic development in the region — the shift to "iron buffalos." There are still live water buffalos in Thailand, but not so many, and few being used as draft animals. The versatile "iron buffalos" now serve as a handheld plow or, with a change of tires and a trailer hitched to the back, a motorized cart taking people and goods to fields or market. By the 1990s, however, most rural people in Thailand already had pickup trucks for the second job.

From 2001 Thailand began another set of policies to further reduce rural poverty, particularly in the north, northeast, and the south of Thailand where rural poverty rates have always been higher. In large part, these policies were to build a voting base for Prime Minister Thaksin's new political party elected to office that year.[19] The policies worked quite well in building that voter base among small farmers *and* to further improve the economic standing of small farmers. (A key reason Thai politics remain volatile today is that Thaksin and his banned political party enjoys continuing strong support among Thai farmers since his government was overthrown in a military coup in 2006.) The most important poverty reduction programs since 2001 include the "30 Baht Health Care System" (about $0.75 at the time), a "People's Bank" with microloans to the urban poor and small farmers, the "One Million Baht" grant program to villages (about $30,000), the One-Tomban One-Product program (a tomban is a district including ten to fifteen villages), and the promotion of small factories with lower skilled jobs in the rural rather than only urban areas. In Thailand and Vietnam one also quickly learns that it is not only the existence of such programs but how the programs are carried out in a less corrupt and more efficient manner that makes Cambodia so different.

A Journey through Northeastern Thailand

Before descriptions of rural Thailand, Vietnam, and finally Laos, the method of selecting villages and whom to interview should be made more specific. First, regions in these countries were selected which have higher levels of poverty. Then, within these areas, subdistricts were selected which had higher and lower levels of poverty. Beyond that, village selection was rather random and usually unannounced. At times local officials were contacted and asked their permission before arriving. Doing this, however, usually meant time wasted being taken to "model" villages by these officials, especially in Vietnam. To minimize such "showcasing," we often simply got into a car or hopped on motorbikes from a base in provincial capitals and drove to selected villages unannounced. Once arriving in a village the headman was usually sought out for the first interview, or sometimes a schoolteacher or head monk who usually know as much about the village as the headman. This procedure, of course, could be an inconvenience to people but it seemed necessary so as not to be misled by local officials who naturally want to put their best foot forward for a visiting foreigner.

The first Thai village selected for interviews was in the center of the Isaan region, the northeast of Thailand. As usual the village headman was the first sought out. On this day, however, this 50-year-old man was out of town for the weekend taking classes for his BA in economics! This northeastern part of Thailand is one of the "poorest" regions of the country, and the stronghold of "red shirts" protesting inequality and poverty in Thailand. But one could see from the beginning it was certainly not like rural Cambodia. With the headman away from the village, interviews began with the head monk of the local wat (temple).

Sitting just inside the temple entrance on an imitation-leather couch, wearing the usual saffron-colored robes, this pleasant middle-aged monk began by saying, "This is such a poor village." After traveling throughout the rural areas and slums of Cambodia, the temptation was to ask, "Are you kidding?" But of course, poverty is relative to what one is accustomed to in their personal environment. Driving through the village one could see new pickup trucks in most driveways, the "iron buffalos" in most barns (they cost about $1,300 each we learned), many head of cattle next to several houses, electric power lines and TV antennas at every house, and houses made of concrete, stucco siding, and tile roofs. There was an electric pumping station in the village to provide irrigation for the rice fields, and every street in the village was paved. This middle-aged monk was too young to have seen the poverty in rural Thailand before economic development policies were launched from the late 1950s.

This kindly monk proved to be well informed about this village of just over 100 families. Their primary economic activity, which was already obvious, is rice farming. He explained how much land the families in this village own on average; a quick calculation between the Thai measure of *rai* and the Cambodian use of the measure hectare indicated these Thai villagers have only a little more land than the average Cambodian farmer. But even so, most families in this Thai village are able to sell a substantial amount of rice every year. Most families also raise farm animals and vegetables to sell at local city markets. Others grow sugarcane which is sold to processing plants not far away. There was obviously no hunger in this village.

When asked if economic development programs started by the government recently disposed by the military coup in 2006 were working well, the monk's eyes opened wider, and he responded with an enthusiastic yes. In his opinion, the "One Million Baht" program and the "One-Tomban, One-Product" programs were working best. The "One Million Baht" program gives each group of villages in the country a grant of about $30,000 to be used for improving the village standard of living. The money must be paid back to the tomban government (a group of villages) at a very low interest rate, with the interest going into the pool of money for future projects. The elected headman of each village and his advisory council make the decision as to how the money is spent. The head monk did not know how all of the money was being used in this village, but did say that the "One-Tomban, One-Product" for this tomban is fish paste. The development idea of this program is efficient production of scale and then a national distribution system. Each tomban all over the country is to select one product that can be best produced in the area, then villages in the tomban collectively contribute to the production. The next step in the "One-Tomban, One-Product" program is the construction of little shopping areas all over Thai cities carrying products from these village groups, with the profits going back to these villages. One can already see the crafts, textiles, and foods in several of these little "One-Tambon, One-Product" shopping malls in Bangkok and Chiang Mai, with many still being built in smaller Thai cities.

As usual, toward the end of the interview this monk was asked about any significant problems thought to exist in the village. According to this monk it was teenage drinking, smoking, and fights at festivals. It sounded like an answer from any preacher in rural America. He then brought up the problem of unemployment for the young people. There is only a finite amount of land which cannot be divided again and again over the generations. Some of the young people must find jobs outside of agriculture. In village after village in Thailand many young people are doing just that, but too often in cities as far away as Bangkok. In this particular village the monk said some 80 percent of the young people have already left the village. In other villages in the northeast of Thailand, to be described below, there are innovative solutions to this problem.

In response to other questions, schools in the area are good and close by, most young people now go to school until 15 years old, and about 10 percent go on to a junior college or university. While there is dengue fever in the area, it is not a serious problem like it is in Cambodia. He didn't think there was any HIV-positive people in the village. And, "Yes, health care is no problem." There is a free government clinic two miles away and a government hospital four miles away which also provides free health care for low-income families. In response to the last question, he thought awhile then said the government should do more to advise these farmers about better care for their farm animals. That was the only other problem he could think of.

At this point the healthcare system in Thailand should be briefly described. In a vast contrast to Cambodia, for many years healthcare was provided free to the poor, and at comparatively low cost in government hospitals and clinics for other Thai citizens. In 2001 the government instituted the "30 Baht Healthcare System" in which all citizens pay no more than about 75 cents for all medical care and medicines, unless they are below the poverty line, in which case it is all free of charge. Soon after the military coup in September 2006 this healthcare system was amended. The new military government figured it cost more than 75 cents to do the paperwork determining if people are below the poverty line, so now initial medical care is free for all citizens.[20]

After a couple of hours the head monk was thanked with the expected bows and *wais* to show respect. A few houses down the street there were the usual interviews with typical families in the village. The first house was of rather traditional design, on stilts (though these were of concrete), rather large and nicely constructed of wood and a tile roof. The usual open air living area under the house was paved rather than dirt and mud. Toward the back of this ground floor patio was a beautifully carved teak staircase going up to the main part of the house. The house above looked almost the size of a standard American working-class home. Of course the house had electric lines coming in, but the house was so large, and with so many rooms, that it was impossible to know how many TVs, stereos, and other such consumer items this family owned. There was a relatively new pickup truck in the driveway, and various kinds of farm equipment in the back.

The mother, two of her children, plus some neighbors, were sitting in the cool area under the house, seemingly quite happy to talk with a *farang*

Typical house in a Thai village.

(Western foreigner) who had just arrived. Everything the monk had said earlier was confirmed. This family grows rice, has several cows, and grows a few other things to sell. Banana and mango trees surrounded the house. She had four children and her mother living in the household. One could not help from being impressed to learn two of her sons had earned BAs at a good university. The only new piece of information gained was their views of Thaksin's village development programs. Asked if better off since his rural development programs began, they discussed the question awhile then decided, "Not really." This family's problem, and that of a few others in the village, is the headman let people in this village borrow money from the One-Million Baht Program to buy extra fertilizer for their rice fields instead of using the money for some kind of collective project that would bring additional income to the village. In 2007 the price of rice went down considerably, they had less income from selling rice that year, and consequently were still in debt.

　　With discussions like this in other Thai villages it became clear that the judgment of headmen and their advisors are very important if these programs are to work properly. In other Thai villages there are innovative programs from the One Million Baht Program which paid off handsomely. The debt problem in this particular village, however, was no doubt solved beginning from 2008 as the price of rice almost doubled. With Thailand the world's biggest exporter of rice, farmers all over the country have enjoyed big profit increases. In reaction to this jump in world food prices, the Thai government began putting more money into irrigation projects so Thai farmers can capitalize by increasing their normal two rice crops a year to three.

With the U.S. financial meltdown coming just a few months later, it remains uncertain how much the Thai government can deliver on this plan. But it is rather certain the 90 percent of Cambodian farmers with no irrigation, and lucky to get one crop a year, will not capitalize on this jump in world food prices. The Cambodian government, in contrast, has allowed more land grabs so the rich and foreign agribusiness corporations can create large-scale farm production which makes small farmers landless. The small increase in jobs for landless peasants on these new plantations will produce only small compensation.

Talking with several other families in this first Thai village, the only new information of significance pertained to sons and daughters working in Bangkok, usually sending money back home. Two issues are involved here; one is the type of work some of these young people are doing in Bangkok, and the other is that they have to go so far from home to find work. There are programs in Thailand to encourage small factories to locate in rural areas. Outside of this first village, in fact, there is a small factory, a shoe factory that employs about 300 young workers. While providing only a small number of new jobs needed for the 12 villages in the area, it is a start in the right direction. Before leaving discussion of this village, and before considering the other kinds of work the young people from this village have found in Bangkok, especially the girls, it is important to elaborate on these small factories in rural Thailand.

One of the most impressive things seen in any country in Southeast Asia is just outside the provincial town of Nang Rong. We should first recognize that the man behind this development project, Senator Mechai Viravaidya, is a true hero in Thailand. A physician who gave it up for politics, Mechai first became famous for helping bring down Thailand's high birthrate in the 1960s and 1970s. There is a simple economic logic; if the birthrate goes up more than the economy expands, the country is getting behind with more mouths to feed. Mechai pushed foreign donors and the government to fund family planning clinics around the country, also setting up his nonprofit chain of restaurants call "Cabbages and Condoms." As the funny name implies, they are vegetarian restaurants also claiming to have the largest selection of condoms on sale anywhere in the world. Back then you could also take your restaurant receipt next door for a free vasectomy. Later, in the 1990s, Mechai focused on reducing HIV infection in Thailand, programs cited by the United Nations as the most successful in the world.

An example of one of these anti–AIDS programs was observed in 1990. A stage had been set up in the middle of the street, in a brothel area called Soi Cowboy. Go-go bars lined both sides of the street. It was a "Miss Anti-AIDS Beauty Pageant." It was a rather bizarre sight: Bar girls on stage were being ranked in the contest by how loud the crowd cheered. The point of it all was a guy dressed as Superman on the stage throwing little cards into the crowd explaining how to prevent HIV infection, while others in his team were handing out free boxes of condoms. After Miss Anti-AIDS was selected, "Superman" went into each bar with assistants who handed out more of these cards and boxes of condoms as "Superman" twirled around the polls on stage with the working girls. There were obviously other educational campaigns about AIDS and HIV infection, and while prostitution is illegal in Thailand, the government sent personnel to the brothel areas to teach the girls to demand customers to use condoms. There was also government pressure on the go-go bars to require periodic medical checks of the "working girls." During the early 1990s, using one indicator of the HIV infection rate, about 10 percent of new army draftees in Thailand tested positive. By the mid–2000s the rate was less than 1 percent.

Back to poverty reduction: University colleagues recommended interviews and a visit with the director of a large NGO compound called CBIRD, Community Based Integrated Rural Development, just outside the provincial town of Nang Rong. The first thing one notices upon arrival to the Nang Rong CBIRD are little signs giving directions on the grounds of this NGO among a dense jungle of tropical plants. These signs are a clear hint to who is behind it; they are shaped like big condoms with happy faces. The next thing one notices is a Cabbages and Condoms restaurant inside the gates. Mechai has branched out to other social problems. The three- to four-square-mile area, looking like a jungle resort is, among other things, the grounds of a big single-story hotel complex for tourists and conventions. All hotel rooms have little happy face condom signs with the room number on the doors. But there was much more. Mixed among the hotel rooms, toward the back, are three fairly large textile factories employing about 3,000 village young people in this area, plus a couple hundred young people running the hotel complex. The employee parking lot was full of new, mostly Honda Dream motorcycles. Also on the grounds are classrooms for various job training programs. One contained a new state-of-the-art computer lab. The manager of this Nong

Rang complex explained that there are 18 of these CBIRD branches in Thailand — five in the north, eight in the northeast, three in central Thailand, one in the east, and one in the south. Others are planned. Information booklets explain they are all extensions of Mechai's PDA, Population and Community Development Association, which he started in 1974 to reduce population growth, then fight the spread of HIV infection. Thailand is a much richer country than Cambodia, but even the Thai government can't pay for all of these development projects. Funding for CBIRD, for example, comes primarily from the Canadian government and foreign corporations operating in Thailand that Mechai so successfully hits up for donations.

Three villages lucky enough to be within 20 miles of this CBIRD operation had been selected for interviews. The headman in one of these villages gave an overview of conditions. This headman's house was not so big, at least compared to the one visited several days earlier belonging to the headman away for the weekend studying for his BA in economics. Still, the house was new, big enough for his current family of three, and stylish by current rural Thai tastes; which is to say, concrete and tile, not on traditional stiles, and clearly not fit for the tropical environment. Many of the other houses in this

The CBIRD grounds.

village were of this type, others of more traditional rural Thai design on stilts. All of the houses had electricity and TV antennas.

This time more questions to the headman were focused on the impact of CBIRD in surrounding villages. In this particular village, some 80 percent of the young people in his village have been working at the CBIRD textile factories for the past several years. Along with the agricultural production of their parents, the approximately $5 per day these young people earn has made a big difference in their standards of living. One could see there were many new houses in this village, and many new cars, trucks, and motorbikes in front of these houses. Among the best outcomes of these CBIRD jobs, they all seemed to agree, is families are kept together, their children are less likely to be in trouble in the big city, and the elderly are taken care of by their adult children as tradition requires.

These travels through northeastern Thailand have led to other insights into Cambodia's problems. Clearly, the Cambodian government is corrupt and dysfunctional, and simply lacks what development experts call "institutional capacity." The problem, however, is not restricted to Cambodia's central government. Visiting village after village in Thailand one cannot help but became more and more impressed with the elected headmen and their advisory councils. An insight slowly emerged during these interviews in both Thailand and Vietnam. A few months later, while reviewing photos and field notes, it hit like a thunderbolt. A person can go into a Thai village unannounced and ask to talk with the headman. They can usually be found somewhere in the village and are happy to talk with a foreigner for a couple of hours or so. When suddenly confronted with detailed questions about the village, such as how many families there are, how much land do they have, what is the rice yield and income from other sources, exactly how they are using money from the "One Million Baht" program, etc., etc, these headmen had quick, detailed answers. They were asked many other questions about government aid programs, which ones were in their village, and how they get this aid. In every case these headmen, despite the unannounced visit and without notes or record books, could recite impressive amounts of precise figures. In short, it became clear that these guys are professionals. These village headmen are on the ground level of what is relatively good governance in Thailand. (We will see more precise measures of good governance by the World Bank and other agencies in later chapters.) Most headmen in Cambodian villages know very little about such things and have very little training.

All of this led to more questions about how local government officials in Thailand are trained, or how they come to know all of this information. Eventually the answers became clear; there are many meetings with higher government officials and training seminars. Visits in the northeast of Thailand for over 10 years helped make it all obvious after more recent contrasting visits in Cambodia. Most of the visits in that 10-year period were spent in the Nong Khai Grand Hotel. About the only hotel in the province with enough capacity for large meetings, it always seems the hotel fills up a couple of weekends each month. The hotel staff would say it was government healthcare workers in the province, army officers, police chiefs, local government officials and headmen (several times), local teachers, provincial Red Cross workers, and so on. They were all there for training and information seminars from higher government officials, usually from Bangkok. Few other Southeast Asian countries are seemingly so fond of meetings. Historians tell us local political and civil organization has never been strong in Cambodia. And what little of it existed was basically destroyed for probably generations by the Khmer Rouge.

A final observation about these Thai headmen: In village after village one can see how important these people can be for poverty reduction and economic development. They have always been responsible for various government programs that get down to the village level, but now have much more responsibility with the many new development programs since 2001. The One Million Baht program is the best example. The training and good sense of the headman and his council of advisors are critical for the success of this program. The $30,000 divided up among several villages in each area can be wasted, mismanaged, or invested toward projects likely to fail. One can find a few failures, some reasonable successes, but also quite a few brilliant projects.

The headman of one village figured they had a lot of plant material and animal manure going to waste. So, they figured, why not use some of the One Million Baht program money to invest in equipment for a little fertilizer factory? When interviewed, this headman was inside a shed about the size of a two-car garage as he and three other men from the village bagged black pellets coming out of two little machines about the size of a washing machine. People in the village take turns making fertilizer in their spare time which they can use in their fields for free, plus sell to other villages at low cost. An exceptional idea compared to simply using the money to buy fertilizer at a feed and seed store in the city. Another village decided they needed something like a little 7–11 store so their people wouldn't have to go so far to the provincial town to buy things. It was being built down the street as the headman was describing the idea on his front porch. In addition to saving the trip into town, they can sell things to their village people at lower cost, and at the same time create jobs for village young people. But even more, the store will have a training component for these young people so they might get such jobs in nearby cities. Other villages have set up fish farms, improved irrigation systems, and many other things that create local jobs and improve standards of living, while at the same time generating a return on their investment which assures the loan will be paid back. Very little of anything like all of this happening in rural Cambodia.

A "Poverty-Reduction" Program, By and For the Poor

Before leaving Thailand we must consider another "poverty-reduction program" somewhat unique in the world, at least on the scale it exists in the northeast of Thailand. It is not a poverty-reduction program that should be highly recommended, but it has had a significant impact on poverty reduction in this region and must be recognized as such.

Before describing it, it should be pointed out that Thailand is one of the most tolerant societies one can find. Most kinds of diversity, if not always valued, are at least accepted in Thailand. A few hundred years ago immigrants from Iran, Europe, and Japan were not only accepted in the society but became important political figures and were even allowed to marry members of the royal family.[21] Today there is much less conflict between various ethnic groups than most other countries in the world. An untypical example is the Islamic separatist movement in the far south of Thailand, untypical because Muslims are accepted throughout Thailand and found in high government positions.[22] With this background information people can perhaps understand why there is more acceptance of marriages between Thais and foreigners than many other societies.

A recent study from one of Thailand's most respected institutions, Mahidol University, found there are *at least* 15,000 Thai women from the northeast married to Western men. A majority of these men are Europeans — with German, Swiss, and British men leading the pack.[23] The poverty-reduction part is that the study estimated about $4 million come into the northeast economy every month, $48 million a year, because of these marriages. Another study found these marriages have generated about 750,000 new jobs in northeastern Thailand. The Thai government's National Economic and Social Development Board estimates that the money generated from these marriages accounts for about 6 percent of the region's economy. There is one small village, not far from the northeastern provincial capital of Roi Et, referred to as the "Swiss Village." Of the 750 households in this village, as many as 200 of the daughters are married to Swiss men, some living in Switzerland sending money home, but many also living part time in the village with nice new homes built by their husbands.[24] A *Bangkok Post* investigation found that "job brokers" were responsible for most of the marriages in this village. The headman said a few village women went to work in Thai restaurants in Switzerland and came back with Swiss husbands. Other village women asked to get jobs in Switzerland and met Swiss men. As these village women returned for visits with their Swiss husbands and friends of their Swiss husbands, other matches occurred, and so on in a snowball effect. These are certainly not "mail-order brides" or anything like it. These are men and women getting together, and if not necessarily falling in love, at least deciding on their own free will that they want to be together. The original study asked the Thai women why they married these European men. One should be skeptical that these women were totally honest about the order of importance. But there is little doubt the top two reasons given are both important — number one, the bad behavior of Thai men; number two, foreign men have more money.

In the previous chapter there was mention of some money coming into Cambodia from Western marriages or boyfriends. But the situation in Cambodia is not even close to what one finds in northeastern Thailand. In the provincial Udon Thani airport (the number one province for these marriages) it sometimes looks like 25 to 30 percent of the travelers are European men and their Thai wives or girlfriends. Interviews suggest these couples have met in many circumstances. One met his Thai wife as she was retiring from her job as a bank executive. Others met while working as Catholic missionaries or teaching English in Thailand during their youth. Other Western men met their Thai wives while they were foreign exchange students in Thailand. There is, however, what most would consider a negative side to many of these marriages.

After years of research and academic work in northeastern Thailand, stories about sons and daughters working in Bangkok, sending money back home, have become commonplace. Village parents often say that their daughters are hairdressers, construction workers, hotel maids, department store clerks, and so on. One must always wonder what they are *really* doing. There are no precise estimates, but recent books on the "profession" suggest a large percentage of the 15,000 northeastern women married to Western men met these men in the go-go bars of Bangkok.[25] Case studies suggest these women are working in these places to make good money to send back home, *and* for the chance of finding a *farang* (Western) husband. If they are attractive, the money they can make is many times more than working in a factory. But it must be made clear that these are not really brothels with anything like the Southeast Asian sex slaves and trafficking one reads about or sees on the TV news. They are in many ways more like marriage markets.

Authors who have researched the subject, along with many case studies, show these girls in the upscale go-go bars of Bangkok are free to come and go, follow rather strict condom rules (pushed years ago by Senator Mechai), and have cell phones with emergency numbers to call for help. The danger of HIV is not as great as it is in other bars, but the danger is still there. These girls are taking a risk of being beaten, and there are cases of girls killed by deranged "customers," which are the main reasons one should not recommend this particular kind of poverty-reduction program.

There is one case in a village observed for this research off and on for about a year. The village is about an hour and a half north of Bangkok where village people also stay in the Pratunam slum in Bangkok to sell farm produce. One young girl had come back to the village with a substantial bank account. A result was another young, pretty girl decided that is what she wanted to do. Village informants said the girl who had just returned from working in the bars tried to talk her out of it. Returning to the village north of Bangkok a few months later we asked about this girl and was told she is now working in Pat Pong, the biggest and most famous of these areas in Bangkok.

None of this, of course, is new in world history, just bigger and more organized in Thailand. A famous American anthropologist in the 1960s, Oscar Lewis, wrote some books from his fieldwork in Latin American countries where he found much the same thing, though on a much smaller scale.[26] His explanation was that in a culture of poverty some things like prostitution are not accepted as much as they are tolerated as a means of survival. After coming back to the village Oscar Lewis found the girl's work in the big city was conveniently not discussed, and she could get married and have children as any other lady. In Thailand, though, with so many mixed marriages that are formed in more common ways, and with such a high regard for women married to Western men in northeastern Thailand, it is quite easy to pass off your marriage as the result of meeting in the "local marketplace" as told by a young Cambodian lady in the village just outside of Battambang.

There is growing disapproval of these *mia farang* (women married to Western men) among middle-class Thais. One editorial in the *Bangkok Post* suggested these marriages are making Thailand appear to be the world's brothel. But there seems to be very little disapproval among the rural northeastern Thais. And knowing Thais are usually quite tolerant of such things (prostitution, as noted above, is actually illegal in Thailand), one doubts the number of *mia farang* in northeastern Thailand is likely to go down any time soon. The "poverty-reduction" money will keep flowing into Isaan for a long time.

Traveling throughout the country there is little doubt anything like this will ever happen in Vietnam. For one thing, the culture is different, and for another, the communist party elite are rather Puritan about such things. Prostitution is present in Vietnam, but more limited and hidden. While Lao culture is much the same as northeastern Thailand, the communist party elite in Laos are more like their Vietnamese brothers. Cambodia has some potential for following this "Isaan poverty-reduction program," but only a potential. While prostitution is rather widespread in Cambodia, it is less open, and much more repressed by the government. The bigger problem in Cambodia is that it has been a haven for pedophiles from around the world. From 2005 the Cambodian government has admirably cracked down on the problem, and with the help of many rich countries who are arresting these men when they arrive back to their home countries, pedophiles are moving out of Cambodia. In the summer of 2008 and throughout 2009 a major government campaign began against the more normal kinds of prostitution. So far, hundreds of girls have been arrested in Phnom Penh and some of the more open brothels have been closed. There are recent human rights NGO and newspaper reports that these Cambodian girls were arrested for prostitution and sent to a terrible prison in Phnom Penh where they are raped and beaten by the police and prison guards.[27]

It is ironic when one thinks about it; in Cambodia poor girls are arrested for prostitution while little is done to stop corruption by Cambodian elites sucking millions of dollars away from programs that could reduce poverty. In Thailand, where prostitution is also illegal, one can walk by go-go-bar areas in Bangkok at the 2 A.M. closing hour to find a dozen or so police trying to sort out the traffic jam. At the other end of the power hierarchy, one Thai government after another falls, at least in part, because of corruption, and studies show reductions in corruption by Thai elites in recent decades.[28] Following events in Cambodia for at least 15 years, one finds it hard to find any reports of corrupt officials arrested or punished in that country despite the fact Cambodia is rated among the top 10 corrupt countries in the world.

Gender Relations in Thailand

Before leaving this subject we should consider some of the relatively unique traditions of gender relations in Thailand that help explain this well organized "poverty-reduction program" through the sex industry. Many scholars suggest a link to the social system established in Ayudhya (A.D. 1350–1767) whereby men were required to spend months each year away from their families on projects for the king, thus leaving women to take charge of caring for their families by whatever means they can find. A more complex cultural interpretation, however, involves the matrilocal system found among lowland rural Thais for centuries. In contrast to the more typical patrilocal system around the world, Thai daughters are expected to take care of their elderly parents and thus it is one of the daughters and not a son who inherits the farmland. Young men marrying a Thai farm girl will move to her land and if he doesn't perform well he is kicked out. This gives Thai women more power and influence in the society than found in most other Asian countries.

This matrilocal system, however, comes with considerable pressure on these young women. Given that they are the responsible party in the family, if the family is poor and their agriculture production is insufficient for family needs, these women are expected to find other means to provide for the family. Small shops run by women selling things in the village are common but bring in little money. There is now the lure of factory jobs in the big cities for these poor farm girls, but the wages will at best be around $5 per day. A young pretty woman can make much more money in the tourism sex industry, with the added benefit that she could possibly strike it rich by landing a relatively wealthy foreign man. Such prospects are simply too tempting for many young women from poor areas of Thailand.[29]

It is time to resume our journey through Cambodia's poor. We will proceed to the other regions of Cambodia, then visit Phnom Penh slums and the many homeless urban people recently dumped in the countryside. Following these tours through Cambodia's poor we can put it into perspective again with comparisons from Vietnam and Laos, in many ways fairer comparisons considering Thailand's huge head start with poverty reduction.

CHAPTER 6

Cambodia's Poor: Slum Clearance, Khmer Rouge Style

While Cambodia's rural poor have been neglected, left to lose their land, and have had hundreds of millions of dollars stolen that were targeted for programs aiding poor village families, the situation for the urban poor has been even worse. For several years residents of poor areas of Phnom Penh have been forcefully evicted from their homes and sent to rural "resettlement camps" with no jobs, no agricultural land, some with nothing but a 5-by-12-meter plot of land to build a straw house, but most with no land at all. One estimate in 2007 alone was that over 5,000 urban poor have been forcefully evicted from their homes, homes to which they often had "something like" legal title. (The problem of legal title to land explained later.) Reviewing information about new land leases currently being obtained by mostly foreign construction companies, Amnesty International estimates about 150,000 poor Cambodians are at risk of being evicted in coming months.[1] If this keeps up, it will approach the forced removal of people from Phnom Penh by the Khmer Rouge between 1975 and 1979.

Rumors of even worse abuses of the urban poor were confirmed in July 2008 when the UN Human Rights Commission and various human rights NGOs released their joint findings. The Phnom Penh police have been secretly rounding up hundreds of "street people" and holding them in two old Khmer Rouge prisons for months without notifying relatives, much less with any kind of judicial proceedings. A high percentage of these people are drug addicts, but also a high percentage of these people simply had to live in the streets. Some of those rounded up and held for two months before this particular prison was discovered were as young as eight years old. In early July

2008 the *Phnom Penh Post* wrote about one of these old Khmer Rouge prisons; "The center had been open for two months but was abruptly emptied on June 24 as reports that the scores of drug addicts, street kids and mentally ill held behind its padlocked gates were being beaten or starved drew the attention of the United Nations and NGOs." The discovery was made when one young boy escaped, though his mate in the escape was killed as they tried to flee the prison. The resulting investigation reveled the existence of the two prisons, including the body of a woman who had been dead for days and left to rot among the other prisoners. The local representative of the UN Commissioner of Human Rights was quoted as saying, "Rounding up people on the streets and locking them up is not the way to address the problem of poverty."

During fieldwork in Phnom Penh slums between 2006 and 2010 there were many interviews with people about to be evicted from their homes. Some of these people showed injuries from recent beatings designed to frighten them into leaving. There were depressing stories in four "relocation camps/villages" from some of the three thousand urban poor who had been dumped in four rural areas after eviction. Despite repeated statements by Prime Minister Hun Sen and the Cambodian government from 2005 that these forced evictions would stop, they continue to this day.

Land grabs and violent relocation of Cambodia's poor are not limited to the cities. There are many stories like this one in the southern part of the country where big estates were recently created through land grabs by Cambodia's wealthy and foreign companies (with the cooperation of the Cambodian government). The *Phnom Penh Post* reported in July 2008: "Armed with assault rifles, axes and knives, more than 300 soldiers from Brigade 31 of the Royal Cambodian Armed Forces (RCAF) cordoned-off hundreds of hectares in an area known as Chey Sena, on the fringes of Bokor National Park in Kampot, and began ripping apart the homes of some 200 families living in Anlong Krom, a small collection of huts." Some villagers were beaten unconscious and arrested when they tried to stop the soldiers from destroying their huts and vegetable fields. These evicted villagers were then put in trucks and taken to another village, where villagers there were forced to give part of their land to those evicted from Anlong Krom. The Cambodian Army put roadblocks across every road in and out of the area hoping to hide the forced evictions, but foreign NGO people had already been able to talk with these evicted villagers. The human rights group LICADHO has reported 98 land-seizure cases involving 5,252 families in 2007, and 51 cases involving 3,275 families in the first six months of 2008.[2] As of 2010 there continued to be reports on NGO web sites such as LICADHO and Amnesty International about further forced evictions, and almost daily on the web site of the *Phnom Penh Post*.

Amnesty International in particular has focused attention on these illegal and violent land grabs in the Cambodian countryside. Their web site contains extensive information from interviews with evicted village people, and a surprising number of photos of Cambodian police and the military caught in the act of beating people and burning their homes. One case involved the forced eviction on April 20, 2007, of 105 families from a fishing village, Mittapheap Village, near the coastal town of Sihanoukville where foreign construction companies are now building tourist hotels. Amnesty International reported, "Some 150 members of the [Cambodian] security forces, including the military, shot in the air and on the ground, while demolishing and burning down houses and beating people with electric batons." Eighteen villagers were injured and 13 placed in prison for resisting police. A full report issued by Amnesty International in February 2008 provides much more detail and gruesome color photos of other village people being beaten and their homes burning.

A report on the Amnesty International web site in June 2008 describes an even bigger disaster looming. "On 6 February 2007 the municipality of Phnom Penh entered into a 99-year lease contract with a company whose development plan risks displacing between 3,000 and 4,200 families, and possibly up to 20,000 people. Many of those affected have lived on the land for a long enough period to have strong claims to formal land title deeds under Article 30 and 31 of the 2001 Land Law. According to the contract, which has been approved by the Council of Ministers, a concession of 133 hectares has been granted to [the] company, including almost 90 per cent of Boeung Kak Lake which is to be filled and dried." The *Phnom Penh Post* reported in July 2009 that many of these poor people along the lake are now being flooded out of their homes. The BBC has also been following the situation on their web news site since that time. The forced evictions of poor people around Boeung Kak Lake are proceeding rapidly. The full report on land evictions issued by Amnesty International on February 2008 provides well documented cases of many other such evictions backed by the Cambodian government so that foreign construction companies (most found to be South Korean or Chinese during this fieldwork) can build luxury hotels, condos, and casinos all over Cambodia. There is no question that many top government officials are bringing in handsome bribes for effectively giving away Cambodian land to big multinational corporations (as will be seen in more detail in Chapter 9). Returning to Boeung Kak Lake in January 2010, there were only concrete foundations of homes along the lake where people had been interviewed during follow-ups to this fieldwork in 2009.

LICADHO (Cambodian League for the Promotion and Defense of

Homes being flooded around the lake and the foundations of others already demolished by 2010.

Human Rights) and Amnesty International have documented the following evictions in rural and urban areas in Cambodia:

- In the 13 provinces in which LICADO works — roughly half the country — more than a quarter of a million people have been affected by land-grabbing and forced evictions since 2003.
- In the capital, Phnom Penh, 133,000 people — more than 10 percent of its population — are believed to have been evicted since 1990.
- In 2008, according to Amnesty International, a further 150,000 Cambodians are at risk of forced relocations nationside.
- As of 2004, it was estimated that 20 to 30 percent of landowners held 70 percent of the country's land, while the poorest 40 percent occupied only 10 percent; in the countryside, 45 percent of families were landless or near landless.[3]

It is important to know that violence is not only directed against the poor. Labor union leaders have been killed, social movement leaders trying to protect Cambodia's natural resources have been killed, as have opposition politicians and journalists. On July 11, 2008, a journalist writing for a Cambodian newspaper critical of government corruption and illegal land grabs was killed, along with his son, in Phnom Penh. Quoting the *International Herald Tribune/ New York Times*, "Khem Sambo, 47, and his 21-year-old son were gunned down in a drive-by shooting Friday. Khem Sambo reported on corruption and other social ills under the rule of Prime Minister Hun Sen for the newspaper *Moneaseka Khmer*, affiliated with the opposition Sam Rainsy Party."

Economic development (or attempts at it) almost always lead to dislocations. Some people benefit more than others, at least temporarily. There will be new shopping malls, hotels, office buildings, and condos that will attract new investment and in the long run, hopefully, create new jobs for local people. The slums which have been, and will be, cleared in Phnom Penh are certainly not nice places to live. But in the places where these evicted people have been forced into trucks in the middle of the night and dumped in rural fields with nothing are in many ways worse. Slum removal does not have to be done as is happening in Cambodia. A government reveals much about its nature in the way it treats its own poor when dislocations must be managed.

As a young social worker in the United States almost 40 years, I had many clients who received eviction notices in the mail. The city embarked on an urban renewal campaign and these poor people were in the wrong place, and easier to move than middle-class families with greater access to lawyers. They were angry, of course. But they were given compensation and new places to live instead of being loaded up on trucks one night and dumped in a completely undeveloped plot of land with no housing structures, no water or electricity, and told "Here is your new 5-by-12-meter plot of land to live on." Throughout Southeast Asia in recent years, one finds in cities such as Bangkok, Hanoi, and Saigon that poor slums slowly disappear, with high-rise condos, hotels, and office buildings taking their place. These people, however, are seldom treated like the slum dwellers of Phnom Penh.

Evictions in Other Southeast Asian Countries

In Vietnam, for example, there are new neighborhoods in Danang where slum people from central areas of the city have been relocated. One new housing area for these people visited in 2007 was 10 years old or less, called Thanh Khe Tay Village, still an easy trip to where most still have jobs in the central part of the city. There are three rows of four-story concrete apartment buildings, looking pretty ugly but no doubt better than what these people had before. They are at least sturdy and relatively clean. They withstood the typhoon that came through this part of central Vietnam in 2006, though people in these new apartments said the city government had to help some of them replace roofs.

Also in these "project houses" are some fishermen who had been relocated there a few years ago. They had no complaints about the housing. Some people in these project houses are renting, but these fishermen took the government up on a very low-interest loan to actually buy their own condo. Since they lost their little fishing boats in the typhoon of 2006, the local government hasn't asked for the mortgage payments. The seven fishermen being interviewed at a sidewalk café outside their apartments that day were mostly upset about the loss of their fishing boats in the typhoon. The local government had recently offered each of them a low-interest loan of about $500 to replace their boats, which these fishermen said actually cost just over $1,000 to replace. They all said they didn't like to be in debt for their new apartments *and* a new boat at the same time. Currently, though, they must work as unskilled laborers and make only about $2 per day. Finishing beers on the sidewalk in front of their apartment complex, however, they finally agreed, "I guess we have to take the loan to replace our boats. We will have to make up the other $500 with help from relatives."

In Hue, the old capital of Vietnam a couple of hours north of Danang, there is a different kind of "slum dweller" in the process of relocation. In an area on the fringe of the Hue city limits lives a group of "boat people," though probably better referred to as "sea gypsies," who have been there for generations. In 2007 there were 2,000 of these people living up and down this river. Each family has always lived on their small boats and survived by fishing. After climbing on and off many of these little boats, these people told their stories. In the past they could make about $1.50 a day selling fish. These sea gypsies confirmed what local Communist Party officials had earlier said; their annual income had been about $200 and they have medical benefits as do other Vietnamese citizens. The problem now is that the little river tributary just outside of town has become polluted and there are no more fish for miles. They simply cannot maintain their old lifestyle. An American-funded NGO was helping with some micro-loans, but it was the city government that provided almost all of the aid to relocate these people. The local "People's Committee" in the area said they are slowly relocating these people to land areas where they can change to farming. These sea gypsies said they do not like leaving their traditional life and know nothing about agriculture. But in contrast to Phnom Penh slum dwellers, they are at least being treated humanely

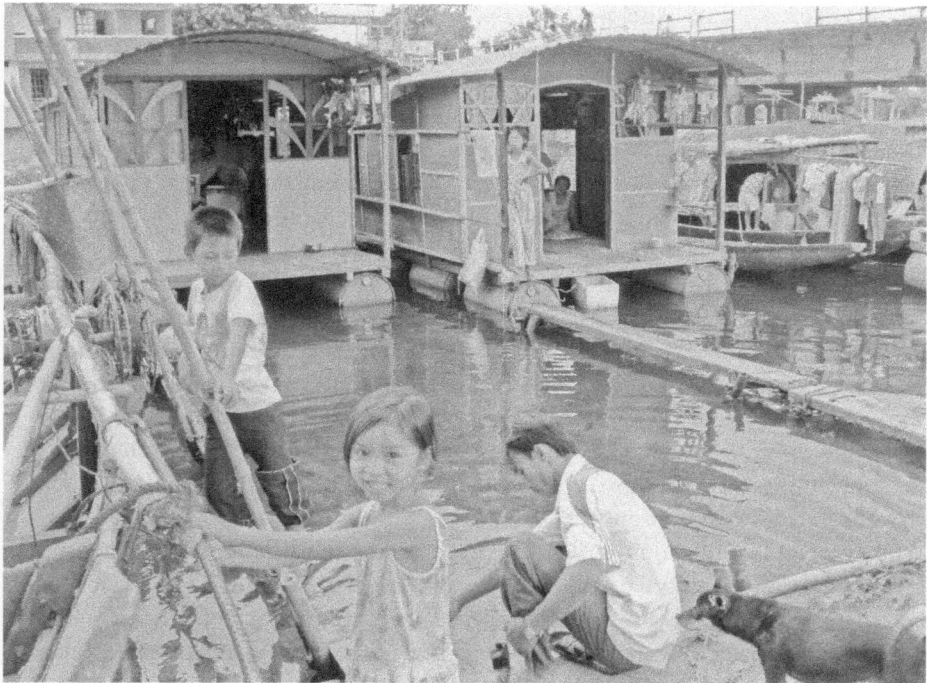

Sea gypsies on their boats.

and will have a livelihood after given their new homes. The process is going slowly, the local Party official said, because it is rather expensive. The cost, paid by the local government, is about $8,000 for each family to provide these sea gypsies with enough land for agriculture and a house built for them. Vietnamese-American NGO people who have been working in this area confirmed the local People's Committee was giving correct information.

There are also land disputes in Vietnam where one side in a conflict over land title wants to develop the land. By one estimate there are some 200 such conflicts in Vietnam today. A primary cause of land conflicts all over Southeast Asia today stem from a history of kingdoms far different from those in the West. In most of Southeast Asia there was not much of what in Europe was called a landed aristocracy who owned almost all land in area, with landless peasants working on huge estates controlled by a landed aristocracy. For centuries in Southeast Asia most land was theocratically owned by a king who allowed peasant villagers to farm the land for minimal taxation and little direct interference. There were seldom clear boundaries between kingdoms so that peasant villages on the fringes were especially left alone (as will be describe in chapters 9 and 10 below). As more modern nation-states with legal systems developed, village people who had farmed their land for generations were suddenly faced with a need for land titles. Governments in the region have tried to settle these conflicts, but usually with great difficulty given their history. On top of this, of course, was the mess created by communist collectivization of all land in Vietnam, Laos, and Cambodia. When land was again privatized in these countries from the mid– to late 1980s, land disputes became even more complex. Vietnam has what appears to be a relatively fair land claims law that puts disputes through civil courts. Even though Thailand never had communism or land collectivization, their history without specific land titles has caused similar conflicts. Thailand too has an effective court system working to settle land disputes in what is usually a reasonably fair manner. As the various reports from NGOs working on these issues in Cambodia indicate, especially those from Amnesty International, the Cambodian court system is *not* preventing the government from giving disputed land to rich Cambodians and foreign corporations.

The fate of slum dwellers in Thailand provide another striking contrast to those in Cambodia. Anyone who has traveled around Bangkok can tell many stories of squatter slums along railroad tracks and in fields away from the main roads. But the squatter slums in Bangkok are, to a large extent, misleading. Unlike the huge slums in Indian and African cities, these people in the slums of Bangkok are mostly part-time squatters; they have a home and rice fields back in their villages and are in Bangkok temporarily to work as unskilled laborers or sell produce grown in their home villages. Be that as it may, they are living in squatter slums around Bangkok that middle-class Thais would like to eliminate.

One of the biggest slums, Klong Toey in the southeastern part of Bangkok, has been there for decades. Visiting Klong Toey a few times since the 1990s to talk with people living there and NGO staff working to help these people, one can see it is not a pretty sight; 100,000 people are crammed into a two- or three-square-mile area next to a flood plain close to the main river running through Bangkok. The "houses" are of plywood, cardboard, and tin, with very little space inside. Stagnant, green, slimy water stands under many of the huts and beside sidewalks, with all kinds of trash and an occasional dead animal floating by. The head of the Thai NGO working to help these people in the late 1900s was a former sociology professor at Chulalongkorn University. He described a fascinating history of Klong Toey.

Over two decades ago when Klong Toey had already been in existence for a while, a middle-class high school girl took an interest in the people there at the time. She began teaching some of the squatter children after her school hours. As this middle-class girl grew older, she wanted to do more. She persuaded some local NGOs to donate money for a little school and clinic. But as the numbers of people in Klong Toey grew, developers attempted to push these people out. There were some cases of shacks burned in attempts to scare these people out. The young lady, who was later elected to the Thai parliament, appealed to NGOs to do something to protect these people. Eventually the most popular daughter of Thailand's revered king took up the cause and made the Klong Toey project one of her own sponsored charities. In Thailand, with the king's backing, that's it. Klong Toey is now untouchable to developers. It exists to this day, still with about 100,000 people going back and forth from villages to Bangkok to make a living. But there is now a fairly nice elementary school on the grounds, a better clinic, and food programs.

Several miles away, in another part of Bangkok, there is Pratunam slum, one of the many smaller slums in Bangkok. This squatters' settlement is along train tracks next to the tallest building in Bangkok. Most of these people are from a village visited earlier about one and a half hours' drive north of Bangkok. Back in Bangkok later we had dinner in one of the plywood and tin shacks along the train tracks.

Pratunam slum.

Most of these people have homes back in their village and come to the slum a few days a week to sell their produce, cutting out any "middle men." Only a few of the families do not have their own homes back in Ongkharak village but certainly close relatives who would take them in if necessary. This was the case with a 20-something-year-old girl living in the Pratunam slum with her young daughter and mother who cooked dinner that night. She worked as a maid during the day to take care of them. Interestingly, while it is an "illegal" squatter village, Pratunam slum huts have mail boxes and have tied into electric lines. In 2005 the Thai government sent eviction notices to these people, giving them two years to start moving elsewhere. In 2010 the slum houses were still there. The government has not followed up on the eviction notices. People still living in Pratunam slum in 2008 said they were not much concerned the government will ever follow up on these eviction notices.

There are many other examples indicating how difficult it is to evict slum people in Thailand. As is typical for national universities in Thailand, Silpakorn University was established with a land grant in the name of an earlier king. The old main campus of Silpakorn University is across from Wat Pra Kaeo, the most important temple in Bangkok, and the Grand Palace on the Chao Phraya River that runs through the city. University officials would like to develop more of the land along the River which belongs to the university under this land grant. But many squatters have been living on this land for generations and the lengthy court process to reclaim this land, they say, is not worth the struggle and would probably be unsuccessful. Instead, the university has expanded its programs on other campuses, the biggest outside of Bangkok in Nakorn Pathom.

None of the above is to claim people are never evicted in the name of progress in Thailand. But they are never evicted the way thousands of families are being evicted in Cambodia today.

Evictions in Cambodia

In Cambodia the evictions, beatings, and burning of people's homes continue as this book goes to press. First interviews with people in one of the infamous Phnom Penh slums were conducted in February 2007. There were more interviews in other slums during April 2008. Most of the people were gone. In several other places around Phnom Penh slums were totally cleared with new casino hotels and condos under construction or already finished. A few other former slums were still vacant in 2008 but with construction equipment ready to build new buildings. We then visited the first slum in the middle of Phnom Penh that we first visited in February 2007, a couple of blocks inland, not far from the huge body of water where the Mekong and Tonle Sap rivers merge.

In 2007 one could find worse slums in Southeast Asia, particularly in Manila, but not many could be described as worse. In a five- or six-square-block area were the partial remains of an old crumbling concrete apartment complex about five stories high. Mold was growing over the outside walls of the remaining buildings, about half already torn down as people were moved out. As part of an old building was torn down the construction company put razor wire around the vacant space to keep people from coming back in. Trash and rubble were everywhere, but almost 700 families were still living there, many in makeshift shacks of plywood and tin on the grounds outside of the old apartment structures. Several families were interviewed then, many of whom had been living there for over 10 years. Several had missed out on the Cambodian land redistribution in the 1980s because they were refugees from the Khmer Rouge in camps in Thailand. Forced back into Cambodia in the late 1980s or 1990s, this was one of the few places they could live. Many of these families had actually been renting a one-room shack of scrap wood and metal for $10 per month. Few of the people had regular jobs, just unskilled laborers when they could find work — many were working for a recycling plant collecting plastic bottles around the city. Some of the children looked more malnourished than any seen in Cambodia. Two women had black eyes and bruises, looking as if they had recently been beaten. Later, Cambodian informants suggested they were probably beaten by customers given that many prostitutes live in this slum area.

About one year later, in the spring of 2008, there were more observations and interviews in this particular Phnom Penh slum, Dey Krahorm. Many of the old crumbling buildings were still there, along with the razor wire and piles of debris and trash everywhere. But there were fewer people. Residents said only 200 people remain, the last resistors to the forced relocation.

The story of a key leader of the resistance movement, referred to as Tima in Chapter 1, has already been told. This very impressive lady survived torture by the Khmer Rouge years ago, and has since been in this slum for more than 20 years. As of April 2008, Tima said the beatings and burnings had stopped for awhile, most likely because of upcoming national elections in late July 2008. She added that Prime Minister Hun Sen and the Cambodian People's Party didn't want the bad press coverage, which is the likely reason Cambodian journalist Khem Sambo (also mentioned earlier) was killed on July 11. After the national elections, which Hun Sen's Cambodian People's Party was sure to win and did, she figured all hell will break lose in her slum area.

Tima and others in the slum provided more details about the Korean company, 7NG, behind the forced evictions in this particular slum, all of which was confirmed by well educated Cambodian informants later. Some government official or officials have given this company land rights and the company was ready to build either a new hotel or condos on the land. Asked where most of these former slum residents are being "relocated," Tima and other remaining slum dwellers gave directions to four areas some 20 to 30 miles outside of Phnom Penh. They described something of the conditions in these "villages." Visits to these four "relocation camps" during the next week showed things were worse than described in three of these "relocation camps."

The first was mostly populated by former slum residents lucky enough to have documents suggesting legal ownership and proper title to their Phnom Penh slum homes. One must remember that after Khmer Rouge farm collectivization and the nationalization of all private property from 1975, the new Vietnamese-backed government in the mid–1980s began privatizing all real estate again, in both the cities and countryside. For a large percentage of Cambodians today there are two problems; either they were out of the country at the time (many in refugee camps in Thailand) and received no property, or, in the haste to redistribute this land, proper land titles were never given. Some slum dwellers, such as Tima, currently leading the resistance, who have some papers claiming title to their dingy and crumbling rooms are in a better position. But even these people much prefer to stay where they are for reasons that became clear after interviews in the first relocation village.

About 20 miles outside of Phnom Penh, looking for this first "village" a few miles off a main road, one first sees a rather large new factory in what seemed like the middle of nowhere. Asking directions to this Borei Santepheap resettlement village, it was finally located just on the other side of the new factory. After driving around the factory, one is met with a rather amazing sight: Also in the middle of nowhere, except for the new factory, are rows and rows of small houses, all attached to houses on either side and behind, each row running for about 200 to 300 yards. Two or three hundred of these houses were completed in April 2008, though many were still uninhabited, with about 150 to 200 others still under construction. Several people living in these houses were interviewed to find out where they came from, conditions in the "village," and what opportunities they had for employment.

Once inside, these little houses are not so bad. They have new tile floors, a front living area, an indoor bathroom, and a sleeping area in back. Remarkable for a rural area in Cambodia, they have electricity. Of course, the factory behind them must have electricity and thus the power lines could be brought

The 7NG company town.

to this housing area with little difficulty. A few people living in the little houses had opened businesses targeting customers in the village. One lady had a little convenience store selling mostly drinks and snacks, down the street was a CD and DVD shop (no doubt pirated music and movies), some had little restaurants, and others little clothing shops. A regular small city was being created.

But this is the deal, as told to us by Tima back in Phnom Penh, and then confirmed by several residents of this "company town." Perhaps it will not be surprising to learn that the factory next to this housing complex is a textile "sweatshop" that just happens to be owned by the same South Korean company, 7NG, forcing people out of Tima's Phnom Penh slum. The name "Williby's" is on the front of the factory, but sweatshop employees in this company town and NGO people back in Phnom Penh confirmed 7NG owns and runs the factory. How else can 7NG get a captive work force in the middle of nowhere when the $2-dollar-a-day wage is about the cost of a round-trip commute from the closest city to this factory? These 7NG managers have created a brilliant system; take their homes in the city and force them to move to a sparsely populated area where 7NG needs sweatshop employees.

While 7NG has created a good deal for itself, huge problems remain for these relocated slum dwellers. First of all, the sweatshop only hires young people, almost all girls between 17 and 21 years old. That is the explicit policy. Even worse, potential employees must pay an upfront bribe to company officials worth about one month's wages to get a job. The vast majority of people in this company town, those who are not teenagers, are out of luck. There are no other jobs unless one can come up with the cash to start his or her own little store in the housing complex. If they do have a teenage daughter in the family *and* can come up with the cash, there is a job paying about $50 per month. (These teenage workers said they are mostly making pants labeled with a price tag of $40 each.) These young employees usually work from 7 A.M. to 10 P.M., though after 5 P.M. is overtime for which they get 25 cents per hour. Asked how they liked the textile job, most interviewees responded with faces of disdain, saying they were told "we are treated like dogs." Well-educated Cambodian informants later pointed out that this concept of "being treated like dogs" has a much harsher meaning in the Cambodian language than in English.

For slum dwellers like Tima having at least some questionable title to their place in Phnom Penh, the deal is also this: if one gives up title to a Phnom Penh abode, 7NG offers about $6,000 to leave. But if the family agrees to move to the new company town, they get one of these little houses free of charge. Residents in this "sweatshop village" claimed the houses have a market value of about $13,000. Some slum dwellers with other options had a better deal; after accepting a little house in the company town they tried to sell it. Those who couldn't sell the house (most cannot we were told) try to rent it out. There are few takers. The woman running a little convenience store said she was renting the two-room house for $50 a month. The rest of her family remained on land in a small village not far away, growing rice in the traditional manner. She was able to bring in more than $50 a month from her little store, thus surviving in the company town and helping out her family back in the village. But she was apparently one of the big exceptions.

Despite the clean new home with a tile floor and electricity in the company town, everyone interviewed said they had been better off in Phnom Penh. And it is important to again stress that these are the luckiest of the relocated slum people. They listed reasons for their discontent; first was always the lack of jobs in the area. If there is no teenager in the household, or they cannot afford the bribe of one month's salary to get the sweatshop job, the closest jobs are back in Phnom Penh which pay about $2 per day. A daily commute to Phnom Penh costs $2.50, even before the doubling of gasoline prices during the summer of 2008. Almost all of these families are substantially worse off because one or more family members must work in Phnom Penh, sleeping homeless while in the capital city, returning to their families back in the company town once every week or two. Many of these people work for a plastic recycling plant in Phnom Penh, as they did before forced out of the city, but now sleep on the grounds of the recycling plant. Another common complaint is that the only primary school is much further away than where they lived in Phnom Penh, and there are no other schools above the primary level around the company town. Then there is a problem with medical care; in Phnom Penh they could get to some of the low-cost clinics run by NGOs (later found to be funded by the Japanese government). In the company town, like most peasant farmers outside of Phnom Penh, they must mortgage their house and borrow money at about 20 percent interest per month to pay for medical care when needed. But as noted above, these former slum dwellers in the company town are far better off than those interviewed in the other three relocation villages.

Conditions in the next two resettlement villages were far worse, though found later to be better off than the forth and final resettlement village visited. Both are about 20 to 30 miles outside of Phnom Penh in another direction from the South Korean company town visited first. There were about 2,000 people in each village at the time, all people relocated from other slums in the capital (that is, slums other than where Tima was fighting to keep her home). Most of the people relocated to the second and third relocation village came from a slum closer to the waterfront in Phnom Penh. It is now a vacant lot, a blue corrugated metal fence around the perimeter, with guards to keep out the homeless. Various kinds of earth-moving equipment were nearby. Another foreign construction company, in this case, Chinese informants said, was ready to build a tourist hotel, expensive condos, or casino.

A key reason people in this second resettlement village are in a worse situation is that they had no clear title to the property where they lived in Phnom Penh. One night police and company guards came with trucks, beat those who attempted to resist, loaded them and their few possessions onto the trucks, drove them out of Phnom Penh, and dumped them where they have been living for the past two years. There was no company house or a $6,000 cash settlement. These people were given a 5-by-12-meter plot of land. That is it. There was no house on the little plot of land, they were given no building material for a house, they have no electricity or fresh water, and they have no agricultural land. There is no city with significant jobs any closer than Phnom Penh, which again would be a daily commute costing over $2. Most of these people had to borrow money to buy building material for a house of wood and straw, using their little 5-by-12-meter plot of land as collateral. A $300 to $500 loan for building materials costs about $7 to $30 interest per month, depending on how much land they could put up for the collateral. Because they have almost no income to repay these loans, interviewees repeatedly said their little plot of land was in danger of being lost. Others couldn't get the loans and were living in what looked more like large straw baskets rather than houses.

Ironically, many of these people are helped by a Korean Christian church nearby which gives out free rice every month. These is a primary school down the road run by this church where the former slum children can attend school. As in other villages, some survive because family members sleep in the streets of Phnom Penh or in temporary huts of plywood and scrap metal, working for $2 a day as unskilled laborers. One woman said they mortgaged their little 5-by-12-meter plot of land for $300 to buy her husband an old motorbike so he can work as a motorcycle taxi driver in Phnom Penh, sleeping in a park most nights.

The first family interviewed in this village had three children in elementary school, plus an elderly mother and father living with them — seven people in their house of wood and straw on a 5-by-12-meter plot of land. An older daughter was working in Phnom Penh. The house was the usual wood and bamboo frame with straw serving as walls and a roof. They attempted to brighten up their little hut by covering the inner walls with color pictures from some old magazine. It was hard to believe seven people could sleep in this house, and probably they didn't. At least when it didn't rain some slept outside.

The father of this household was sitting on the bamboo floor, looking quite sad, wearing black shorts and no shirt, a traditional checkered Cambodian cloth scarf over his shoulder, his gray hair cut short. His wife, mother, and father, sat further back in the little hut. As usual, toward the end of the interview, the children were given gifts of notebooks and colored pencils. One would think they had been given a rare treasure; within seconds the children were happily drawing pictures. One pretty girl about eight years old, wearing an old pink dress, her long black hair half hiding her face and bright eyes as she leaned to one side, was drawing a picture of the visiting foreigner. She giggled and hid her face when that was noticed. Her younger brother, perhaps six years old, wearing blue shorts and no shirt, was sitting in his mother's lap, a big smile on his face as he drew something else. The other little girl sat further back in the hut as she drew. Despite the obvious cheer generated with gifts, it was in reality a rather depressing scene: Here were three little children almost overwhelmed with joy because of a few notebooks and colored pencils. Looking around their house, one could see that aside from some old clothes, these notebooks were about their only possessions.

Their parents were first asked why they left Phnom Penh. With looks as if it was a dumb question (which it actually was, but the answers had to be confirmed), the father finally responded, "We had no choice, we were afraid for our lives." Their story was rather typical: They were in refugee camps when land was privatized in Cambodia during the 1980s, so they missed out. They said they now survive on the free rice from the Korean church plus money brought back by one daughter working in the Phnom Penh plastic recycling plant, sleeping on the grounds most nights.

At the end of the interview the mother said something which sparked a little discussion with the translator. The wife was surprised her husband had opened up so completely during the interview. It was the first time she had seen him do so with anyone in many years. He was beaten by the Khmer Rouge before they escaped to Thailand, Thai soldiers in the camps were not to be trusted either, and more recently he was beaten by the police forcing them out of their Phnom Penh slum. She said that in all those years he was afraid to talk about such things with anyone outside of his family until today.

After a couple of hours with this first family, the next family interviewed lived a few huts down the dirt road. Amazingly, this family had 14 people of varying family relations living in a similar hut on their 5-by-12-meter plot of land. Their story was much the same. But members of this family were able to get privatized land in a village back in the 1980s. However, due to illness in the family, they had to mortgage that land to pay for medical bills, finally losing the land in 1994 after they couldn't repay the loan. They ended up in the Phnom Penh slum, but there was enough work for unskilled laborers to pay the $10-a-month rent and buy food. Now in this relocation village they are surviving on donated rice and the little money two family members can make as unskilled laborers back in Phnom Penh. Driving to this relocation village one passes a small factory about three or four miles away, and a DHL collection warehouse where trucks leave to make their deliveries. Asked about potential jobs in those places, the first response was that there were no job openings, and secondly, as in other factories, one must pay the boss a bribe of one month's salary upfront before getting a job. Asked about their health, the mother responded quickly. Their kids get sick a lot, she thinks because of not enough food. But in one way they are better off than slum people taken to the company town; not far down the dirt road was a low-cost clinic, funded by a charity (they didn't know by whom). If hospitalization was needed, the mother said they would try to get back to the Japanese-funded hospital in Phnom Penh.

There were similar stories from other families in this relocation village. Some, however, were in worse situations. During a downpour from the early start of the rainy season that year, a very old lady who had trouble walking came up to a hut of another family in order to get out of the rain. She was soaking wet, and totally homeless. She was given land after the Khmer Rouge years but lost it after becoming ill. She used to live with two adult children in Siem Reap but said they are now too poor to take care of her, she explained. While living homeless around the Phnom Penh slum that was cleared, she was forced onto the truck taking people to this village. She now lives on donated rice and sleeps with different families around this relocation village who invite her into to their little huts.

Two days later there were interviews in the forth and largest resettlement camp. Taking several wrong turns down muddy roads almost impassable by car, asking again and again where the Andong Thmei resettlement village was located, there finally appeared a well surrounded with people pulling up buckets of water. Next to the well was a big mud pond where a dozen or so little boys were splashing each other in the water. People at the well pointed toward a vacant field where in the distance we could see a line of straw huts. Leaving the car next to the well and walking across the open field toward the straw huts, we could see more clearly what resembled a fortress of straw a few hundred yards away, a fortress of perhaps one hundred straw huts with their backs to the outside, forming a square about a quarter-mile wide on each side. Walking completely around one side of the "straw hut fortress" there was finally a space to squeeze inside. Suddenly appeared something like a whole city, but a whole city with only small walkways between straw huts covering almost every foot of space inside the straw hut fortress. It was like one of those life-sized mazes farmers in the U.S. and Japan cut through their corn fields where people can pay money to become utterly lost. After talking with several families that day, there was in fact need to ask directions several times before finding the way out of this straw fort maze.

Various families in different parts of this "relocation camp" were interviewed that day. A middle-aged man who was apparently an informal headman said this village started with 1,000 people over two years ago and has since grown to over 3,000 people as more and more Phnom Penh slum people are dumped here. This information was later confirmed when checking the Amnesty International web site which details some of the history of this relocation village, including pictures from the first year to 2008. People in this worst resettlement village were given no rights to land and have no idea when they are likely to be evicted again. Asked why these people were not at least given little 5-by-12-meter plots of land like the previous two resettlement villages we had seen, the village "spokesperson" said he didn't know. He assumed the construction companies that kicked them out of Phnom Penh were simply

Andong Thmei relocation camp.

not as "generous." It was discovered later through informants that most of these people had no title to the land or huts where they were living in Phnom Penh and could therefore be evicted without any potential claim for compensation. Various charities have donated building materials for their little huts, other charities donate food, while others are working to create some sanitation for this area. Anyone can imagine what it is like for some 3,000 people crowded onto the small plot of land with no running water, no toilets with any kind of septic system, and electricity to only one small part of the straw fortress. Just before leaving the straw fortress there was a sign on a building holding construction material used to improve sanitation in this relocation camp owned by a California branch of Habitat for Humanity. No Americans were there at the time but a family next door said Habitat for Humanity was involved with several projects such as building gutters throughout the straw village so it wouldn't flood during the rainy season. Returning to this village in January 2010 there was a new French NGO office for micro-loans mentioned earlier. But little else had changed.

Except for being packed together with about 3,000 other people, and lacking even rights to a 5-by-12-meter plot of land to build a straw house, the stories of families in this straw fortress were like those in other resettlement villages; there were no jobs in the area, it was too expensive to commute every day for jobs in Phnom Penh, so some were homeless in the capital city while they work to bring a little money back to family members. None had legal title to any property in Phnom Penh before being dumped into this place for the usual reasons; they were either refugees in Thailand when land was given out or they lost their land because of debts. There was a little Christian school not far away. It would be impossible for even a small percentage of the children from this straw fortress to fit into that school so one must assume very few get any schooling.

After walking through this resettlement camp one can only be amazed that these ingenious people have somehow created a semblance of civilization out of the mess. They have no government aid, and only a little aid from various NGOs. They have just done it themselves out of necessity. The huts packed together in this huge slum transported to a rural area are of dirt floors and wooden polls covered with straw. It seems to fit into some kind of mosaic pattern or maze which may have some logic if viewed from a few hundred feet above the ground. Spaces between many houses are covered with stagnant, green, slimy water which flows into the huts during the rainy season. But despite it all, this packed area of humanity has taken on the slight appearance of a city. In a small area on one side of the resettlement camp someone had strung up electric lines. A few enterprising residents have established little straw hut grocery markets, or fish markets, still others have little meat markets, the usual raw meat hanging in the tropical heat with proprietors constantly swatting flies. There were five or six "restaurants" and even a couple of very small pharmacies with the basic array of pills.

Because of its size and the appalling manner of its origin, this huge kind of concentration camp has attracted the attention of a few charities and NGOs from around the world. As noted above, returning for more interviews and observation in early 2010, we found a new NGO from France helping out with micro-loans of $100 to $200 for the little shops catering to the needs of people in this massive relocation village. There are the beginning of projects to store fresh water in large blue plastic tanks, some NGO was constructing little concrete outhouses with septic tanks underground, and as also noted above, people from the USA Habitat for Humanity have been building gutters in an attempt to control flooding. But none of this is adequate considering how many desperate people are packed into the area. We could find no health-care workers in the area, and it is hard to believe the rate of illness and disease is not extremely high, especially among the children.

Considering what one sees throughout Southeast Asia today, except for the poor in Burma, it seems clear that the slum people and village people losing their land in Cambodia are among the most abused people in the region. What is being done to these people is just pure and simple brutality. After describing what can be seen in Cambodia there is a common response; "that sounds all too familiar." One should not belittle the Khmer Rouge genocide by comparing it to what is happening now. But today there seems to be a similar mentality among the Cambodian elite that allows this to happen, and in many cases makes it happen by calling in the Cambodian police and military to round up people in the middle of the night and dump them into relocation camps so South Korean and Chinese companies can have their land. These slum dwellers from Phnom Penh are intentionally violated by greedy people in high places who participate in the violation of their own citizens so they can enrich themselves when foreign corporations came calling with money. Cambodian people trying to bring this to the attention of the country and world have been killed. The slum people themselves are being beaten and their homes burned down if they try to resist.

For the other poor of Cambodia, mostly in rural areas, it is more like criminal neglect. Most people in rural villages around Cambodia are not actively violated. They are simply left to their poverty by a corrupt and dysfunctional government where money for infrastructure improvement and medical care that could improve their lives is siphoned off a little here, a little there, so very little actually gets down to help these people. It is difficult to say which government is worse; Burmese military dictators who refuse aid agencies entry to their country when more than 100,000 of their people die and thousands more need aid after a typhoon in 2008, or a government which pretends to be a democracy but year after year does little to help its citizens, except those who have become rich from corruption and can pay bribes to get what they want.

To put the continuing tragedy in Cambodia into further perspective we need to consider conditions in Vietnam and Laos. These two countries were in similar conditions of poverty some 20 years ago. Vietnam is now reducing poverty faster than almost any other country in the world. And while still much poorer, little "sleepy," landlocked Laos is doing much better as well. Once the contrast to Vietnam and Laos is made clear, we can return to more specifics about current conditions of corruption and the dysfunctional government in Cambodia today.

CHAPTER 7

Cambodia Compared with Vietnam and Laos

In many ways Vietnam and Laos are better comparisons to Cambodia than is Thailand. Unlike Thailand, just 15 years ago Vietnam and Laos had levels of poverty and economic development comparable to those of Cambodia. Vietnam has since left Cambodia far behind and is closing in on Thailand. Poverty levels in Laos have moved lower only recently. But in a key contrast to Cambodia, and more like Thailand and Vietnam, Laos is beginning its development policies with a more equal focus on rural and urban areas. If Vietnam, Laos, and Cambodia continue on their current course for a few decades, Vietnam will look more like Thailand does today, while Cambodia will look more like one of the smaller, highly unequal Latin American countries falling into stagnation. Laos is moving in the right direction, but it is too early to tell how steadily economic growth and poverty reduction will progress.

A History of Poverty in Vietnam and Laos*

Percent of Vietnamese population below the national poverty level

1988	1993	1998	2002
75%	58%	37%	28%

Percent of Lao population below the national poverty level

1993	1998	2005
46%	38%	31%

*Source: Dollar 2004; World Bank 2008a; World Bank 2007b.

Anyone who has visited Vietnam since the early 1990s is amazed every time he or she returns. Much like China, though on a smaller scale, the country has been transformed. Every year Ho Chi Minh City (Saigon) seems to have new high-rise hotels and office buildings. Where none had existed before, there quickly appeared "industrial parks" outside both HCMC and Hanoi, full of factories built by big-name corporations from North America, Europe, Japan, and South Korea. In Hanoi the big hotels and office buildings have been kept further from the center of the city to preserve the charm of the Old Town, a few hundred years old. Just outside the center of Hanoi, though, are many new office buildings, hotels, and industrial parks much like those in HCMC/Saigon. On roads into the heart of Hanoi, by the late 1990s, there were already small shop houses bulging with TVs, washing machines, refrigerators, and stereos.

Contrasts between the Vietnamese and Cambodian countryside are far greater. The World Bank *World Development Report* for 2008 tells us that only 9 percent of rural people in Cambodia have electricity. That figure is 73 percent in Vietnam. Only some 7 percent of villages have water control or irrigation in Cambodia, while the figure is over half in Vietnam. Cambodia cannot adequately feed itself and is a net importer of food (though rice exports are rising fast). Vietnam had extensive malnutrition and hunger at the end of the 1980s; today they are the world's second largest exporter of rice and coffee, with virtually no one starving in Vietnam today. Cambodian farmers are able to afford an average of just 3 kilograms of fertilizer per hectare of land under cultivation; in Vietnam that figure is 245 kilograms per hectare. The average annual increase in agricultural production between 1990 and 2004 in Cambodia was basically flat, just 0.8 percent; in Vietnam it was about 4 percent, and of course has averaged much higher than that in the last 10 years.[1] Vietnam is certainly not without problems. But in contrast to Cambodia, the country is following development policies that will lead to sustainable economic development and poverty reduction.

Transition from a Communist Economy

Both Vietnam and Laos remain communist countries since North and South Vietnam were united under a communist government in 1975, and Laos fell to the communist Pathet Lao that same year.[2] Soon after communists took over in both countries there were the usual "reeducation camps" where thousands of the former enemies were rounded up and kept in prisons for a few years. But there was no "blood bath" like there was in Cambodia between

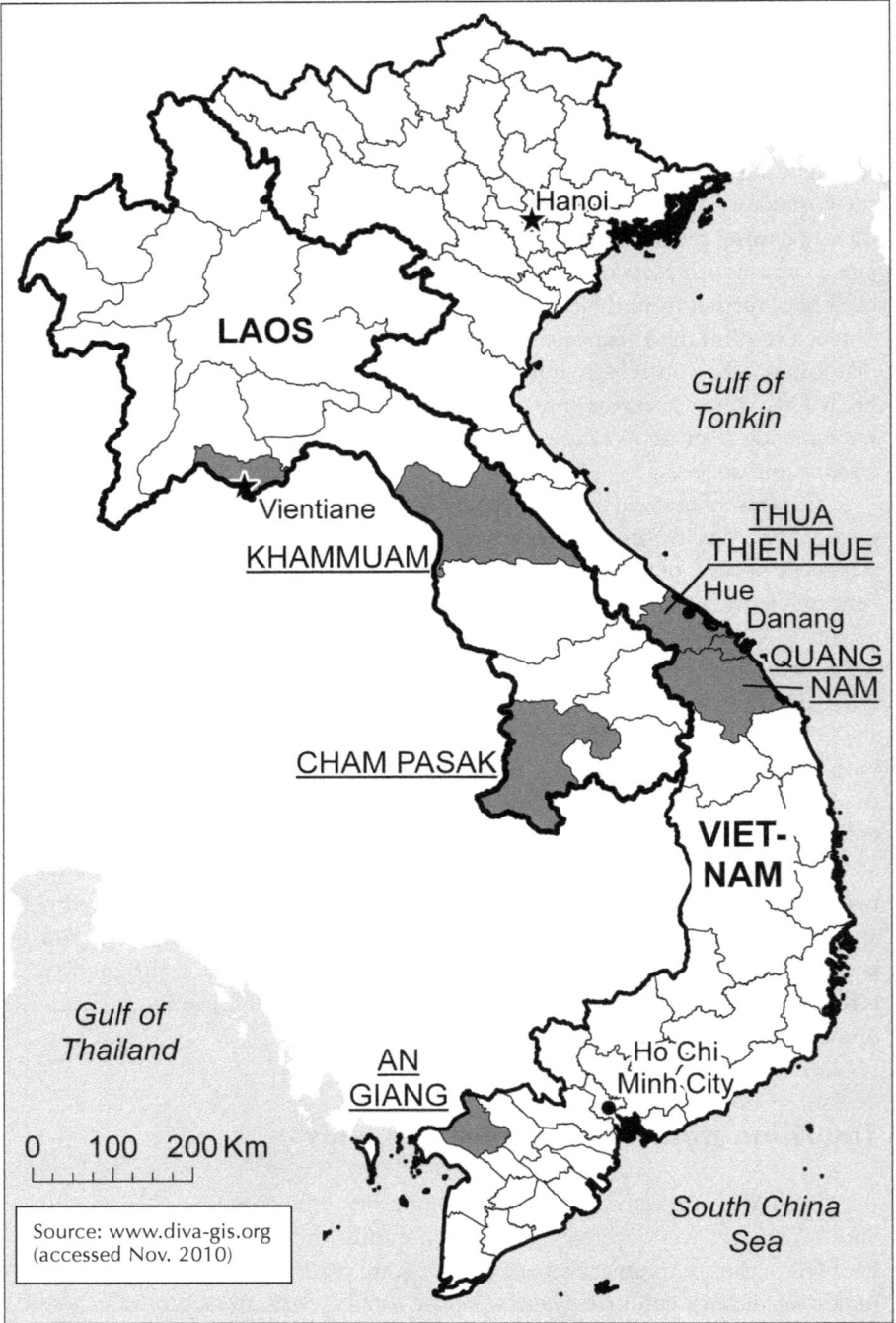

Map of Laos and Vietnam.

1975 and 1979. Both Vietnam and Laos had very repressive states for the first couple of decades. In recent years, however, the extreme political repression has given way to a greater concern for economic development. Neither country has anything like the human rights found in most Western countries. But there are more freedoms in Vietnam and Laos than most people in the West realize. In both countries one sees Christian churches operating quite openly, with many of these churches packed on Sundays in Vietnam. There is no more police or military presence than one finds in the United States.

In Laos people can travel through the flat Mekong River Basin with the same freedom as in Vietnam. Laos does have some travel restrictions; there is a low-level war still going on with the hill tribe Hmong who were organized by the CIA to fight communists during the American part of the Vietnam War. A few thousand of these Hmong remain in mountain areas, still being attacked by the Lao military. Every couple of years a Western reporter is arrested for a couple of days when caught sneaking into or back out of the area.

The first time, Western tourists are surprised. They have seen how repressive these communist countries are on TV and movies. In both Vietnam and Laos one can sum it up this way; in 1975 they won the war but quickly lost the peace. The old Stalinist policies put in place after 1975 were mostly failures. By the mid–1980s in Vietnam, much of the country was starving. During the second half of the 1980s the Vietnamese communist party finally wised up to these failures. And Communist Party officials are fully aware that the Vietnamese people have a long history of rising up against governments that don't take care of their people. By the late 1980s, the Vietnamese Communist Party began economic reforms called *doi moi*. Today these economic reform policies have progressed to the point where one can suggest that Vietnam has a capitalist economy, but with a continuing communist political system.

Yes, there are a few remaining state-owned factories, but far fewer as a percent of the overall economy than in China today. In essence, the Vietnamese Communist Party made a pact with their people, saying something like, "We will do things to help improve your economic opportunities and leave you alone to get rich, as long as you leave us (the Communist Party) alone in return." This pact with the people means things such as it being okay to be an active Christian and build up church membership all over Vietnam, but not to use the church podium to preach for the downfall of communism. At present, the Vietnamese people are mostly okay with this arrangement.

Forms of Government and Economic Development

We also need to understand that numerous studies by the World Bank, United Nations, and the most respected scholars on the subject show there is *no correlation* between democracy in poor countries and economic development.[3] Such conclusions are rather obvious when one thinks about it; Vietnam and China certainly do not have democratic governments, but their economies are booming. India is always described as the biggest democracy in the world, but only recently has India started to have some economic development, and in contrast to Vietnam and China it is economic development with almost no poverty reduction. While more democratic today, both South Korea and Taiwan were highly repressive dictatorships while they were "Asian Tigers," moving out of poverty and close to an economic level with the richest countries today.[4] During the late 1800s to World War II, while rising to rich-nation status, Japan was certainly not a democracy.[5] Across the Pacific from these Asian countries we find higher levels of democracy in many Latin American countries, but we also find higher levels of poverty, income and wealth inequalities, and economic stagnation.

For poor countries (as we will see in more detail in the final two chapters) the key to economic development is not democracy but *government efficiency* in developing good economic policies *and* the ability to carry out these policies. Equally important, and more allusive, is the motivation of political elites to help their people. There are dictators who seemingly don't give a damn about their people, such as those in Burma and North Korea, and there are dictators who are more motivated to improve the lot of their people than many elected officials in formally democratic countries. It is obvious that political elites in China and Vietnam today fall to the side of the latter, while many "democratically elected" leaders in Latin American countries have been on the side of the former. But it is not simply that some dictators care more about their people; there is also self-interest involved in many countries because they know their people might throw them out in mass protests if things don't get better.

What the above also implies is that simple statistical measures like democracy (having elections, competition among political parties, etc.) don't always get it right. Most people will be surprised to learn that there is more of a civil society in Vietnam (a society in which various interest groups are organized and demanding the government improve things for their group) than exists in many countries labeled democratic. This is certainly the case compared to Cambodia. Thailand provides another good example: The most respected political economist in Thailand today has referred to Thai peasants as "a wild and unruly lot." Throughout the second half of the 20th century, through dictators and democracy, Thai peasants have been well organized to push for their interests.[6] During the economic boom years of the 1990s, for example, one estimate was an average of two organized protests by rural people per day. The rural-based Assembly of the Poor (also translated as the Forum for the Poor) is one of the most powerful interest groups in the nation. Since the 2006 military coup which took out a prime minister highly favored by Thai peasants because of his policies there have been massive protests by "red shirts." The rural poor in Thailand may not always be well represented in parliament, but woe to the prime minister who completely ignores their interests. This is not what one finds in Cambodia.

We will return to these issues again in the next chapter with a focus on the Cambodian government, but before leaving this issue it should be noted that over time there *is* a correlation between economic development and some form of democracy. But the causal correlation is the reverse of what most people think; high levels of economic development (which also means higher levels of education) cause democracy, not the other way around.[7] Once people have enough to eat and become economically more comfortable, secure, and better educated, they then start thinking about freedom and human rights; this is what eventually brings some form of democracy. Vietnam and China, for example, will be more like democracies in a couple of generations or so if their strong economic development remains on track. Laos has been moving in the same direction as Vietnam, but much more recently and so far more slowly. A younger communist leadership has been pushing reform because of potential unrest as the Laotian people watch others becoming more prosperous on either side of the country.

Vietnamese Economic Development and Poverty Reduction

Something like Vietnam, smaller territories under different names, has existed for more than 2,000 years.[8] During the first 1,000 years Vietnam was dominated by China, and for a few hundred years afterward Vietnam went back and forth between Chinese dominance and independence. A result of this history is that Vietnam has more Chinese cultural influence than does Thailand, Laos, or Cambodia. Like Laos and Cambodia, Vietnam was increasingly dominated by the French from the early 1800s, then became a formal French colony before the end of the 1800s. In contrast to Laos and Cambodia, Vietnam was more of an economic prize for France, and the French subsequently put more money into Vietnam to develop the economic infrastructure and offer Western education to the Vietnamese. In part because Vietnam was such an economic prize to the French, the war to gain independence was more prolonged. Laos and Cambodia became free from France in 1953, as did the south of Vietnam. The American part of the Vietnam War came into full force from 1964 until 1975 (though there was a secret war run by the CIA based in Laos from the late 1950s). But by 1970 both Laos and Cambodia had been sucked back into the American war and became communist as well in 1975. After 1975 Cambodia received the most devastation at the hands of their own people, the Khmer Rouge, while Vietnam and Laos "only" wrecked their economies with unrealistic Stalinist communist policies. By the late 1980s both Vietnam and Laos were giving up the communist economic policies, however slowly in Laos.

The most important economic reforms coming out of *doi moi* from the late 1980s were the elimination of collective farms and reinstating of private family farms, a free market for selling goods rather than having to sell to the state (especially for farm products), allowing for privately owned corporations, and slowly selling shares of state-owned companies to achieve the goal of privatizing these state-owned companies, as well as opening the economy to the global market for foreign corporate investment.[9] None of this happened overnight; it was a gradual process of two steps forward and one step backward because opposition within the Communist Party would mount to delay or temporarily reverse some of the policies. People arriving in the international airport outside of Hanoi in the later 1990s would see an amazing sign along the road halfway to the city — "Ford Welcomes You." The U.S. automaker was building a new plant. About three or four years later that plant and others from American, Japanese, and European companies were up and running, in the case of Ford, pouring out small pickup trucks. But before that new Ford factory was in operation there was a reversal of some *doi moi* policies. A year after that "Ford Welcomes You" sign was displayed, billboards advertising Western products had all been painted over. A conflict within the Communist Party led to restrictions on Western imports, Western business deals, and advertising. A year later the billboards were back up as if nothing had happened, and Western business deals were moving ahead.

Extensive research (to be detailed later) has shown that an influx of foreign investment is not always good for a country's economic future. There is no direct correlation between foreign investment and future economic growth and poverty reduction. It all depends on how the host country is managing the foreign investment. If foreign corporations are allowed to do whatever they want to do in the country, the resulting low wages, low or non-existent taxes, and the free movement of foreign capital in and out of the country can leave an economy worse off in the future. The North American Free Trade Agreement (NAFTA) in Mexico is a good example. When NAFTA came into effect many foreign corporations poured investments into Mexico for factories that could sell products freely in North America. Some 10 years after NAFTA was signed almost half of those factories were closing, with many moving to China where infrastructure development was better, there was a better educated workforce, and wages and other production costs were even lower.

The point is that the host country must have a government which puts limits on what these foreign companies can do; these foreign companies must pay taxes so the country can improve infrastructure, and even better, the foreign corporation should be made to form partnerships with domestic firms (old ones or newly created) so that profits and technology know-how remain in the country. Less developed countries with weak and/or highly corrupt governments are often unable to make such demands on foreign corporations. Other countries have a ruling class concerned with only their own short-term profits and not the future economic prospects of their citizens (as is apparent in Cambodia). In such cases foreign corporations are allowed to do as they want to exploit workers, avoid taxes, strip the country of natural resources with little future benefit to the country's economy (only to benefit the ruling elites with bribes), and destroy the environment.

There will be more details about all of this in the last two chapters, but a key point is that Vietnam, like China, Thailand, and all other booming Asian countries, have governments willing and able to protect the long-term national economic interests of its people. For example, until recently Vietnam had a 51 percent domestic ownership rule for foreign corporations as in Thailand. This Vietnamese law has recently been amended, but the fact remains that there are many rules placed upon foreign corporations coming into Vietnam that protect national economic interests. Foreign corporations bitch about these regulations in China, Vietnam, and Thailand. They would prefer to do as they please in these countries. But in the end these foreign corporations see there are long-term benefits for them to invest in these countries so they do so, and their investments benefit the foreign corporation *and* the long-term prospects of the host country.[10]

A Tour through Rural Vietnam

As noted earlier, fieldwork in Vietnam was mainly along the central coast and in the Mekong Delta. The rural fieldwork began at a Vietnamese-American-

Thuy Tan Village.

funded NGO outside of Hue, FESR (Funds for Encouraging Self Reliance). Their office in Hue is quite impressive. About a dozen Vietnamese young people were working away at computers keeping track of micro-loans and doing research on the potential for other projects funded through micro-loans. FESR was established by Doan Le Phung, a Vietnamese American who earned an American Ph.D. in engineering and became rich. His $1 million endowment to FESR has meant over 10,000 families in central Vietnam have received micro-loans of $300 or so, with 8,000 families currently with one of these loans. Almost 100 percent of these people repay the loans which require no collateral and come with a very low interest rate. While visiting the FESR office in Hue after months in Cambodia, one can only think how badly poor Cambodians could use such help. But one is even more impressed by what has already been done by the Vietnamese government.

Some FESR staff were on their way to visit Thuy Tan village about 15 miles outside of Hue, on a big river. Approaching the village one drives over a levy perhaps three quarters of a mile in length helping to control water. Along the way are pumping stations getting the water into their rice paddies when needed and out when not needed. There are electric lines coming into the village and reaching every household. There were paddy fields as far as the eye could see, all brightly green with new rice sprigs. Once in the village to observe the big river on the other side, one can see dozens of poles sticking up, holding nets for the fish farms. Every farm house had at least one or two new motorbikes, TV antennas, fresh water, and various electronic consumer goods inside. After spending time in rural Cambodia it is a very impressive sight.

There were 996 families in the village, about 4,500 people, 23 percent of them below the Vietnamese national poverty line. Even though each family has about the same amount of land as village families in Cambodia, almost all can sell some rice every year, with most families also making an extra $1,000 per year selling fish from their fish farms. Other families sell ducks, chickens, and cows to add to their income from rice. This village was, of course, a collective farm from 1975 to the end of the 1980s. With *doi moi*, though, all families now own the land around their homes and have 50- to 100-year individual family rights to their rice land, unless they don't use the land for three years in a row. It will be several years before the Vietnamese government decides if it should make all land completely private with families having the rights to sell the land. Given Cambodia's experience, Vietnam's current policy keeping land in the hands of small farmers is probably a good one, though it is doubtful the Vietnamese government would allow for massive illegal land grabs such as those going on in Cambodia. Also important is that all village families in Vietnam have some kind of government-sponsored health care. It is certainly not as good as what Thai peasants get, but much better than in Cambodia where families must sell their land to pay for emergency health care.[11]

Over 250 households in this village are currently receiving micro-loans from FESR. The micro-loans are used for such things as more pigs for the little pig farms, fishing nets, fertilizer, and so on. Impressive NGO work, but most impressive is the physical infrastructure funded by the local Vietnamese government to make these micro-loans pay off. Those concrete levies with pumping stations one drives over when coming into the village are about 10 years old. About 70 percent of the construction was funded by the government, with the other 30 percent funded through a government loan to the village to be paid back with profits from increased rice yields. The electric lines and fresh running water lines are totally paid for by the local government.

After the first interviews in central Vietnam there were more in the Mekong Delta area south of HCMC/Saigon. Another Vietnamese-American-funded NGO, Co-Vietnam, has been funding many scholarships for young

Binh Hoa village.

children, mostly but not exclusively for girls at risk of falling into the sex industry in this Mekong Delta area close to the Cambodian border. There have been over 450 scholarships given to girls in the fifth to ninth grades, with funding continued through the twelfth grade for girls who stay in school. Arriving in the area, we first attended a graduation ceremony for some of these girls at a little school run by another Vietnamese-American NGO in partnership with the large and rather powerful Women's Union in Vietnam.

The next day there were interviews in the poorest village in this area, Binh Hoa, poor primarily because these people do not have Vietnamese citizenship, and have been in a kind of no-man's land for generations, going back and forth between Cambodia and Vietnam. With no land of their own, they exist by making and selling crafts such as straw brooms and incense. They earn from $1 to $1.50 a day making brooms as they had for 20 years. Some families in the village are a little better off, such as one whose father is from time to time able to make a little money as an unskilled construction worker in the nearest city. But that is as affluent as it gets in this village of "stateless peasants." With Cambodia just a few miles away, a gateway to the booming sex industry in places like Thailand, it was easy to understand the concern about young girls of this village.

After this tour with Co-Vietnam there were more interviews in villages back in central Vietnam. As World Bank poverty maps suggest, villages in these four provinces tend to have higher rates of poverty than all but three other regions of Vietnam. The fieldwork was now back to unannounced visits to avoid party officials giving "showcase tours," and also to avoid the time-consuming welcoming speeches and lunches with Party officials. The first villages visited were in Quang Nam province where levels of poverty are as suggested by poverty maps, though still better than the average village in Cambodia. Only a few typical villages in these provinces are described here.

Approaching the first village in Quang Nam province one sees healthy rice fields with plenty of water from irrigation pumps. All houses had electric lines and motorbikes parked in front. The first family interviewed was apparently well liked in the village, with the father something of an unofficial headman. After a couple of hours with his family he insisted on walking, providing information on every household passed, introducing any family that appeared along the way.

This unofficial headman's family turned out to be one of the poorest. With just over 100 households in this village, he estimated 15 families are poor, adding, "and one is mine." Two rather old motorbikes were parked outside of his house, and a new TV with DVD player was inside. As in almost all Vietnamese villages, his house was very Chinese in design, made of brick and mortar covered with a kind of stucco, a tile roof, and concrete floor. He and his wife have three children, 13, 10, and 6 years old. After sitting down in this house he brought out a big stack of merit certificates their 13-year-old daughter had won in school. Mother and grandmother were looking on with big smiles, while their daughter looked shyly to the floor while sitting on her father's lap. A few minutes later he sadly said they can't afford to pay the extra money it takes for high school. They were living and working in a small city during *doi moi* and land redistribution, only later deciding to live in this village where they have several relatives, thus missing out on the land redistribution.

As his two young sons came into the house, one sitting on his father's lap, he explained that he rents the old beaten-up truck parked outside to make money hauling things for people in the village, mostly their rice crop. The family also raises a few pigs which they sell for $200 or so per year. Almost all other village households have land and grow enough rice to feed their families and sell a good amount every year. Other than having no land nor owning the truck he uses for his main livelihood, there is the problem of his wife's health. She had a small heart attack a year ago so can't work much. They couldn't afford a long hospital stay, but she did get medical care and medicine, with relatives helping to pay the additional charge not covered by the government.

Among other people interviewed in this village, some were quite elderly and living alone. After so many years of war and so many younger people now working in urban areas, a rather high concentration of elderly people in rural Vietnam is understandable. The impressive side to this concentration of elderly people is how they are cared for. The first elderly lady in this village interviewed in the living area of her small brick house was surviving because she had her own small plot of land which other village people worked for her with no charge, giving her all the rice yield. Another elderly woman next door was introduced as neighbors were arriving to cook her dinner, the elderly woman described earlier who lost her husband and three sons fighting against North Vietnam on the side of Americans. It was again admirable to see how the village takes care of their elderly, but this old lady highlighted one of the serious shortcomings of Vietnam today. With no land and no relatives, she

An old war widow in her home.

is completely dependent upon neighbors for food and such things as repairing her roof after a big cyclone the year before. She lives in the usual Chinese style house of brick and mortar with tile roof and concrete floor, though with nothing inside but a table, a couple of chairs, and a bed.

Over the next few weeks, and again after more time in Thailand and Cambodia, more villages were visited in Quang Nam province, closer to the Lao border, then other villages in Danang and Thua Thien Hue provinces. There were many remarkable families with stories of tragedy and survival during the war years, and stories of hard work and new opportunities that have made their lives much better since the mid–1990s. With the focus of this book on Cambodia these stories must be left for another time. Before leaving Vietnam, some additional observations are useful.

Recent World Bank and United Nations reports pertaining to economic development and poverty reduction in Vietnam seem reasonably accurate. Poverty *is* dropping rapidly. Almost all families interviewed said they are much better off than 10 and 15 years ago and are very positive about their futures. All the villages visited had electricity, most had some kind of water control for their rice paddy, good roads, some government health care (but far less than in Thailand), and nearby schools. Very few people in Cambodia said they are any better off than 10 or 15 years ago, 90 percent have no electricity, government health care is virtually nonexistent, and the rather equitable redistribution of land some 20 years ago is being reversed with "land grabs" by the rich and debts for medical care.

Traveling through central Vietnam and the Mekong Delta, however, shows varying levels of poverty. One cause of the varied poverty levels has to do with where village families lived in Vietnam before *doi moi*, and the second pertains to local government aid and support, which varies throughout the country today.

When *doi moi* economic reforms began in the late 1980s, some of the collective farms/communes had better land, more infrastructure development, and fewer people per area of land than others. This is to say that village advantages and disadvantages, along with communist economic policies *before and after doi moi*, have affected conditions of poverty today. If the collective farm had more land per person, and had more infrastructure development, then families in that commune were better off after privatization. Land privatization progressed village by village, with households in each collective farm getting an equal amount of farm land. It was the luck of the draw as to where you were when privatization began. Some villages simply had more and better land at the time than others.

Secondly, much government aid today comes from provincial and local governments. Some provinces are richer, less corrupt, and do a better job at helping villages. Opening markets, allowing families to work their private plots of land, and such things brought about by *doi moi* were key factors in helping rural people. But much of the government help now comes in the form of money for new irrigation projects, farm equipment, rice seed, and fertilizer which must be repaid with future profits. Village-wide projects like irrigation, water control, better roads, etc., come in the form of government funding and government loans (about 70 percent government funding to 30 percent from government loans according to informants), with villages paying back the 30 percent from increased profits from their future rice yield. Quite simply, some provincial and local governments have more resources and better local officials to carry out these benefits. Again, it is the luck of the draw as to where peasants were before *doi moi* kicked in.

Finally, it will be useful to end this review of Vietnamese poverty reduction with some background on the president of the country in 2008 and his accomplishments. In vast contrast to Cambodia, most people around Vietnam had considerable praise for their leader. At the beginning of *doi moi* years (late 1980s), Nguyen Minh Triet was appointed governor of Binh Doung district just west of Saigon, the district which includes the famous tunnels of Cu Chi (the huge underground city built by the Viet Cong under the noses of the American military during the war). The land in this area is hard (thus the tunnels) and poor for agriculture. But with intelligent analysis he helped create a model of rural economic transition for the area. Mr. Nguyen figured that rapid economic growth in Saigon could lead to new opportunities for nearby rural people despite such poor soil. Considering what resources they had and could develop, given the emerging markets in Saigon, he hit upon the idea of diary farms, then went about getting funds to help farmers in his district shift to dairy farms. His economic success in the late 1980s came to the attention of higher communist party officials, and Mr. Nguyen was promoted to mayor of Saigon/Ho Chi Minh City. During his eight years as mayor he was in charge of extensive economic planning, with his plans for industrial parks around the city to attract foreign corporations especially successful. One could watch these industrial parks slowly fill up with American, European, Japanese, Korean, and Taiwanese factories in the 1990s and 2000s. After eight years as mayor, Nguyen Minh Triet shot up the party ladder to his current position of president of Vietnam where he is helping further economic development and poverty reduction for the whole country. Unfortunately, one is told of no such cases like this in Cambodia. A large percentage of high government officials in Cambodia are people who have attained their positions because they are loyal to Prime Minister Hun Sen and able to make the rich richer, with little motivation or actions that actually bring much benefit to the rest of the people in Cambodia.

Economic Development and Poverty in Laos

Again and again one hears that Laos is a "mysterious and sleepy" country "seemingly lost in time." Indeed, even in Vientiane, the capital, life seems slower; there is less traffic, people walk more slowly, shop owners seldom hustle customers to sell their merchandise. With only 6 million people in the country, about half the total population of Bangkok alone, it is hard to imagine Vientiane is a national capital. Most provincial cities in Thailand and Vietnam are larger, more developed, and bustling with economic activity. Many roads in Vientiane are still unpaved, there are no buildings over three or four stories tall, no railroads, and a dusty, rotting, old two-story building continues to be the central shopping mall. Aside from the old capital of Luang Prabang, among the few reasons tourists visit the country are for the great European restaurants (a colonial holdover) and excellent duty-free shops just across the Mekong River from Thailand. In his book, *The Bottom Billion*, Paul Collier includes statistics showing one of the world's main "poverty traps" is being landlocked with bad neighbors. Laos remains landlocked, but her neighbors (primarily China, Thailand, and Vietnam) are rapidly becoming good economic neighbors. The communist government of Laos, though, remains more insecure and secretive compared to their communist big brothers to the north and east.

Laos actually did not actually exist before the French created it out of smaller kingdoms along the Mekong River.[12] And unlike Vietnam, Cambodia, and Thailand, the government of Laos rules a country in which a large percentage of people don't even identify themselves as Lao. Only 60 percent of the population are lowland people of Tai origin who have been in the region for a few thousand years. The other 40 percent are people of various hill tribes who continue to move rather freely across the mountainous regions of northern Southeast Asia and China. These hill tribe people hold no allegiance to the country, remain mostly untouched and far away in the vast mountain regions that dominate Laos.

Compounding this situation is the history of the Indochina wars. The largest hill tribe in Laos, the Hmong, were organized by the CIA to fight Vietnamese communists from the late 1950s, and then the Lao communists from the 1960s. A few thousand of these rebel Hmong remain in the mountains, now hungry and without many arms, posing no real threat. But that old threat is kept alive in the minds of the Lao communists by Hmong outside the country. A few years ago former Hmong rebels now living in California were captured coming across the Mekong River into Laos with a boat load of military weapons. More recently there is the sad case of Vang Pao, the Hmong leader of the CIA secret war. In June 2007, this man who helped save hundreds of American pilots downed in Laotian jungles, was arrested in the United States, charged with "attempting to buy arms for a new revolution in Laos."[13]

A more realistic threat to the Laotian communists was a series of bombs that hit Vientiane in 2000. They began in a restaurant favored by foreigners in May 2000. Several people were injured and one died. Other bombs followed: In July 2000 there was a bomb at the central post office, in September a bomb thrown into a hotel, in November a bicycle bomb at the international airport, and finally a bomb at the Friendship Bridge connecting Thailand and Vientiane over the Mekong River. These were *not* the serious bombings which have become commonplace in Middle Eastern countries and India these days. Only 40 people were injured and one killed in Laos. The interesting part was that no one claimed responsibility for the bombings. Despite the limited damage, Laos was no less shaken. By the spring of 2001 one could find Vientiane a bit like a fortress; government buildings and banks had fences around them, with guards checking everyone who entered.

Many Laotians assumed rebel Hmong were behind the bombs. Most informed speculation, though, cited turmoil within the Lao Communist Party, with junior party members responsible for the bombings. At the time there was something of an internal rebellion in the Communist Party, mostly against the ruling politburo where the youngest member was 70 years old. People inside and outside of the Communist Party were angry that their communist brothers in China and Vietnam had booming economies with rapid poverty reduction while virtually nothing seemed to change on the dingy, dusty streets of Vientiane. But the old guard held on until the 82-year-old Khamtay Siphandone stepped down after the Party congress in 2006. A more reform-minded group was finally in charge of the Lao Communist Party. Ironically, compared to the anti-globalization protests and attacks on symbols of big capitalism beginning from the 1999 World Trade Organization meeting in Seattle, these Laotian bombs in 2000 were probably against an old communist elite, making it difficult for these symbols of big capitalism to build new factories in the country.

A few things were happening before the new Party leadership took over in 2006. In 2004 one could see some renovation in the central restaurant and market area of Vientiane. In 2005 there were a couple of new industrial parks under construction on the fringes of the capital. By 2008 a few of these Japanese, South Korean, and Chinese factories were up and running.[14] The biggest development could be seen just outside the capital in 2008. A huge Olympic-class sports complex was under construction for the upcoming Asian Games, financed mostly by the Chinese who have been increasingly moving into Laos and Cambodia for economic advantage.

Rural Laos

Visits to the lowland villages in Laos began in mid–2007 by traveling on newly paved roads leading out of Vientiane. The first village was about one hour from the capital called Ban Champa. About 70 households were living in wood, bamboo, and rice-straw huts much like those all over Cambodia. But throughout this village and others one could see new brick homes, some already finished, others still under construction. All of the lowland villages visited outside of the capital (Vientiane) and all the way down the Mekong River, almost to Cambodia, had electricity. Most houses had TV antennas, motorbikes parked in front, and "iron buffalos" in back. There were quite a few actual water buffalos around, but in keeping with my "water buffalo indicator of economic development," one could see few of these animals plowing or pulling carts compared to rural Cambodia.

Arriving at this first village outside of the capital (Ban Champa) it was already rather mountainous, making rice cultivation more difficult. Most peasants were growing vegetables and raising various farm animals, especially goats. Hunting wild game in mountain jungles around these villages had been a major economic activity in years past, but game was now scarce so they turned to domesticated farm animals for sale in the city. As usual, each village family was asked if their economic conditions are better compared to five years ago; families in every village responded with a resounding yes. In this particular village, electricity was brought in six years ago, with an all-weather road to Vientiane built about the same time. While pipes bringing fresh water to every house was not yet common, there was a new electric pump and well supplying water to the village. When asked about government programs to improve the village economy, considering that poverty levels were not much different than those in Cambodia a few years ago, it was surprising to hear these people describe several seemingly well designed programs. Government officials in Vientiane and Phnom Penh described the need for such programs, but here in rural Laos one could see *these programs really do exist*. Many families had received government micro-loans with no interest for farm improvements such as new animals and vegetable fields. There are new clinics in these lowland Lao villages, though according to calculations from the information provided, costs are a bit more than in Vietnam and certainly more than in Thailand. But compared to Cambodia, health care for these people is much more available and affordable. Like other villages visited in Laos, there was a new elementary school. One family was so proud of this new school they had their 10-year-old daughter provide a guided tour through the forest to see it. After two years of fieldwork in the region it was not surprising to find a little plaque saying the school building was funded by the Japanese government.

A few people in these first villages not far from the capital had relatives working during the day in Vientiane. One might assume these jobs in the capital must explain their higher standard of living compared to rural Cambodians. In coming months, visits to other Lao villages far down the Mekong River proved this assumption wrong.

The next set of interviews in rural Laos were in the flat plains around the city of Pakse, about 150 miles down the Mekong River from Vientiane. In village after village one could see they had much the same standard of living and government aid as in the villages outside of Vientiane; all villages

Village near Pakse.

had electricity, most had irrigation for their rice paddies, new iron buffalos and motorbikes, and even some light trucks coming into the farm areas from Pakse. Later, much further down the Mekong River, in the larger flat plain around Savannakhet, it was much the same. The easiest way into this area is a border crossing between Nakhon Phanom on the Thai side of the Mekong to Thakhek on the Lao side, in a very old boat. There is yet no bridge over the Mekong for many miles in this area. Once in the little city we could see a couple of new hotels under construction, though little other new economic activity. But in the countryside we could see much the same level or rural development as further up the Mekong River, with electric lines going to all lowland villages, new motor vehicles and iron buffalos everywhere, and lush rice fields with enough rice to sell on the market.

As noted earlier, the overall statistics on economic development and poverty in Laos presented in annual reports by the World Bank and United Nations are in one way misleading. About 40 percent of the Lao population are from various hill tribe people mostly living in remote (and many in very remote) mountain areas. For example, the most recent country assessment by the World Bank published in 2007 using data collected in 2005 indicated that poverty in Laos had gone down from 46 percent of the population in 1993 to 31 percent in 2005.[15] Like most other reports it makes no distinction between the 40 percent of the population who are hill tribe people and the majority lowland people. However, a more recent study supported by the Asian Development Bank conducted by an American anthropologist, a long-term resident of Laos, indicated progress among the lowland people compared to remote hill tribe peoples still relatively untouched by the outside world.[16] This report published in December 2006 found poverty among lowland people is down to about 25 percent compared to over 50 percent for hill tribe people. It is primarily in almost inaccessible mountainous hill tribe areas of Laos that conditions are more similar to most rural people in Cambodia.

The most recent World Bank country report praises Laos for opening to the international community in recent years and working more effectively to reduce poverty. The UN Human Development Report for 2009 shows that while Cambodia was ahead of Laos in its human development ranking in 1995, by 2000 Laos had moved to about an equal rank with Cambodia, then ahead of Cambodia by 2005, and further ahead by 2007. Vietnam was already ahead in 1995 and has pulled even further ahead of both countries by 2007. Even with its large number of remote hill tribe people, Laos has less malnutrition than Cambodia, with 19 percent for Laos compared to 33 percent for Cambodia. Income inequality in Laos is among the world's lowest, while it is much higher in Cambodia. Despite all of this, as a percent of GNP per capita, Cambodia is exporting over twice as much agricultural and manufactured products (mainly textiles) compared to Laos.

There are looming problems for Laos, many related to increasing investment by its neighbors, especially China, in hydroelectric power plants and extraction of its minerals. With the country mostly covered by mountains, the many rivers coming down from these mountains are ideal for dams providing electricity. Thailand, Vietnam, and especially China are now funding such dams. Some 30,000 Chinese have poured into Laos in the past few years, many involved in these hydroelectric projects. If not well managed, the Lao environment could be severely damaged and future poverty reduction, especially among the hill tribe people in these remote areas, could be doomed. As natural resources are taken out of Laos by these neighboring countries there is also the danger that corrupt government officials will siphon off funds that could go to national economic development. But while closed and rather incompetent in the past, and still behind Vietnam in government efficiency and the ability to establish and carry out policies for economic development and poverty reduction, Lao government officials have recently shown themselves to be more responsible than those in Cambodia. The 2006 corruption index, published by Transparency International, ranked 163 countries, including Cambodia for the first time. While Laos was less corrupt than 50 countries, Cambodia was among the most corrupt.

Conclusion

The main point of this chapter analysis of Vietnam and Laos is that both countries are achieving more economic development with poverty reduction compared to Cambodia. Again, one sees only Burma not surpassing Cambodia in these important areas of progress. The advancement in Vietnam will be less surprising to most people given greater media coverage and World Bank and United Nations reports that in some ways are less misleading. There is a rather unique situation for Laos; its very small population includes 40 percent who are very primitive and isolated hill tribe people living much like they did hundreds of years ago. It is understandable that a poor country like Laos cannot yet provide electricity, agricultural market access, medical care, schools, and other infrastructure development to people in such remote areas. As we have seen earlier, Thailand now has a good record of reducing poverty and providing infrastructure development for its smaller population (as a percent of overall population) of hill tribe people. But this progress came after the majority lowland Thais had achieved much more poverty reduction. Cambodia, with a much lower percentage of its population in rather inaccessible mountain areas, has no excuse.

It is time to return to Cambodia. The next chapter will first delve further into the problems of corruption in Cambodia, going beyond impersonal statistics about corruption to understand how widespread the problem is, and its impact on individuals and the future of Cambodia. The following chapter will take up the interrelated subject of inefficient governmental institutions, or what is often referred to these days as "institutional incapacity." Institutional incapacity does not simply equate to government corruption. Even if Cambodia was seriously trying to reduce corruption as in Thailand and Vietnam, Cambodia would still find it difficult to carry out rational policies for economic development and poverty reduction. We must understand how Cambodia's past has weakened the country's institutions, as well as social networks, personal trust, and mental health.

CHAPTER 8

Corruption
in Cambodia

At a conference on economic development at one of the leading universities in Phnom Penh a few years ago, the keynote speaker presented a paper critical of government corruption in Cambodia, among other things, giving corruption data from the World Bank and Transparency International. During the question-and-answer period, a high-ranking official in the Ministry of Education stood up for a question, starting by saying how he was shocked that people could think there was corruption in his Ministry. It was much like the Iranian president telling people after a speech in the United States that there is no persecution of homosexuals in Iran because there are no homosexuals in Iran.

Cambodian Prime Minister Hun Sen tends to get upset when outsiders criticize his government. (He gets upset with insiders, too, but in the case of insiders there can be various forms of legal action and persecution instead of only an angry verbal response. For example, opposition politicians and union leaders have recently been jailed for slander.) When a UN Human Rights Commission official criticized Cambodia for severe human rights violations in 2006, Hun Sen went into one of his long, furious speeches, with the BBC quoting him as saying, "Cambodia is not hell." He called UN envoy Yash Ghai "deranged," then added, "human rights groups in Cambodia failed 'to reflect the facts' about Cambodia."

A couple of years earlier the World Bank finally had enough with the Cambodian government and charged them with corruption. In a rare move, the Bank demanded repayment of loans where there was clear evidence of corruption and threatened to cut off future funds to Cambodia. This kind of action is almost unprecedented for the World Bank. Indeed, according to World Bank insiders, the Bank usually "budgets in" a certain percentage for corruption loses when assessing the costs of their funded projects.[1] In Cambodia, though, the World Bank decided the level of corruption was getting way beyond "normal bounds."

Informants have told of a business providing faked birth certificates in Cambodia. As in most Asian countries, government officials, including schoolteachers and professors, must retire at a comparatively early age. This forced retirement is a significant problem for many people in Asian countries with ever increasing life expectancies and pension systems much less generous than the U.S. Social Security System. But it is an especially serious problem for top government officials in Cambodia. Some government officials claim, and two separate foreign NGOs confirmed, that by 2011 there may be something like $1 billion a year coming into Cambodia from the recently discovered oil deposits off the southern Cambodian coast.[2] Working for one of the world's most corrupt governments, this means a huge income loss for government officials who must retire before 2011.

As noted earlier, in 2006 Transparency International was able to include Cambodia in its annual ranking of corruption in governments around the world. This annual survey of people doing business in countries around the world ranks these countries from 10 (no reports of corruption) to 0 (the highest level of corruption).[3] Finland, Iceland, and New Zealand were tied for the least corrupt at 9.6, the United States was tied with three countries at 7.3, and Cambodia scored a 2.1, ahead of only eight other countries in this study of 163 countries. In another report issued in 2007 by Transparency International, firms doing business in these countries were asked what percentage of government procurements included bribes.[4] Cambodia led countries in all regions of the world with over 90 percent. A World Bank report issued in 2007 included a Cambodian survey of foreign business managers who were asked about the most important problems limiting economic development and poverty reduction in the country.[5] Over 80 percent said the number-one problem is government corruption in Cambodia. The second-ranked problem, with a 55 percent ranking, was government inefficiency. The next two problems were an uneducated workforce and inadequate infrastructure (both 46 percent). Toward the bottom of this list of impediments to economic development were street crime and theft (18 percent), and, unsurprisingly for these foreign companies, restrictive labor regulations (17 percent) and tax rates (14 percent). In 2009 Transparency International released another report on corruption and bribes around the world. Surveys in most countries asked the question, "In the past 12 months have you or anyone in your household been asked to pay a bribe?" In the 12 Asian countries included in the sample, the average answering "yes" was 11 percent. In Cambodia it was 47 percent. Following Cambodia in second place was Indonesia, but with 29 percent answering "yes." Only in sub–Saharan Africa and some states newly independent from the old Soviet Union do we find countries on par with Cambodia.[6]

Western and Asian newspapers are full of stories about corrupt government officials in China, Vietnam, and Thailand. The stories are of bribes being paid, embezzlement, evading rules pertaining to labor and consumer safety, and the list goes on and on. One would think these countries are among the most corrupt in the world. Following the same logic, comparatively few news articles about corruption in Cambodia would suggest a low level of corruption. Closer analysis, though, suggests the opposite. Most of the news articles about corruption in China, Vietnam, and Thailand are about people *caught and convicted* for various types of corruption. There are few news articles like this for Cambodia because comparatively little is being done about corruption. There are few government crackdowns in Cambodia like we have seen in China and Vietnam, nor would we expect there to be a major crackdown when it is top levels of government involved in some of the worst cases of corruption in Cambodia.[7] As one would expect, World Bank indicators of corruption levels show no change in the high level of corruption for Cambodia between 1996 and 2006 compared to other Asian countries.

During interviews in Phnom Penh in 2007, one middle-aged woman, second in command at one Cambodian government agency, replied to the usual question about the greatest problems facing Cambodia today with, "Lack of business law, government and corporate corruption, and illegal land grabs."[8] She went on to explain, "with almost no regulation of business by the government, people are being taken advantage of by both Cambodian and foreign companies. The situation invites more corruption and rapidly growing inequalities in Cambodia." Another middle-aged man in another government agency said, "Corruption is a central problem." He added, "Cambodia has a very good economic development plan for 2006 to 2010, but the big question is, can they carry it through with so much corruption and disorganization?" As for related problems, he said, "Government salaries are so low they cannot attract talented people into government; all the best go into private industry." He continued, "the extremely low salaries among government civil servants almost forces them into corruption or jobs on the side where they actually spend most of their hours each week."[9] This man was doing just that. He admitted that he spends most of his time working for an international NGO that pays pretty well by Cambodian standards.

NGO leaders and academics tend to be much more critical. Everyone interviewed pointed to corruption at the highest levels of government, starting with Prime Minister Hun Sen and his wealthy friends. Several of these people added that when the Cambodian government approves some new investment from domestic or foreign corporations, top government officials, and Hun Sen himself, always get a big cut. Another informant added that "the prime minister has a small clique of friends who are his strongest supporters who are the biggest beneficiaries of the corruption." Another informant said some of these friends of the prime minister are amassing huge land holdings in the countryside. On a trip from Phnom Penh to the southern coast, a Cambodian academic informant pointed out a large plantation in southern Cambodia recently acquired by one of the prime minister's friends. (There will be more details on this at the end of this book.) The land grabs and slum clearance going on around a large lake north of Phnom Penh were described in Chapter 6. Solid evidence uncovered by a European NGO indicates that the developers taking this land are from a joint Chinese and Cambodian corporation. With a permit from the highest levels of government (in a deal that was at first secret), they acquired this large track of land worth an estimated $2 billion for only $78 million. It turned out the head of the Cambodian side of the deal is the wife of a top politician, and good friend of Prime Minister Hun Sen.[10]

In 2004 Transparency International came out with a study of the most corrupt government leaders of recent decades.[11] Suharto of Indonesia topped the list with as much as $35 billion stolen over a 30-year period. Marcos of the Philippines was second with as much as $10 billion stolen, and Mobutu of Zaire, now Democratic Republic of the Congo, was third with $5 billion stolen. With a little more time Hun Sen could be up among these champions, especially after the oil money starts rolling into Cambodia.

Other interviewees, though, added that corruption, while on a more petty level, is actually worse in the lowest levels of government in the capital, and especially in the provinces. A young Cambodian woman doing poverty assessment research for a foreign NGO explained, "This is why it is very difficult to change anything in Cambodia." Foreign aid comes into the country to develop infrastructure or improve health care, education, or agricultural production, but only a fraction of that money ever gets to the actual program.

Toward the end of the fieldwork in Cambodia there was an interview with an Cambodian academic who had just finished her Ph.D. in agriculture economics at one of the best universities in Japan. She already has a rather high academic position in one of the best universities in Cambodia because of the scarcity of people with Ph.D.s. She admitted she already has much less youthful optimism and drive to help her country compared to when she was a student in Japan. She looked distracted for a while, watching a gentle rain falling on palm trees and other tropical plants, then said, "When I was a PhD student in Japan I had so much hope for Cambodia. That's what motivated me to study hard." She again stopped talking for a few moments while looking out at the falling rain, then added, "Now that I have been back a couple of years everything seems so hopeless." Officials of top government agencies, she continued, "consider only their selfish material interests. There is like, you know, a net between the donor money coming in and the people it is actually supposed to help." She gave some of the usual examples, such as Hun Sen demanding payment up front before any corporate investment or foreign aid money can be spent. "It always ends up in his pockets, and those of his close supporters." She gave some specific examples from other levels of government. One was a recently discovered case where the director of the National Museum in Phnom Penh had demanded and received personal payment for artifacts that were sent out on loan to a European museum. "These people treat national property as if its their own," she added with a look of destiny.

Toward the end of the interview she gave an example of one of her relatives. He wanted a promotion to a higher position in the government agency which handles customs. The promotion, he was told, would cost him $20,000. The relative got in touch with some contacts in that office, did the math, and figured he could make up the cost of his promotion in about a year. He borrowed the money and took the job. The story was similar to ones heard in small villages, though, of course, at a much lower monetary level: One must usually pay a bribe to get a job in both the public and private sectors. Parents of teenagers in the resettlement "village" next to the South Korean sweatshop said the going rate was a bribe of one month's salary before their daughters could get a job there. This academic informant agreed the practice is very common.[12]

At this point she became equally critical of the World Bank; "The World Bank just wants to get its money spent. They have little concern with corruption, and little oversight." Reminded that in 2006 the World Bank had finally demanded some money be repaid when they found corruption, she responded with something like, "That was only the tip of the iceberg." Given her Ph.D. in agricultural economics, the questions turned to the village poor. Again she used the phrase, "There is a net between the foreign donor money and the poor people." She was not surprised when told there seems to be very little government or foreign donor programs in the villages throughout Cambodia. She brought up the issue of growing land inequality. The World Bank and United Nations figures, she said, "show land inequality is raising very rapidly [as noted in chapters above].... At least after the Khmer Rouge days, these poor people could grow their own food. What happens when they can no longer do that?" Since this interview, there have been several articles about

Hun Sen going to oil-rich Middle Eastern countries for economic deals. Several Middle Eastern countries have been granted huge tracks of farmland in Cambodia in exchange for loans or investments. For example, Kuwait was granted 124,000 acres of land and Qatar is investing some $200 million for its own agricultural production in Cambodia.[13]

The "Big Man" Government

It is tempting, and, unfortunately, somewhat accurate, to draw parallels between the common form of organized government corruption in many sub–Saharan African countries and Cambodia today. This is not simply because almost all the other countries making the most corrupt status in Transparency International's annual survey are sub–Saharan African countries. It is how the corruption operates in Cambodia. African specialists often call it the "big man" form of government.[14]

The "big man" form of government is much like the name implies.[15] The goal is to control as much of the country's wealth and other resources as possible so the "big man" can hand it out as rewards to supporters, who in turn are to protect the "big man" from any opposition. One objective in the "big man" form of government is to flaunt your wealth and power so that everyone knows you have it, and thus this particular "big man" is the one the others should be attaching themselves to for a cut of this wealth.

The key, of course, is the ethnic divisions in Africa. The European grab for colonies in Africa during the late 1800s resulted in a continent divided into countries/colonies with no regard for ethnic divisions. Most of these sub–Saharan African countries ended up with boundaries that included many ethnic groups which have historically hated each other and been at war. In fact, the details of history show that in most cases the European colonists used these ethnic divisions in African to divide and rule.[16] Today in sub–Saharan Africa there is competition within these ethnic groups to be *their* "big man," and then to have supporters against challenges from the other ethnic groups. In the case of Cambodia, though, the divisions are almost exclusively class divisions, Hun Sen's rich friends in opposition to all others.

The next chapter will delve more into why this "big man" form of government developed in Cambodia, but here we can consider a preview of three reasons. The first, and probably most important, is the total collapse of political order and the previous government during the Khmer Rouge years, 1975–1979. Not only was the previous government dissolved, but most former government officials were massacred in the killing fields. Combined with this collapse of political order was the fear and mistrust of fellow Cambodian citizens after the Khmer Rouge killing fields. The stage was set for this kind of "big man" form of government under Hun Sen. Secondly, as pointed out by the most respected historian on the subject today, David Chandler, there has been this strain of patron/client form of government in Cambodian history to a much greater degree when compared to Cambodia's neighbors, particularly before the Angkor civilization changed from Hinduism to Buddhism.[17] The patron/client form of political organization was then enhanced after the old Angkor empire fell apart about 600 years ago, pushing Cambodian kings and local leaders into something like the "big man" form of government to survive the internal divisions within the country and attacks from Thailand and Vietnam. After the collapse of governmental institutions during the Khmer Rouge period (1975–1979) the situation became more conducive to something like a "big man" form of government. Thirdly, there is abundance of natural resources in Cambodia, which means there is a lot for a "big man" to control and hand out to supporters. Newly discovered oil wealth provides a good example.

Coming Attractions: The Great Oil Ripoff

A few years ago foreign oil companies discovered large pools of oil and gas a few miles off Cambodia's southern coast line. The average estimate is that by 2011 something like $1 billion a year will be coming into Cambodia because of this oil and gas.[18] At first thought, one might conclude that poor Cambodia has found its savior. But that first thought is likely wrong.[19]

In one of the most insightful books on world poverty in recent years, Paul Collier's data show there are "four main traps" that tend to make and keep a country poor.[20] In the countries where the one billion poorest people live, 73 percent have been in a recent civil war, 29 percent have abundant natural resources (particularly oil or diamonds), 30 percent are landlocked with few resources, and 79 percent have had a long period of bad governance. Three out of four is not good; at least Cambodia is not landlocked.

There are several problems for poor countries with abundant natural resources. The export of these valuable natural resources can cause the local currency to rise in value, thus making other exports less competitive. Also, local services and food become more expensive, thus diverting more economic surplus to pay for and produce them. Poorer countries rich in natural resources also tend to think in the short term and neglect sound economic policies that will lead to the development of other, more sustainable industries for economic development. But, of course, one of the key problems is a frenzy of theft among government officials in countries where transparency is limited and corruption is rife.

One of the most important cases in sub–Saharan Africa is Angola. Only six other countries in the world produce more oil than Angola. At 800,000 barrels of oil a day, Angola is ahead of Kuwait. But despite this oil wealth, about three-quarters of Angola's population live in extreme poverty and some 2 million would probably starve without food aid from international agencies. The United Nations estimates that 2.7 million Angolan children are mal-nourished. Like many sub–Sahara African countries, Angola has been in a civil war for years, 27 to be exact. About half of government spending had gone to cover the costs of this war, including half of its oil revenues. Thus, there is some hope with relative peace coming to the country. But the cor-ruption is huge. In 2001 it was estimated that international oil companies paid Angola about $900 million for exploration rights. Half of that money went to the war, but $450 million went missing. The International Monetary Fund estimates that about $1 billion was missing from all state revenues. Over the last five years the IMF figures that about $4 billion has disappeared from state revenues. Two years ago one outside auditor estimated that Angola spent more money on cars for cabinet ministers, legislators and their wives than on health care and education for all its people.[21]

Another case is from Equatorial Guinea, a small country on the Atlantic coast north of Angola. A few years ago Equatorial Guinea was found to have huge oil reserves on shore and offshore. Still, except for a few elites, almost all of the people in this small country live on less than $1 per day. In 2003 it was discovered that $300 to $400 million dollars of the government's oil rev-enues had been hidden away in a small bank in Washington, D.C. Later it was discovered that the dictator of Equatorial Guinea has $16 million in another account, and he and his family have a home in Washington, D.C., worth $2.6 million and another in Beverly Hills worth $7.7 million, plus dozens of expensive sports cars. Mobil Oil recently admitted to paying him personally hundreds of thousands of dollars to drill for oil in his country, plus a cut in much of the profits.[22] With a population of about 500,000, that $400 million alone (and there is no doubt much more is hidden away) would have put about $800 into the hands of each person in the country, putting everyone way above the $1 day extreme poverty line, and even above the $2 per day line. Among other examples is that of Nigeria; the country has brought in $280 billion in oil revenues over the last 30 years with almost no economic development or poverty reduction to show for it.

One possible solution to all of this corruption suggested by the nonprofit agency, Global Witness, is to pass laws in rich countries like the United States requiring their oil companies to disclose publicly all payments made to governments for such things as oil exploration in the country. At least people in the country and agencies like the United Nations and IMF could then keep better track of what happens to this money. Such laws could help reduce the level of corruption in places such as Angola.

Another approach recently began in Chad, a landlocked country in the heart of sub–Sahara Africa. Like countries around it, Chad is one of the poorest in the world and has a highly corrupt government dominated by one ethnic group. Per capita income in Chad is just over $1,000 and Chad ranks 165 out of 173 countries on the UN Human Development Index. About 80 percent of the population is estimated to live in poverty. Huge amounts of oil have just been discovered in Chad, and American and Canadian oil companies are rushing into the country. In this case, however, the World Bank has set up its first ever agency to manage the oil investments itself.[23] The first oil royalties have brought about $100 million to be controlled by the World Bank agency, though another $100 million in taxes from this oil wealth is still controlled by Chad's government. So far about $6.3 million has been distributed directly to local villages by the World Bank agency, though it lacks control over how the village elders spend the money. There have been some small improvements in these villages, but the overall impact is yet to be determined. The American oil companies like the project because it helps clear them of any responsibility for the corruption. But the situation for the World Bank agency is still difficult and conflict with the Chad government is increasing.

There are some exceptions to this rule of natural resource money being stolen and mismanaged in sub–Saharan Africa, but very few. One is Botswana which is rich in diamonds. The difference, Collier explains, is that Botswana has a government with transparency, relatively good governance, and checks and balances in government which work to prevent widespread theft of natural resource wealth.[24] But it is not democracy per se that matters. As we will see in the next chapter, and as Collier's data show in the case of natural resource theft around the world's poorest countries, some democracies in less developed countries have good governance and low corruption while many democracies have terrible governance and very high corruption. The same can be said for nondemocratic countries in the developing world; some have highly corrupt governments while others have good governance and are able to use money from natural resources and foreign investment for economic development and poverty reduction.

To gain information on the situation in Cambodia, a British national was interviewed who is in charge of a well-known foreign NGO office trying to convince the Cambodian government that its natural resource laws need to be considerably improved. The key goal is to make sure money from natural resources will actually be used to benefit the country. This, of course, means making the root of this natural resource money transparent so as to prevent the money from disappearing. He was one of the most pessimistic NGO officials interviewed in Cambodia. After just a few minutes of talking with him, he said, "It's going to be stolen. We don't have time to do anything about it."[25] As one might imagine after what has been written above, the British man's agency found their appeals to top government officials were being ignored.

More recently the *Far Eastern Economic Review* has found secret offices and accounts already set up by Cambodian government officials who will be dealing with this future influx of oil money. Quoting the *Far East Economic Review,* "Given the potential for profit, the country's leaders have set up secretive institutions that will let them cash in on the oil when production begins."[26] A few lines down from this quote, given what has already been indicated in this book, the following should come as no surprise: "The Cambodian National Petroleum Authority, which has been placed directly under the control of Prime Minister Hun Sen and Deputy Prime Minister Sok An has established a secretive institution that resembles a prison rather than an oil bureaucracy. Te Duong Tara, director general of the CNPA, allegedly keeps oil-related documents at home rather than his office to prevent staff from seeing them, according to the Global Witness report."

This British NGO informant and some of his staff were interviewed for about two hours during the first meeting, with followup email questions for a couple of months. After two months he wrote that he was leaving the agency and going home. There was nothing he could do in Cambodia, he wrote. A few months later, there was another email from one of his Cambodian assistants saying this agency must "lay low" for a while, then the emails stopped completely. A few months later, an American working with another NGO in Phnom Penh trying to do similar work was interviewed. His agency was more focused on other natural resources, such as timber, bauxite, copper, and gold being found in the rugged northeast of Cambodia. In his opinion these natural resources, all being taken out of Cambodia now, are worth more than the offshore oil and gas. He and other foreign NGO officials interviewed later had various sources of information indicating that much of the money is going to corrupt government officials. He added, "Yes, most of the oil wealth will be stolen as well."

During that first meeting with the British NGO official in Phnom Penh, there was a little brainstorming when he asked opinions about what could be done. The case of a West African country with oil wealth was brought up. The mostly American and European oil companies drilling for the oil in that country's coastal waters were pressured by the World Bank to put all oil royalties into an agency run by the World Bank that would then distribute the money to the government agencies and domestic companies involved with the drilling operations. The question was, "How could anyone get the foreign oil companies to agree to such a system in Cambodia? It is obvious top Cambodian officials wouldn't like it."

A public campaign in the United States and Europe to shame the oil companies into a similar deal was suggested so that the Cambodian government would have to go along with it. There is also the example of an American oil company that was shamed into making sure its pipelines were not being built by slave labor in Burma. The British head of this NGO office brought out a map of the leases already settled over this pool of offshore oil in Cambodia.[27] On the map one could see that a lease to one track was held by Chevron, while the others were held by state-owned oil companies from Thailand, Malaysia, China, and Indonesia. All agreed a public campaign of shame wouldn't work on these Asian state companies.

Conclusion

Before leaving this subject it should again be stressed that corruption in Cambodia is not just limited to the top echelons of government. This corruption permeates all levels of society, or at least all levels with any authority to take advantage of a position for personal gain. The health care system is so full of corruption it has become dysfunctional. At best, only 40 percent of money spent for health care by the Cambodian government, mostly from foreign NGOs, actually gets down to patients. The system is so defective that foreigner donors are starting to give money only to healthcare providers run by international NGOs, with studies showing they have been much more effective.[28] One academic informant described personal experience in a Phnom Penh government hospital. "To get decent medical attention," she said, "one must bribe one of the doctors. If that doctor is not at the hospital or on call when a medical emergency occurs, other doctors will not treat the patient."

There are similar problems in the educational system.[29] Many interviewees said that that bribes go along way in helping students pass entrance exams to get into a university. At the secondary and primary level, parents must usually pay a small bribe to the teacher if their child is to get any attention from the teacher. Many poor village families said they could not afford to keep their children in school because of these required bribes. The going rate, according to villagers, is about $0.10 per day, a hefty sum for people with more than one child and making less than $1 per day. The situation has grown so bad that there was recently a rare protest by parents in Phnom Penh.

With this kind of corruption in the medical and educational institutions, one can imagine how rampant it must be with the police and courts. Nor are the prisons excluded; interviews with families of inmates, for example, tell us they must pay a $25 bribe to the warden each time they want to see their family member in jail. Corruption and bribery is not limited to the public sector; promotions in the private sector come primarily with bribes. There were a few small factories not far from two of the "relocation villages" for slum dwellers forced out of Phnom Penh. When asked why they could not find jobs in these nearby factories instead of sleeping in the streets of Phnom Penh for days to work at the old plastic recycling plant because they couldn't afford the $2 per day commute from the "relocation village" to Phnom Penh, these former slum dwellers said they could not get a job in these nearby factories because they could not afford the bribe.

The next chapter will explore some explanations for the dysfunctional Cambodian government and high levels of corruption. But here we can conclude with a simple one. Everyone with much education interviewed in Cambodia — foreign NGO workers as well as Cambodians at all levels of government — agreed that most of the corruption is because of extremely low salaries for government officials.[30] Several academics from top universities in Phnom Penh — one with a Ph.D. from a top Japanese university, another with a Ph.D. from a good American university — said they receive about $200 per month from their university salary. Their salaries are somewhat higher because most university faculty do not have Ph.D.s. Doctors make about the same in government hospitals, with nurses making only $50 or so per month. Village schoolteachers also get a salary of around $50 per month.

There is a vicious cycle at work; the educational system doesn't work well because teachers must take bribes and/or spend most of their hours working at some other job to put food on the table. It is much the same for government healthcare workers and government officials in all agencies. A result is that Cambodia cannot replenish the physical and human capital (roads, electric power, as well as human talent) destroyed by civil war and Khmer Rouge genocide. Because Cambodia cannot replenish the physical and human capital, it is very difficult for the country to move out of its current poverty. Because it is difficult to move out of poverty, the corruption continues on almost all levels.

Most of the blame, however, must be placed on top government officials. They certainly do not need more bribes to put food on the table for their families; they have gotten rich. A bigger question then is how the top levels of government have become so corrupt and government agencies have become so inefficient and dysfunctional. It is time to turn to this question.

CHAPTER 9

State Incapacity
*Why Nothing Gets Done,
and the Poor Stay Poor*

The new buzz words coming out of the World Bank these days are "good governance" and "state capacity" or "institutional capacity." By good governance they mean government efficiency and low corruption. By state capacity they mean the ability and even the existence of government institutions to do the normal things governments are supposed to do all over the world. There is no question these buzz words are right on track. Many social scientists have shown that various measures of government efficiency are strongly related to poverty reduction and economic development in less-developed countries all over the world.[1] One research team of UC Berkeley sociologists created a "Weberianness scale" named after the famous German sociologist, Max Weber, who about 100 years ago wrote the definitive work on the nature of bureaucracies and how they should function.[2] Using this scale to measure efficient government in developing countries, this Berkeley team and others have shown such scales to be strongly related to GNP growth in less-developed countries, with other studies showing it is also related to poverty reduction. A key reason economic development and poverty reduction is higher in Asia than Latin America or Africa today is that many Asian countries have some of the highest scores on measures of government efficiency.

Few of these scales measuring government efficiency have information from Cambodia. The disruption of civil war and continuing Khmer Rouge attacks until well into the 1990s prevented data collection. Studies around the beginning of the 21st century show Thailand and Vietnam score fairly high, and even Laos is about average. A 2007 World Bank report was finally able measure government efficiency in Cambodia.[3] The country ranked among the bottom 10 to 25 percent of countries all over the world, with only Burma and North Korea ranking lower in East and Southeast Asia.

As described earlier, Cambodian government officials provided several documents containing development plans and ministry data on poverty conditions. Most valuable, however, was the inside information about problems within this government agency. In one of these meetings a neatly dressed man with a rather pleasant smile and quiet voice spoke impeccable English though his college education was in Belgium. The meeting began in his somewhat academic-looking office with small talk that eventually, as usual, got around to the Khmer Rouge years. He was in his early 20s when the Khmer Rouge took over in 1975, and like all others living in Phnom Penh, he and his family were captured by young boys wearing black "pajamas" and carrying big AK-47s, then marched for days into the countryside before they reached an empty field where he spent his next four years growing rice. Like others, he told stories of eating lizards and all sorts of bugs when he could find them, drinking water from muddy ponds, and being watched constantly by those young Khmer Rouge boys carrying big AK-47s. Many people were killed before his eyes, mostly those who did not work as hard as these boys with the big guns thought they should, or showed some form of disrespect. And like others, he told of the attempts by the Khmer Rouge to determine his background and education. He survived by convincing the Khmer Rouge he was from a family of unskilled laborers with no education. His father disappeared during the Khmer Rouge years, and after the Vietnamese invasion in 1979 he returned to Phnom Penh with his mother, homeless and looking for some way to make a living. He was also lucky to hear that the new government, backed by the Vietnamese, was looking for anyone with a college education for new government positions. As noted earlier, with approximately 300 people left in the country with a college education the new government was desperate to find people to help run the government, or what was emerging as such in those early years in Cambodia without the Khmer Rouge. He was bitter toward the United States for blocking needed aid during the 1980s, but neither was he happy with the Vietnamese in the background directing his country during that time.

As we moved into the primary questions, like other Cambodian officials had done, he pulled out various government documents showing what his agency had determined must be done to improve economic development in the countryside and reduce poverty. He knew that economic development in Phnom Penh must go along with development and poverty reduction in the countryside, and knew all too well what people in the countryside needed.

Toward the end of interview he again asked not to be quoted by name and then offered a familiar story; "I feel like I'm wasting my time. We develop these plans, get some foreign donor to help with money, and then nothing happens. The plans never get implemented and the money seems to disappear." He added, "And government claims of poverty reduction in Phnom Penh are not to be trusted. They don't include homeless migrants in the city, though figures of high poverty with no change in the countryside since the early 1990s are accurate." His agency was told a couple of years ago that 65 percent of development aid should be spent in the rural areas and the rest in urban areas. In reality, he said, what little aid money is actually spent rather than stolen goes for urban projects. Asked to name the most important problems in Cambodia today, like others, he began with government corruption and no government regulation of what foreign corporations are doing to people in the country.

During another interview with a well-educated woman in a relatively high government ministry position, there was much the same information. She admitted that she seldom actually works for the government. She was in her office at a branch of one of the most well known international aid agencies. Many government officials like her, she said, work in their official ministry offices only when foreign donors come up with money for some project. (Some 50 percent of Cambodian government funds come from foreign donors.) Research indicates that *local* government incapacity is also one of the biggest problems in Cambodia.[4] The specific project which she currently headed for the international NGO was focused on training local government officials to better understand their duties, perform their jobs more efficiently, and with less corruption. In short, they were trying to build what the World Bank and UN call "government capacity" among local government officials in Cambodia. As noted in the previous chapter, after interviews with "commune" and "tombon" (a local government district covering about 10 villages) officials in Vietnam and Thailand, one could easily see the contrast of professionalism and efficiency compared to their counterparts in Cambodia. When asked if her work with local government officials was doing any good she responded, "Probably not." With very little education and almost no experience among these rural officials, her agency was making little progress. Their NGO funding was about to run out and the training program was to conclude after covering a very small part of Cambodia.

"Yes," she said, "most people with any education outside of Phnom Penh were killed," but then added, "those who are left have mental scars and can think only about the short term." During the Khmer Rouge years and throughout most of the 1980s, she said, all most Cambodians could do was worry about day-to-day and week-to-week survival. She added, "They have lost much of their trust in fellow citizens that existed before the civil war and

Khmer Rouge days." Much the same was said about a year later in Cambodia's second largest city by a young psychologist working for a European-funded Transcultural Psychosocial Organization. It was their task to somehow identify and treat Cambodians alive during the Khmer Rouge years who have lingering or post-trauma mental disorders.

Asked to list some of the biggest problems in Cambodia today, she came up with the usual, but added some interesting new problems that were later cited by other Cambodians. For example, there are many small foreign and domestic NGOs, perhaps 2,000, doing various things in Cambodia, with few of their projects coordinated or following a broader organized plan. In her view, foreign aid agencies do what they know how to do from their past experience in other countries, but what they are doing now is often not what Cambodia actually needs. And many domestic NGOs she said are fake; "they are trying to attract foreign money for their own economic survival and doing very little for the country."[5]

Asked how her Cambodian government agency could best help the country, she listed several ideas for rural development projects, such as organic contract farming, eco-tourism, and environmental projects, as well as a long list of things that should be funded through micro-loans.[6] There are relatively few agencies offering micro-loans in Cambodia compared to the other Southeast Asian countries, she said, though a large Cambodian bank is offering micro-loans. However, the Cambodian bank she mentioned requires significant collateral, usually the farm family's land, and charges a higher interest rate compared to other countries in the region.

These observations and interviews closely matched the various reports about government inefficiency and incapacity in Cambodia. But what to do about it? What causes government inefficiency and incapacity? Studies by the World Bank and many academics show that "good governance" and "state capacity" are keys to poverty reduction and economic development, *but no one has devised effective ways to produce good governance and government efficiency if a country does not already have it!* The World Bank and United Nations have programs in countries around the world to give better training to local government officials in hopes of producing better governance, but with little success. The head of "Seila" in Phnom Penh, of one of these UN agencies charged with this task, was interviewed. He said their training programs for local government officials have probably had very little impact in Cambodia. And the UN was closing his office down in 2008.

It is time to put the above observations into a broader historical perspective. There is both potential good news, but perhaps more bad news for Cambodia.

Another Little History Lesson: If You Didn't
Have It Then, You Probably Ain't Got It Now

A team of social scientists at the University of Zurich have put together a large data set measuring dozens and dozens of characteristics of less-developed countries today and going back a few hundred years.[7] As the World Bank focus on "good governance" and "state capacity" would suggest, this Zurich data set indicates a strong correlation between several measures of "government efficiency" and sound GNP growth per capita in a country, while other figures show the same correlation to poverty reduction.

As noted above, the World Bank, United Nations, and development scholars are trying to come up with ways to promote "good governance" in countries that don't already have it. One can log onto the World Bank web site and click on the subject to find many discussion papers and conferences. The United Nations also has some programs in place attempting to train local government officials, such as Seila mentioned above where a Cambodian government official was "moonlighting" in Phnom Penh to keep food on the table. To date there is little evidence these programs are working. The Zurich data set is now able to tells us much about where "good governance" comes from, and unfortunately has some bad news for many less-developed countries today. Countries were ranked on their levels of "government complexity" (the presence of national, regional, and local governments) 200 years ago, in other words, before the European colonials took over most of the world.[8] The bad news: if less-developed countries didn't have at least some government complexity 200 years ago they are unlikely to have it today. Put another way, there is a quite strong relationship between having some government complexity 200 years ago and a higher rank on government efficiency and good governance *today*. Countries which currently have good GNP growth and poverty reduction, such as China, Vietnam, and Thailand, are ancient civilizations with long traditions of government organization. Everyone recognizes China in that category: Though China collapsed into civil war and revolution during most of the 20th century, in large part because of the negative impact of colonialism, it was gradually able to regain government efficiency over the last 25 years of the 20th century. Thailand's political organization goes back to the 1200s (without the disruption of colonialism), and Vietnam had it much earlier than Thailand.

In Hanoi, for example, one can find the "Temple of Literature" in the tourist maps and guide books. Europe, of course, prides itself on its old universities like Oxford and Salamanca in Spain founded a few hundred years ago. When one reaches the Temple of Literature in Hanoi one will learn it was actually their first university, founded about 1,000 years ago! Plaques, looking much like tombstones, from the first graduates cover much of the temple grounds. Vietnam, too, was in chaos, civil war, and revolution through much of the 20th century, but after the first failed Stalinist economic policies began from 1975 throughout Vietnam, they got their act together by the end of the 1980s to mount an amazingly successful program of economic development and poverty reduction since then.

So what about Cambodia? Their ancient Angkor civilization goes back more than 1,000 years. In an earlier book and academic papers, I wrote that Cambodia could probably pull out of its current situation of rampant poverty and corruption because it had an ancient civilization with something of a complex government many centuries ago.[9] Like Vietnam, one might reason, Cambodia was disrupted by French colonialism and then the long Indochina Wars involving the French and then Americans. Given a few years to recover from these traumas, like Vietnam, Cambodia should be able to spring back. After more study of Cambodian history, then fieldwork in the country for almost two years, *the situation for Cambodia appears much less optimistic.* The historical evidence suggests that long before 200 years ago Cambodia had already lost most of the influence from its ancient civilization and government traditions. It seems that to the extent this ancient civilization and tradition of government complexity still had some influence on Cambodia 200 years ago, first French colonialism and then the Khmer Rouge finished it off far more than French colonialism, the Indochina Wars, and then communism harmed these ancient traditions in Vietnam. It is likely that Cambodia's ancient civilization and tradition of government complexity were already eroded centuries before. The Zurich data set described earlier shows Cambodia is one of the main exceptions among countries having an old civilization and somewhat complex levels of government more than 200 years ago and more economic development and poverty reduction today. Cambodia is one of the major "underachievers"; almost all of these other old civilizations have higher levels of government effectiveness measured by the World Bank in 2008. Cambodia is rated rather high in government complexity more than 200 years ago, but lags way behind other countries in government efficiency today. Other interesting cases of countries lagging behind are Afghanistan and Burma. China, Vietnam, India, and Thailand had about the same level of government complexity as Cambodia more than 200 years ago and currently have much more government effectiveness today. Major "overachievers" are Malaysia and Botswana; they had much less government complexity more than 200 years ago but have more government effectiveness today.[10]

One of the most respected historians of Cambodia, David Chandler, describes how it was increasing bureaucratic centralization and the ability of kings to organize people and policies to get things done around 1,000 years ago that are in large part responsible for that impressive civilization.[11] How else could they have built the huge temples of Angkor Wat? Many thousands of people had to be organized for these tasks, and thousands more had to be organized and controlled to grow the food which fed the world's first city of one million inhabitants back then. According to Chandler, these were not simply brutal kings beating their subjects into submission and controlling them like slaves. Certainly there was some of that, but there was also a "web of rights and responsibilities" to maintain the cooperation of their subjects. In other words, 1,000 years ago the people would respect and obey the king as long as the king took care of things so the people were fed and protected from outside threats.

All of this began to unravel, we have seen, when ecological disruption made it more and more difficult to feed a city of one million people, and then the Thais began attacking over 600 years ago. Cambodian kings began losing their legitimacy and support to such a degree that the old Angkor civilization began to crack. The Thais put another nail in their coffin, so to speak, when they sacked and burned Angkor Wat in 1431. The Angkor Kingdom had to be repeatedly moved further away from Thailand, until finally the capital was moved to Phnom Udong, closer to the Mekong River, and then down to the meeting of the Tonle Sap and Mekong Rivers at Phnom Penh where the capital remains today. Along the way the kingdom split apart, then reemerged, but never as it had been during the Angkor Wat days before the 1400s.

To the extent one could say there was still an Angkor civilization after the 1400s, though, the kingdom had changed. With less and less ability to assure basic needs for all their people, Chandler describes how Cambodian kings fell into a kind of "patron-client system" in which the king would highly reward a small group of supporters in return for their support against the mass of people who were falling into further misery, *not unlike the "big man" form of government* described above which is more common in fractured and dysfunctional sub–Saharan African countries today. The ancient Angkor civilization was so far gone that by the early 1800s when the French started taking over the country, few Cambodians even knew that Angkor Wat had ever existed. The temples were in essence rediscovered by the French who at first thought it impossible that the weak and disorganized Cambodian people they were coming to dominate could have ever built anything so grand.

Some recent historians, however, question the degree to which the Angkor civilization ever had benevolent kings or efficiently organized government to hold the allegiance of its people like the other kingdoms which later emerged in this part of Southeast Asia. John Tully, for example, claims early Angkor kings had always ruled more harshly and with their own interests in mind compared to Thailand, Vietnam, or the kings of Europe.[12] After the 1400s, Tully argues, this harsh, brutal rule increased. Another factor was possibly the earlier dominance of Indian Hinduism in the Angkor civilization compared to Theravada Buddhism which was the dominant religion in Thailand, Burma, and the smaller kingdoms in what is now Laos. Theravada Buddhism, even more than other branches of Buddhism, preaches that good karma and nirvana will be attained through personal merit based on good deeds to other humans. Early, as well as recent, Thai kings have been devout Theravada Buddhists, sometimes spending a few years as monks in strict Buddhist monasteries before becoming kings. Soon after the high point of the Angkor civilization about 1,000 years ago, Theravada Buddhism began making inroads on the dominance of Hinduism, with one king converting to Buddhism only to be replaced by another king who was Hindu. Eventually all Cambodian kings came to accept Buddhism. But from a few hundred years ago up to the present, few Cambodian kings have been as devoutly Buddhist as Thai kings often have been. Whatever the importance of religion for Cambodian kings compared to others in the region, though, it is clear that the bureaucratic organization that helped build and maintain the Angkor civilization 1,000 years ago was slowly eroded over the centuries after 1400, so much so that it was almost gone when the French began taking over in the second half of the 1800s.

As noted earlier, French colonialism in Cambodia, in fact, began in a rather strange manner. Soon after the mid–1800s the Cambodian king of the time *invited* the French to come in and take over the country as a "protectorate." This king knew all too well that without French protection his country was likely to be gobbled up by his more powerful neighbors to the west and east. As the French slowly came into to Cambodia, eventually declaring the country their colonial possession, they realized there was little effective government organization that could be co-opted to run the country for them as the British were doing in India and the French were doing in Vietnam. But rather than putting much effort into training Cambodians to help them run their colonial possession, *the French brought in Vietnamese* who they thought could do a much better job.

Then, of course, the Khmer Rouge finished off any functioning government Cambodia had before 1975. As noted earlier, there were only some 300 college-educated Cambodians left alive in the country after the Vietnamese pushed the Khmer Rouge to the fringes of Cambodia after 1979. A new book written by an American lawyer, Evan Gottesman, who was part of the United

Nations team trying to rebuild Cambodian governmental institutions during the early 1990s, shows this all too clearly.[13] Gottesman discovered discarded records kept by the Vietnamese from the beginning of the 1980s when the Vietnamese were trying to bring Cambodia out of anarchy. The Vietnamese occupiers estimated there was only 15 percent of the remaining Cambodian population with any significant education at all, and almost none with any government experience after the Khmer Rouge genocide. There were a few Cambodian refugees who had fled into Vietnam before 1979 which the Vietnamese trained to some day take over the Cambodian government. One of the most important was the current prime minister, Hun Sen, who was a former officer in the Khmer Rouge Army until he realized it would all self-destruct. But this handful of Cambodians guided and sponsored by the Vietnamese to form a new government from the early 1980s was not enough. That is when the Vietnamese began searching the labor camps for anyone with enough education to help run the new Cambodian government. And this is how they found a few talented Cambodians now in government. But neither the Vietnamese in the 1980s nor the UN task force in the early 1990s could find enough educated and talented people to build anything like an efficient government to bring Cambodia out of its current desperation.

Asian Bureaucratic Ministries: A Cambodian Failure

State capacity and good governance are key reasons economic development and poverty reduction in many East and Southeast Asian nations are proceeding way ahead of other world regions. One rather common element among these Asian countries is an independent and efficient government ministry.[14] By "rather independent" it means these government ministry officials are not closely controlled by elected politicians. Corruption among elected politicians is fairly high to moderate in Asian nations with good economic development and poverty reduction today. But with a somewhat independent government ministry running things, as long as these rather independent unelected government ministry officials are not equally corrupt, corruption among elected politicians is much less of a hindrance. As described above, the modern Asian model of a government ministry somewhat autonomous from elected politicians emerged first in Japan from the second half of the 1800s and is worth further consideration.

From the early years of Japan's "*Meiji* Restoration" beginning in 1868, a bureaucratic ministry was established with a constitution giving elected politicians little influence over the ministry.[15] With Japan's defeat in World War II there was a new constitution written by the American Occupation forces under General MacArthur. This post-war constitution continued to allow for extensive bureaucratic power by unelected civil servants. Indeed, the American Occupation Force unwittingly made it almost certain that the bureaucratic elite would not only maintain its power, but actually expand it. First, because the American Occupation Force did not fully understand the pre-war Japanese political system, it was assumed that the military and elected politicians had most power before the war, and were therefore responsible for the war. These people were promptly purged. Of all purges, over 79 percent involved military officers and 16 percent involved politicians — less than 1 percent involved the unelected bureaucratic ministry elite. Second, the remaining, untainted politicians placed into positions of power by the American Occupation Force were comparatively inexperienced. The resulting power vacuum was filled by the bureaucratic elite.

During the second half of the 20th century the most important Japanese government ministries were the Ministries of Justice, Foreign Affairs, Finance, and International Trade and Industry. The elected prime minister of Japan selects the top minister for each of these ministries, as well as the heads of a few other agencies. These people then make up the prime minister's cabinet, much like those of European democracies today. However, it is the unelected administrative vice-minister in each of these ministries in Japan who is most knowledgeable and powerful. As politicians and political appointees formally heading the ministers of these bureaucracies, they are inexperienced, outsiders to the agencies, and to a large extent at the mercy of the vice-ministers and their vast civil servant staff. The vice-minister of each agency in Japan has spent his whole career in the ministry, working his way to the top since college graduation 30 to 40 years before. The vice-minister, therefore, has wide experience and training in the agency, extensive knowledge of the particular aspects of the Japanese society the agency is to regulate, and the loyalty of thousands of other civil servants below him.

Japanese government ministry officials have not always followed the best policies for economic development. And they have certainly made mistakes. But while there has been fairly high corruption among elected government officials in Japan in the second half of the 20th century, studies have shown corruption in the government ministries has been much lower, resulting in one of the most efficient governments in the world.[16]

After the Japanese gained rapid economic development and poverty reduction with this new style of a relative autonomous bureaucratic ministry dedicated to national interests, the next to follow suit were the South Koreans and Taiwanese. During the 1960s Americans on the left hated the "fascist" dictator Park in South Korea. He did so many despicable things in his country during his rule. Taiwan in the early 1980s looked like a police state with no democracy, the military everywhere, with the heirs to General Chiang Kai-shek stifling all decent. But one must admit that both South Korea and Taiwan have achieved high levels of democracy today, as well as prosperity, poverty reduction, and a high level of economic equality.

Next to follow was Thailand and a few other Southeast Asian countries. Since the 1932 military coup that overthrew the absolute monarchy, the Thai government has mostly been headed by the military. There was some democracy in the 1970s, only to be overturned in another military coup. Then again from the 1990s there was more democracy until another military coup ended that in 2006. One September morning in 2006, Thai and foreign business people in the country woke up with a shock to see the tanks and soldiers had taken over the streets of Bangkok. After breakfast these business people went to work as usual with little concern for the Thai economy. The Thai stock market showed its agreement; there was only a little downward blip before the market returned to its usual upward trend. These people knew who would continue to run the vital functions of government.

While the Thai military was mostly out of politics during the 1990s, as noted above, the civilian government introduced a new constitution in 1997. This constitution brought a higher level of democracy and handed elected politicians more government influence in relation to ministry bureaucrats. Another constitution was written under military influence in 2007, and as one might guess, this new constitution reduced the level of democracy, primarily by bringing back a Senate which is mostly appointed by ministry bureaucrats rather than popularly elected. Then followed new events from 2008 that have amazed people in Western democracies. With the military back in their barracks, and a newly elected government in place from early 2008, there were massive protests, first primarily by urban, well-educated Thais, against this newly elected government, and mostly because of fear corrupt politicians are again running the government, then by "red shirts" (mostly rural and working-class Thais). The main faction leading the protests among urban and educated Thais ("yellow shirts") have called for a new constitution that will further reduce the level of democracy and give unelected government civil servants even more control over the government.[17]

One should not get the impression that Thai politicians have been more corrupt than those in other less-developed countries with at least some level of democracy. We have in fact already seen that Transparency International ranks Thailand as only moderately corrupt compared to other countries below the world's most wealthy. But to the extent Thai politicians have been corrupt, like most other Asian nations with good rates of economic growth and poverty reduction, there has been a strong and somewhat independent bureaucratic ministry elite in Thailand that is less corrupt, well educated, with long civil service careers running the most vital functions of government.

As we have also already seen, Transparency International, the World Bank, and many other international agencies rank Cambodia among the most corrupt in the world. But unlike most other Asian nations, *Cambodia does not have an efficient and independent government ministry running vital functions of government.* This is what every Cambodian ministry official and academic said in private. To recap what has been written above, to the extent there was something like an efficient bureaucracy 1,000 years ago, Cambodia lost it along the way. With the disruption of colonialism, the Indochina Wars, and then the Khmer Rouge disaster, the chance of any semiprofessional bureaucratic ministry in the near future was wiped out. What Cambodia has today is a corrupt, dysfunctional government run in a dictatorial fashion by Hun Sen and his friends enriched through a kind of "big man" system of government, *without the counterweight of a professional, somewhat independent government ministry* to actually take care of the real business of helping the country. More than anything, this is the essence of what the World Bank and development scholars refer to as "government incapacity."

A Missing Civil Society

Despite the above, one must be careful not to present an overly simplistic view of Cambodia's problems today. Yes, the government is corrupt and needs a more professional and relatively independent civil service as a counter. But Cambodia is also lacking another counter to government corruption found in many other developing countries in Asia, what is mostly referred to these days as a *civil society.*

A civil society is one in which many different interest groups are at least somewhat organized and relatively free to organize without *extensive* government repression. A civil society also requires citizens and interest groups who are aware of their interests and what government is doing in relation to their interests. The opposite of a civil society is what the American sociologist, C. Wright Mills, called a mass society in his famous book *The Power Elite* back in the 1950s. Put another way, power is always relative to the various interest groups in a country. Without a civil society, government elites are much more powerful simply because there are few counters to what they want to do in the country. Compared to almost all other Asian nations, including those that still have communist governments (except North Korea), Cambodia has a very weak civil society. As always there are exceptions in Cambodia, but in this case very few compared to other countries in the region.

One representative of these exceptions was introduced by a young American NGO worker. She is a leader of Cambodia's strongest labor union, about the only strong labor union. I will call her Sina.

It turned out that Sina was one of the most impressive young Cambodians anyone could meet in the country. About 30 years old, somewhat attractive, and dressed in the usual Levi's and T-shirt with political slogans that activists must always wear, Sina is one of the leaders of the biggest labor union in Cambodia, one that represents low-wage garment workers. Sina grew up in a small village in central Cambodia, had only four years of education, and left the village when she was 20 to help her family by working in a new foreign garment factory in Phnom Penh, the usual sweatshop. She was popular with the other girls, and obviously smart. Then a fortunate thing happened for Cambodia.

A few years ago when the legislation for a new quota system for textile imports to the United States was going through Congress, under American labor union pressure, there was a clause added which said the higher quotas for Cambodia would be rescinded if Cambodia failed to allow free organization for labor unions in the Cambodian garment industry.[18] So far it has worked, and has been monitored by American and international labor unions later interviewed. As a result, the biggest and most influential labor union in Cambodia is this one representing garment workers. When this labor union was given new life by this American legislation, Sina was in the right place, and obviously one of the right people to move to the top of this union.

Sina told her story while having a couple of beers in the tourist area along the Tonle Sap River one evening. Soon after she joined the labor union she started moving up the ranks because of her smarts and popularity. With only four years of schooling, she taught herself English in her spare time. She said there were invitations for her union to speak at various union meetings around the world and she knew English would be mandatory. Her last international meeting was in conjunction with the World Trade Organization meeting in Hong Kong, where she proudly said she had time to get into the protest action.

Asked about the impact of the American legislation requiring free union organization in the garment industry, her response was very positive. To begin with, she said, the union would not be able to exist without it. People like her would be intimidated, likely beaten, and quite possibly killed without the legislation. Some leaders of labor unions representing other industries have in fact been killed in recent years. As for the garment workers themselves, she said wages quickly came up from an average of $2 per day to $3. Soon after this legislation came into effect, a private, EU-funded research institute in Phnom Penh estimated it had a slight impact on reducing poverty in Cambodia because 30 to 40 percent of the workers' wages are sent home to families in villages.[19] This particular garment union was currently threatening to strike if wages were not doubled. She admitted wages were unlikely to double, but two days before, company representatives agreed to go back to the negotiating table on threat of her union's strike.

Knowing that Hun Sen's government is not going to give up so easily when the wealth of his rich friends are at stake, the discussion with Sina moved to the topic of the government's reaction. Most importantly, Sina said, without monitoring from outside labor unions and international labor organizations it would all fall apart, and her life would likely be in danger. But as usual, she said, there was a counterplan by Hun Sen's government. Knowing they would lose a lot of foreign investment if they went against the U.S. legislation, the government's strategy has been to sponsor several counter labor unions in the garment industry, spreading out the number of members and thus reducing membership of the real labor union. Poor uneducated girls from the countryside working in these sweatshops don't really understand what is going on, so her more legitimate labor union has had to work hard to enlighten them, so far with fairly good success.

Before the end of the interview with Sina, the influential social movement organization in Thailand, Assembly for the Poor, was brought up. As noted earlier, this organization sprang up in the early 1990s to lead many protests on the part of poor farmers.[20] This Thai organization has probably been the most effective in all of Southeast Asia. They have blocked or reversed some legislation deemed harmful to the interests of poor Thai farmers, they have blocked the building of dams that were expected to take away farm land and hurt fishermen. "Yes, of course," she said, "I know all about them." She went on to explain how the Assembly for the Poor was the envy of all activists for workers and poor farmers in Cambodia. But she admitted something like this would be impossible in Cambodia today. Asked "How could the government stop it?" her reply was, first, if a person were trying to organize something like the Assembly for the Poor, as some have tried in Cambodia, the Cambodian government would verbally threaten him or her. The next step is to beat the person trying to organize such a movement. If none of this works, then people's families are harmed, homes are burned, and finally in some cases people have been killed. Without the American legislation, she said, such would likely be the fate of her fellow union activists in the garment industry.

Historical and Psychological
Impediments to a Civil Society

As usual, one must recognize that things are rather more complex; it is not only government repression restricting a strong civil society in Cambodia compared to its neighbors. There are historical power arrangements and more recently psychological impediments. First, a little more history.

As alluded to earlier in this chapter, peasants in Cambodia have been more repressed and controlled than in either Thailand or Vietnam.[21] During Angkor times, for example, Brahmanical families were more like feudal lords controlling the land and their peasants. In neighboring countries like Thailand, there was much less of what could be called a feudal elite of landowners.[22] In theory the kings of Thailand and the little kingdoms in what is now Thailand and Laos owned all the land. There were few big landowners. The practice was for the king to allow village people to use his land for growing their own food, with some tribute, of course. However, until well into the 19th century, there were many separate kingdoms in what is now Thailand, Laos, and Burma, with each of these kingdoms vying to expand their domains. The shifting fringes between all of these little kingdoms were often no-man's land where village peasants were mostly left alone to grow their food without outside intervention. As a result, in the words of respected Thai historical economist, Pasuk, "Thai peasants are a wild and unruly lot." These peasants have a long tradition of relatively independent political action.[23] In contrast, Chandler writes, there has been almost no organization among rural people in Cambodia outside of the family or across villages.

More recently, Tully has provided some more detail to this lack of civil society in Cambodian history. The early Angkor civilization, he argues, more accurately fit Marx's description of an "Asia mode of production" than elsewhere in Southeast Asia. An Asian mode of production is one with a highly centralized and bureaucratized state because of wet rice agriculture. Wet rice agriculture required extensive canals and irrigation projects if a large civilization was to exist, which the Angkor civilization certainly was with about 1 million people in the capital some 1,000 years ago. However, when the Angkor civilization went into decline and eventually was moved close to what is now Phnom Penh in 1432, this highly centralized state had fallen apart because of internal conflicts.[24] Under the highly centralized and repressive state in earlier centuries, in contrast to countries like Thailand, a village civil society could not develop, and never did as in neighboring countries.

The psychological impediments to a civil society in Cambodia came up in interviews with several NGOs. One was mentioned earlier, the Transcultural Psycho-social Organization, funded by European governments to treat rural victims of the Khmer Rouge. But other NGO people had spoke of this psychological impediment earlier.

An earlier interview was in an old two-story house in the heart of Phnom Penh, the headquarters of a small, Cambodian-run NGO funded by grants from Canada, Holland, Italy, Norway and Denmark. In what was the living room when the old house was a family residence, there were posters on the walls about various farm projects and cultural events, antique farm implements on display, and traditional Cambodian crafts. After a few minutes a young man who is the director of this Cambodian NGO drove up in an old jeep. We can refer to him as Virak. This impressive young man had just finished his Ph.D. in agricultural economics in one of the leading universities in Europe. He had recently returned full of fire and optimism to help his rural people.

As we sat sipping more tea in the old living room, Virak, wearing the usual blue jeans and political T-shirt, explained the mission of his NGO. Their primary task is educating poor farmers about better ways of growing their crops and protecting their animals; in essence his NGO is a little agricultural extension station like those run by the USDA around the United States. (And like those operated by other Southeast Asian governments, even Laos, but none were found operated by the Cambodian government.)

After a presentation of the techniques and problems of farming in Cambodia, the questions turned to village organization, specifically mentioning the Assembly for the Poor in Thailand. "Nothing like that could happen here" was his first response, "the government wouldn't allow it." As others had explained in Cambodia, along with many other interviewees to come, Virak said Hun Sen's political party, the Cambodian People's Party, is very active on the village level. Any attempt to form a social movement among farmers against the government would be quickly repressed. Repression, however, is seldom necessary. Cambodian villagers have always been rather passive, he added, and even more so since the Khmer Rouge days. "People are still frightened, have lost trust in other people." In essence, his explanation was that it is hard to stick your neck out when you never know for sure if you can trust your neighbor.

While not a social scientist, this young man trained in agriculture explained what can be found in new studies about economic development and social organization among rural people in developing countries. Trust in fellow villagers, or fellow citizens in general, is a cultural advantage some developing countries have over others. Trust in others is a basic requirement for agricultural cooperatives, as well as cooperation to form interest groups to press for common needs and protection. Whether or not there was much of this in earlier Cambodian culture, it is quite likely the Khmer Rouge had killed it off. Studies of Cambodian refugees from the killing fields published in Western countries indicate posttraumatic symptoms of withdrawal from social interaction and depression.[25] As noted earlier, mental health workers from the Transcultural Psycho-social Organization in Battambang claim there are various studies that indicate 50 to 60 percent of the people over 30 years old have mental problems (the Khmer Rouge generation). The studies of Cambodian refugees in the North America agree with this estimate. As mentioned earlier, signs of this withdrawal of social trust appeared when interviewing an old man in one of the resettlement camps for evicted slum people. His wife said she was amazed that her husband had opened up in the interview. She hadn't seen that in him since they fled the Khmer Rouge.

Conclusion

The legacy of Cambodian history, from the decline of the Angkor civilization more than 600 years ago, to the horrors of the killing fields most recently, weighs heavily upon Cambodia today. The hand of history never completely dictates the fate of a people, but it does shape options, opportunities, and roadblocks. Few countries in recent centuries have faced such complete political and economic breakdown as that faced by Cambodia because of the Khmer Rouge. Out of the void, and under the tutelage of the Vietnamese from 1980, the current government controlled by Hun Sen and his Cambodian People's Party slowly emerged to consolidated power. There was optimism at first, especially when the United Nations finally came into Cambodia in the early 1990s with a mission of economic reconstruction and rebuilding government institutions. But much like the optimism spreading through sub–Saharan Africa when newly independent governments were led by young, bright, idealistic Africans in the 1960s, it was short lived. The fiery rhetoric of a new generation such as Lumumba and then Mobutu in the Congo quickly faded into pessimism and despair when the barriers erected by African history were realized. Mobutu degenerated from a passionate savior of the Congo into one of the three most corrupt men in the world toward the end. He left the country with personal wealth of some $5 billion stashed away in various bank accounts, mansions in Europe, a private Boeing 707 reserved for overseas shopping sprees for his wives, along with palaces back home in the Congo.[26]

Will Hun Sen follow? Will Cambodia continue on its path of unsustainable economic development like most sub–Saharan African countries today? Or will Cambodia be able to make necessary policy changes, reduce corruption, and build more efficient governmental institutions to produce more sustainable economic development with poverty reduction like most of its Southeast Asian neighbors?

CHAPTER 10

Cambodia's Future in the Global Economy

After the massive, "mysterious" temples of Angkor Wat, Bayon, and Ta Prohm, children and amputees begging in the streets are probably the most striking images taken home by tourists. During the 1990s in Hanoi and Ho Chi Minh City/Saigon, one could say much the same for Vietnam. For example, one old peasant lady, bent over from probably 70 years of work in the rice paddies, her tattered clothing looking almost as old, followed colleagues and me with outstretched hand from the northern to the southern shores of Ho Hoan Kiem Lake in the center of Hanoi. One feels guilty for not giving money to a person so obviously poor, but one also learns quickly that if money is given, there is a mob instead of one miserable old lady. In recent years there have been fewer and fewer people begging in Vietnam's cities compared to Cambodia. In coming years one may see fewer of them in Cambodia as well, but if so it will more likely be because the Cambodian government has rounded them up and put them in prisons or "relocation camps" rather than taking care of the problem with economic development accompanied by poverty reduction.

The Evictions and Land Grabs Continue

Contacts in Cambodia, articles in the *Phnom Penh Post*, and another brief visit to Cambodia in early 2010 indicate the arrests of village and slum people trying to keep their homes and land has expanded. Predictions made by people met earlier, such as Tima, the impressive lady leading a resistance among her fellow slum dwellers in Phnom Penh, have come true. Tima said that would happen after the summer elections of 2008: Unlike Burma, the world has again forgotten about Cambodia, and there is no world condemnation as the arrests, beatings, and land grabs increase.

As noted in Chapter 6, there were additional interviews around Phnom Penh slums in December 2008, including another visit Dey Krahorm slum, hoping to meet Tima for an update. The slum was much smaller than before, with only 100 families still holding out. There were almost 700 families in January 2007. By December 2008 there were large spaces between the plywood and tin shacks where others had been torn down, the usual trash and razor wire covering empty spaces. Inquiring in a few households about Tima, no one knew exactly where she was. About 50 of these slum people had been arrested since April 2008 and were probably still in prison. Tima was most likely one of them. A feisty old lady of 70 with closely cropped hair like a Buddhist nun said she is one of the leaders of the protest now. She and the others were ready to hold out at all costs. She had served in the Cambodian Army during the 1980s to fight the Khmer Rouge and was determined to

Bayon Temple

battle to the end again. A couple of weeks later, at the end of 2008, the government imposed a last deadline for their eviction — December 30. A few weeks later the police and paramilitary force moved in with the usual beatings, loading the remaining people onto trucks, burning their shacks. Dey Krahorm slum is now gone. In January 2010 there was a new construction site where Dey Krahorm slum use to be, like many other places around Phnom Penh were thousands of families used to live and work. The first building completed on this Dey Krahorm site was a gym and spa where the employees of 7NG, the South Korean company that evicted these people, could work out.

The next big round of evictions in Phnom Penh is being called "the battle of Boeung Kak Lake." Boeung Kak Lake is a large body of water just north of central Phnom Penh, and home to about 20,000 people. As noted earlier, most people are poor vendors and small farmers who settled around the lake since freed from Khmer Rouge camps after 1979. Many others are small business people operating restaurants and low-cost hotels catering to young "backpacker" European tourists. Some of the lake's poor residents were able to obtain "title" to their land, but that makes little difference to Cambodia's elite. During early 2008 these people heard they would be evicted. Some construction around Boeung Kak Lake had already begun, with parts of the lake being filled in by late 2008, already flooding the homes of hundreds of poor people.[1]

More interviews were conducted with some of these people around Boeung Kak Lake in December 2008 and early 2010. The lake is massive, covering several square miles, just north of Phnom Penh and north of the road leading to the airport. Metal fencing keeps anyone on the road from seeing what is happening. Mostly crude slum homes surround the lake, except the southern area where development has already started. The simple houses along the lakefront have little porches going out to the lake where families have netted fish farms and water plants growing. Most residents are venders, motorbike taxi drivers, or unskilled construction workers. On the east side of the lake are the cheap backpacker guesthouses and the usual cheap restaurants and shops catering to these young tourists. There are a few homes that could not be described as shacks, but no hotels or restaurants above the backpacker level, or, one should say, not yet. One restaurant on the west side of the lake is the typical outdoor place found all over Thailand and Cambodia. Though crudely made, with a rickety little boardwalk and tables over the water, the excellent food draws in both the rich and poor.

Four families on the west side of the lake were interviewed. Their primitive homes were along the lake shore, with part of the house on stilts over the water. They knew they were being evicted, but no one had given them official notice, told them when they would be forced to leave, where they would go, or what compensation if any they would get for their little homes. For those on the waterfront, however, these were moot questions. They were intentionally being flooded out.[2] Across the lake one could see the Chinese-Cambodian construction company had a massive pipe bringing in sand to fill in part of the lake for a new resort hotel. Muddy water with green slime and trash had moved to a couple of inches below the floor of slum houses. When it rains their houses have already flooded, making these people sleep next to the road in front of their homes.

On the east side of the lake there were interviews with some managers of cheap backpacker bungalows. The story was much the same. They had no idea when they would be forced out, where they would go, and if they would receive any compensation for their small businesses. They were also being forced out because of flooding. It was not far from this backpacker area where private paramilitary guards working for the Chinese construction company decided a foreigner should not be taking pictures. A machine gun was used to motion the way out of the lake area. A positive indication of this action, however, was to show this must be the right place to interview people and take pictures of what is happening to slum people in Phnom Penh, interviews and photos that had already been completed. The same thing happened on the south side of the lake about an hour later when armed guards saw a Western foreigner taking pictures of the big pipeline pumping sand into the lake which was flooding out many of the poor residents.

The day before there were interviews with some American and British human rights activists and lawyers trying to defend the rights of these slum people. It was a little surprising to find that the American USAID had been funding some of these people, along with a grant from the American Bar Association for another, throughout the Bush administration. Unlike other slums being cleared in Phnom Penh, the evictions of people around the lake are being more actively challenged in the Cambodian courts. The American lawyer supported by the Bar Association said there is almost no chance of success given the corrupt legal system and the power of Cambodian elites.[3] Like other slum residents, none of these poor people actually have real title to their land that would hold up in court, he said. Around the lake area, and in Dey Krahorm slum which was cleared in January 2009, what some of these poor people have is a "special decree" given by Prime Minister Hun Sen before a national election in 2003 saying they could stay in their slum houses. The 70-year-old lady leading the resistance in Dey Krahorm slum interviewed in December 2008 had provided a copy of the "decree." The American lawyer said it was just a political stunt and had no legal status. In late December

2008 the people of Boeung Kak Lake lost their court appeal. There is still the Cambodian Supreme Court as a final appeal, but their chances of winning are almost zero.

As noted earlier, investigation by foreign NGOs turned up a typical story. A Chinese-Cambodian joint venture has gained rights to land around the lake in return for some $79 million, for land actually estimated to be worth $3 billion.[4] There was no open bidding for this land or even public information about the leases before Prime Minister Hun Sen and his Deputy Prime Minister approved the contracts. The Cambodian partner with this Chinese development company is owned by the wife of a Cambodian senator who happens to be a friend of Prime Minister Hun Sen.[5]

These evictions, however, are not just in urban areas or areas targeted for tourist resorts along the sea coast. Most of the land stolen from village farmers goes to rich Cambodians or foreign corporations who exploit the natural resources or create large plantations. For example, Kuwait has invested about $546 million for some 124,000 acres of farmland, and Qatar has recently invested about $200 million.[6] American and British human rights officials interviewed claim that Prime Minister Hun Sen is directly involved. One NGO showed maps indicating that Hun Sen's Pheapimex corporation has recently acquired some *10 percent of all land in Cambodia.*[7] As noted earlier, in 1993 only 3 percent of Cambodian peasants were landless. It is now 23 percent, with an Amnesty International study claiming 45 percent are "near landless," meaning they have less than one-half hectare of land.[8] As more Cambodian peasants become landless, food produced on these large plantations goes to the world market instead of to hungry Cambodians.

Foreign Investment with Bad Governance

The damage to Cambodia's future is not limited to land grabs. Foreign investment benefitting primarily the short-term interests of Cambodia's rich will be more damaging. There is now a rich body of literature and research indicating that foreign investment from rich corporations can actually have more long-term negative than positive effects on a less developed country with a government that is corrupt or simply lacks the institutional capacity to protect national interests.[9] In other words, as also indicated by data from the "Zurich data set of least developed countries," there is no simple correlation between the level of foreign investment coming into a less developed country and sustained economic growth or poverty reduction; in some countries this foreign investment helps, in others it is detrimental. For example, these data measure "foreign direct investment" (FDI) in 1990 and levels of GNP per capita in 1999 to give this foreign investment time to help raise standards of living. There is no relationship today between these two measures. We have done the same analysis with foreign investment in 1990 and the percent of people in the country living on less that $1 per day in the country in 1999. Again, there is no relationship.[10] Earlier studies using data from the 1960s and 1970s actually showed a significant negative relationship between foreign investment at one point in time and later long-term economic growth in less-developed countries around the world.[11] In other words, the more the foreign investment the less there is long-term economic growth and poverty reduction. The difference between the earlier studies and those today seem to be that more of the world's foreign investment is now going to Asian countries. A majority of the Asia countries have more functional government institutions, comparatively less corruption, and governments which put more restrictions on foreign investment which help long-term economic growth compared to other less-developed countries in the world. Thus, worldwide there are important differences in government effectiveness or good governance between most Asian countries and other less developed countries. Cambodia, unfortunately, is not among the Asian countries able or willing to protect long-term national interests.

The reasons that foreign investment in many countries around the world does not promote long-term economic growth and poverty reduction are rather simple. When corrupt and powerful elites are able to shape government policies they often invite foreign corporations into the country with few safeguards protecting national interests. Such foreign investment brings short-term gains for the rich, but a bleak future for everyone else. For example, with no restrictions or stipulations, foreign investment coming into a poor country can just as easily leave the country, as happened to Mexico after the first years of the North American Free Trade Agreement. A rush to attract foreign investment without safeguards often allows these outside investors to send most of their profits back home without a reasonable level of taxation helping infrastructure development in the poor country. As described earlier, Cambodia needs revenues to pay higher salaries to teachers and healthcare workers, to build new roads that don't fall apart, and to provide rural areas with electricity and irrigation. Very limited tax revenues, along with corruption, are not allowing sufficient human and capital infrastructure development for Cambodia's future.

In addition to this, one must realize foreign investors are usually in a country like Cambodia because of low-wage labor. The two biggest industries generating economic growth in Cambodia are tourism and low-skill textile manufacturing. When wealthy elites in the host country are able to dominate government policy, they are almost certain to do all they can to keep wages low. Again there is a simple logic: Foreign investors are in the country for low-wage labor, local elites are getting rich from the foreign investment, thus, local elites have no incentives to raise wages for low-skilled laborers.

Finally, foreign investment related to natural resource extraction is usually of the worst kind.[12] With potentially huge profits from natural resources in a country that is unable to control corruption, the resources will be offered to foreign companies for a fraction of the real value in return for bribes going to local elites. But there is also another simple (and legal) economic logic to the damage. Natural resources which could be processed within the country to create more jobs and profits are often simply extracted and shipped out of the country, creating more jobs and profits in foreign countries instead of the host country.

All of these negative results from high levels of foreign investment are compounded when only two or three countries account for most of the foreign investment.[13] Such a dominant position in the economy can allow outside investors to have more pressure on government policies for short-term interests benefitting themselves and rich domestic elites against the long-term interests of the poor country. Thailand, for example, has worked to avoid this situation by manipulating investment terms to favor countries with less foreign investment in Thailand as a counterbalance to others.[14] Nothing like this is happening in Cambodia. At the moment, China is the largest foreign investor in Cambodia, with Thailand and South Korea in second and third position. South Korea is coming into Cambodia primarily for big construction projects. China is in primarily for the natural resources, and taking them out cheaply.

None of the above is to suggest that all Cambodian government ministry officials who kindly granted interviews are corrupt or unconcerned about their country. These government ministry officials who told their stories are deeply concerned about their fellow citizens. They know all too well many of the problems described above. In contrast to their counterparts in other Southeast Asian countries such as Thailand and Vietnam, and especially in Japan, South Korea and Taiwan in East Asia, however, these Cambodian ministry officials have little influence. And even if they had much influence, the ministry bureaucracies they help guide have so few well-trained and -educated staff, with salaries that are even close to providing basic necessities for their families, that their ministries would not come close to what counts for "good governance" or government efficiency. In Cambodia it is not uncommon to hear from well-meaning government ministry officials what one scholarly, middle-aged man said sadly, "We have these good development plans, but they never seem to get implemented, and the money seems to disappear."

The Future for Cambodia

World Bank projections suggest that poverty in East and Southeast Asia will be reduced by more than 60 percent in the first 15 years of the 21st century, including or excluding the massive impact of China's population.[15] Poverty in South Asia, mostly because of India, is expected to drop by around 20 percent. Poverty reduction in Latin American countries is expected to be flat, while poverty will *increase* by some 30 percent or more in sub–Saharan African countries. These projections may be somewhat off given corrected poverty measures issued by the World Bank in 2008 and the global recession that began in the same year.[16] But however off these World Bank projections might be, the pattern of massive poverty reductions in East and Southeast Asia will almost certainly stand. The only major exceptions in this part of the world are North Korea, Burma, and Cambodia.

Why is Cambodia more like the troubled countries of sub–Saharan Africa than most of its Southeast Asian neighbors? This is a major question that has been implied throughout much this book. There is no single answer. But there are *some* answers, and that is at least a beginning. Once we have a clearer picture of what is wrong in Cambodia we have better ideas about how to fix the problems.

Corruption

Government corruption in Cambodia is one answer, and it is a big one. We have seen that Cambodia is in the major leagues when it come to corruption, among the top 10 countries in the world. And unfortunately this corruption is at the highest levels of government down to the lowest. If the higher levels of government were less corrupt and intent on reducing corruption in the country, as in China and Vietnam, there would be much more hope for Cambodia. Such is not the case. If used wisely for infrastructure development, for example, that expected $1 billion per year in oil money could go a long way in pulling Cambodians out of poverty. Few people think this is very likely to happen.

Institutional Incapacity

We tend to assume that when a country is a country, listed on all of our maps, etc., that such a country has a government. This is not always the case. Somebody, some big man or group, will always be somewhat in control, or there is civil war. But that is not the same thing as what we think of as a government. A real government has various institutions or bureaucracies to more or less rationally deal with all kinds of management issues for people of the nation — courts, economic planning, education, police protection, building and maintaining roads, and so on. Only a few extremely poor countries in places such as in sub–Saharan Africa lack some of these institutions. These governmental institutions may exist on paper, and perhaps have a few people working in offices for these issues, though very little really gets done. Cambodia is closer to this situation than its neighboring countries, especially Thailand and Vietnam. A major contrast, as we have seen, is that most East and Southeast Asian countries usually have somewhat strong traditions of rather competent and relatively independent government bureaucratic ministries. If elected politicians are corrupt and/or incompetent, these relatively independent government ministries can still keep the country running. This is not the case in Cambodia.

A Lack of Human and Physical Infrastructure

The richest countries in the world have gotten there in large part because they have an abundance of human capital (talent) and physical infrastructure. There must be educated, well-trained people to take care of running the economy, educational systems, government functions, and so on. There must be physical infrastructure — good roads, bridges, electric power, school buildings, communication systems, waste management, and so on. After spending time in other Southeast Asian countries, one sees very quickly that Cambodia is way behind in both human and physical infrastructure development.

The lack of "human capital" is harder to observe in a tour of Cambodia, but after many interviews with Cambodians who complain that few people are educated or trained well enough to do their jobs, one begins to get the picture. A recent World Bank report cited above showed that Cambodia has made good progress in putting elementary schools within a few miles of every village. Another World Bank report two years earlier, however, found that the gap between the official primary school enrollment rate and the literacy rate in Cambodia is among the highest in the world.[17] School buildings don't always mean education is being achieved.[18] Village primary schoolteachers say their children often don't attend classes. University professors admit they do little actual teaching because they must moonlight in other jobs to put food on the table. These professors also say getting into one of the noted universities in Cambodia requires more bribe money than intelligence. They add it is pretty much the same to actually graduate from a university. We have seen how few educated people were left in Cambodia after the Khmer Rouge years. Cambodia is not making strong progress in filling this void.[19]

A lack of human capital and physical infrastructure both make it difficult to attract foreign corporate investment. This also makes it difficult to set reasonable rules on this foreign investment so that foreign investment profits the country's future rather than just the foreign corporation. Thailand and Vietnam can tell foreign corporations that if they invest in the country these companies must adhere to something such as the 51 percent joint venture law described above. Foreign corporations will complain about such rules restricting their profits, but they still come to countries like Vietnam, China, and Thailand because of the good physical infrastructure and human talent. These countries also have rapidly growing domestic markets as well as good records of exports. Such is less the case in Cambodia. Cambodia has much fewer restrictions on foreign corporations coming into the country. They can be fully foreign owned, taxes are low, and wages are low. But there is still comparatively less foreign investment coming into Cambodia. And with the exception of a few factories coming in to make, for example, Honda motorbikes, most of the foreign investment is in very low-skill textile "sweatshops."

Lack of Civil Society

A country's political and economic elites seldom sacrifice their own self-interests to help other citizens without a push. This is the old wisdom, "power corrupts, and absolute power corrupts absolutely." The masses of people must have at least some organization and cooperation among themselves to further their common interests. This is the essence of a civil society. A formal democratic government generally helps promote a civil society, but a civil society can also exist, at least to some extent, without formal democracy. Day after day in the 21st century we hear about one or another group of angry people protesting in China. The same can be said about Vietnam. They are both, of course, one-party communist states. But the people of these countries keep communist party officials on their toes. These communist parties came into being with people's revolutions, and these communist party officials know from their own countries' past, and now from the old Soviet Union and former East European communist countries, they can be taken right back out again.

Democracy makes the actions of civil societies more orderly, but the lack of democracy does not mean some sort of civil society cannot exist. On paper, Cambodia is a multi-party democracy. But this is not the reality. Hun Sen has been in power since made head of the government by the Vietnamese in the early 1980s, and his Cambodian People's Party has been in power since the first UN-sponsored elections of 1993. Any significant descent is strongly extinguished in Cambodia.

This is another fundamental problem for Cambodia. We have seen that some historians claim Cambodia never had a civil society to the extent we find them in Thailand or Vietnam. We have also seen that to the extent Cambodia had a civil society, the Khmer Rouge reduced it considerably. We have also seen studies on the mental damage of the killing fields. Some 50 to 60 percent of Cambodians over 30 years of age have mental problems. A civil society requires trust in one's neighbors. That trust is difficult after what Cambodians over 30 years of age have been through.

Throughout this book I have described how these problems are a legacy of Cambodia's history. Cambodia was in the wrong place in history during its regional decline when the European colonials came in. Cambodia was also in the wrong geographical territory when the Indochina wars were fought, first against the French and then Americans. And Cambodia was in the wrong time in history when poor countries had come to believe communism and communist economic policies were the answers.

With the Cold War over, the United Nations could finally come into Cambodia with help in nation building in the early 1990s. The UN has been much criticized for its failure in Cambodia. But given the situation and what we now know about "nation building," the UN probably did the best it could do.

I had envisioned ending this book with a chapter entitled something like "What We Can Do." I have decided against it. It is a very complex subject involving when foreign aid should be given, in what form, and at what level. There are many issues about how, and even if, corrupt and dysfunctional governments can be reformed without a revolution throwing out government elites. And there are many issues related to how rich countries' trade policies hurt less-developed countries and how these trade policies should be changed. There are other books with details about what we in rich countries can do.[20] In the specific case of Cambodia, there are the obvious problems of a corrupt government, very little infrastructure development, and the human toll of the Khmer Rouge years. One of the most effective ways to help reduce poverty in Cambodia would be to prevent the coming oil wealth from being stolen. But no one seems to believe anything like that will happen.

For now, my primary goal has been to make people aware of what has been happening in Cambodia compared to other Asian countries, and why without basic change Cambodia's future is bleak. If I have achieved any of this goal then I have not let down those poor people who thanked me for coming all the way from America to hear their stories and asked me to please tell other people about their plight.

Appendix.
Village Locations and
Summary of Characteristics

Cambodian Villages

village	families	economic activity	average land	electricity	fresh water	health care	government aid	important needs/problems
Central Cambodia — Kompong Chhnang Province								
Sraskeo	140	rice farmers some fishing	hectare	no	no	very little, clinic far away	some vaccinations	health care, irrigation, water control
Agnchang Roung	45	rice farming, chickens, frogs	hectare	no	no	very little, clinic far away	no	health care, irrigation, water control
Tuol Thlok	40	rice, some fishing, pigs	hectare	no	no	very little, clinic far away	no	health care, irrigation, water control, no school beyond sixth grade
Tolroka	153	vegetables, some rice, low-skill labor	hectare	no	no	very little, clinic far away	no	water control, health care, better roads
Kan Your	60	can sell some rice, low-skill labor	hectare	no	no, NGO wells	very little, clinic far away	no	health care
Southern Cambodia — Kompot Prefecture								
Tropaing Ropao	45	fishing, rice, vegs	hectare	no	no	very little, clinic far away	no	health care, water control okay, fewer fish now
Prek Kreng	35	fishing, some rice, vegs	hectare	no	no	very little, clinic far away	no	health care, water control okay, fewer fish
West Central Cambodia — Battambang Province								
Sam Dach	700	rice	big variation, high inequality, rice exported	no	no	very little	some say micro-loan but can't pay	health care

village	families	economic activity	average land	electricity	fresh water	health care	government aid	important needs/problems
Odam Bang, more like suburb	1,000	unskilled labor	none	some	no	very little	no	health care, jobs in city
Pailin								
Ochial Lech	200	ag laborers	none	no	no	very little	no	need jobs, land, health care, land mines
Boo Tang Su	300	many crops	3–10+ hectares	yes	yes	very little	free land, former KR	health care, better roads to markets, land mines
Otavoa	200	veg crops, fruit	2–3 hectares	some	no	very little	land after war	roads, health care, land mines
East Cambodia — Kampong Chan Province								
Prampi Makara	40	vegs, ag labor	hectares	no	no	very little	no	losing land to foreign corps, health care, jobs
North Cambodia — Stung Treng Province								
Kamphan	60	rice, veg	1–5 hectares	10%	no	free! good	health care (NGO) planning irrigation	water control on Mekong, irrigation, fishing banned due to dolphins
Samkhouy	35	rice, vegs	1–2 hectares	no	no	free! good	just health care	irrigation, water control
Sre Krasang	60	rice, vegs	1–2 hectares	some	no	free! Interviewed at village clinic	just clinic	better roads, water control
Damrei Phong	165	rice, vegs	1–3 hectares	no	no	free clinic 2 miles away	just health care, offer to help fish	water control, fishing banned because of dolphins
Central Cambodia — "Relocation Camps"								
Borei Santepheap II	300+	sweatshop	none, shop house	yes	no	very little	no	jobs! Land, health care

village	families	economic activity	average land	electricity	fresh water	health care	government aid	important needs/problems
Trapeong Angchang	500	none, some back in PP in low-skill jobs	5×12 meters	no	no	very little	none, Korean church gives rice	jobs, building material for home, medical care, everything
Khmer Leu Thmei	200	none, some back in PP in low-skill jobs	5×12 meters	no	no	very little	no, Korean church gives rice	everything, jobs, health care, ag land, material for house
Andong Thmei	800	none, some back in PP in low-skill jobs	no land, not even legal title to land here	some	no	very little	no	everything

Vietnam Villages

Central Vietnam — Danang Province

village	families	economic activity	average land	electricity	fresh water	health care	government aid	important needs/problems
Hoa Lien	35	low-skill labor in Danang, some vegs	less than hectare	yes	yes	fairly good	health care, micro-loans	more micro-loans for pigs, schools okay, more industrial parks in Danang for jobs
Thanh Khe Tay	60	low-skill labor in Danang, fishing	just govt. apt.	yes	yes	fairly good	health care, micro-loans for new boats lost, govt housing	more micro-loans for boats, schools okay, more industrial parks in Danang for jobs
Thanh Ha near Hoi An	80	fishing, pottery for tourists	just homes	yes	yes	fairly good	health care, micro-loans	more loans for boats

Hue Province

village	families	economic activity	average land	electricity	fresh water	health care	government aid	important needs/problems
Thuy Tam	280	rice, fishing, various animals	3–4 hectares	yes	yes	good	extensive irrigation, micro-loans for boats, fish farms	flooding still problem

village	families	economic activity	average land	electricity	fresh water	health care	government aid	important needs/problems
Phu Binh	500	fishing, venders in Hue	none, "sea gypsies"	yes	yes	good	few fish in area now, $30,000 per family to relocate to ag land, micro-loans for venders	better sanitation before move
Central Vietnam — Quang Nam Province								
Tu Cau	100	rice, vegs, farm animals	hectare, some no land	yes	yes	good	micro-loans, irrigation, new roads, schools	more land, flooding
Phong Nhat	200	rice, vegs,	2 hectares	yes	yes	good	micro-loans for irrigation, new roads	
Diem Tay	100	rice	<2 hectares	yes	yes	good	micro-loans, irrigation	
Mekong Delta								
Binh Hoa	60	crafts	none	yes	yes	good	some micro-loans, special schools, women's union craft training	landless, stateless on border

Thai Villages

village	families	economic activity	average land	electricity	fresh water	health care	government aid	important needs/problems
Northeast (Isaan) — Buriram Province								
Ban Kok Pet	100	rice, sugar cane, vegs	3–5 hectares	yes	yes	very good	ag extension, micro-loans, 1 million Baht program, One–Tombon program, etc.	jobs for young people leaving, water control
Nong Paong	140	rice, peanuts, vegs, etc., work in Bkk factories	2 hectares	yes	yes	very good	ag extension, micro-loans, 1 million Baht program, One–Tombon program, etc.	jobs for young people leaving, water control

village	families	economic activity	average land	electricity	fresh water	health care	government aid	important needs/problems
Kok Plai	115	rice, rubber, vegs, work in BKK	3 hectares	yes	yes	very good	ag extension, micro-loans, 1 million Baht program, One-Tombon program, etc.	jobs for young people leaving
Ban Kok Sri Pattna	220	rice, vegs, farm animals, work in Bkk, CBIRD factory close	2 hectares	yes	yes	very good	ag extension, micro-loans, 1 million Baht program, One-Tombon program, etc.	jobs for young people leaving, water control
Kok Pluang	115	rice, animals	1–2 hectares	yes	yes	very good	ag extension, micro-loans, 1 million Baht program, One-Tombon program, etc.	jobs for young people leaving, water control
Kok Rae	70	rice, animals, garment factory near	2–3 hectares	yes	yes	very good	ag extension, micro-loans, 1 million Baht program, One-Tombon program, etc.	
Nong Prue Yai	150	rice, animals, work at nearby CBIRD	2 hectares	yes	yes	very good	ag extension, micro-loans, 1 million Baht program, One-Tombon program, etc.	

Nong Kai Province

village	families	economic activity	average land	electricity	fresh water	health care	government aid	important needs/problems
Ban Suka	50	rice, vegs, textiles in NK	1 hectare	yes	yes	very good	ag extension, micro-loans, 1 million Baht program, One-Tombon program, etc.	

Lao Villages

village	families	economic activity	average land	electricity	fresh water	health care	government aid	important needs/problems
Bhun Bang Fai	110	rice, vegs, factories in NK	1–2 hectares	yes	yes	very good	ag extension, micro-loans, 1 million Baht program, One-Tombon program, etc.	water lines, better roads
Vientiane Province								
Ban Champa	70	vegs, animals factories in city	1 hectare	yes	no	some	ag extension, new electric lines, micro-loans	
Ban Phon Tong	60	rice, animals	1 hectare	yes	yes	some	ag extension, new electric lines, micro-loans	
Ban Dong Bang	225	rice, factory	1 hectare	yes	yes	some	ag extension, new electric lines, micro-loans	
Khammuam Province								
several villages	N/A	rice, vegs, iron buffaloes in all villages		yes	some	some	ag extension, new electric lines, micro-loans	
Pakse Province								
several villages		rice, coffee, vegs, iron buffaloes in all villages		yes	some	some	ag extension, new electric lines, micro-loans	

Chapter Notes

Chapter 1

1. See for example, Tully 2006.
2. Sedara, Sopal, and Acharya 2002.
3. The name for Burma was officially changed in the United Nations a few years ago, and for a while the military dictators threatened to bar journalists from the country if their newspapers continued to use the name Burma. Many Western writers like myself continue to use the name Burma for the country until another name is chosen by an elected government rather than the current military dictatorship.
4. See, for example, BBC online news, July 2008.
5. See, for example, *International Herald Tribune*, May 2006 and November 2007.
6. For more details on this, see Kerbo 2006.
7. Also see the BBC online news, January 22, 2009.
8. *Phnom Penh Post*, June 18, 2010.
9. Coates 2005.
10. See, for example, *The Economist*, June 11, 2009. However, most of my information such as this comes from personal interviews with NGO personnel, Western journalists in Cambodia, or from stories in the English-language *Phnom Penh Post* on the web. I was surprised to read such open criticism and details of government wrongdoing in the *Phnom Penh Post* given that some Cambodian journalists who have written critical articles about the government have been "mysteriously" killed in recent years. When asked about this, foreign NGO personnel would smile and tell me the newspaper only publishes on the web and in English, so 95 percent of Cambodians have little access to this news. Besides, they told me, when the Cambodian government is criticized by Western governments and agencies for their human rights record, the Cambodian government can point to the *Phnom Penh Post* as an example of a free press.
11. See, for example, *International Herald Tribune*, July 2008, BBC online news, January 2004.
12. Clarke, Sack, and Goff 1993; Carlson and Rosser-Hogan 1994; Carlson and Rosser-Hogan 1991.
13. Anbumozhi and Bauer 2010. Available: http://www.adbi.org/workingpaper/2010/07/08/3933.impact.global.recession.dev.poverty.linkages/
14. Tuot and Vutha 2007.
15. Yamagata 2006; also, *Phnom Penh Post*, Nov. 2008.
16. More detail will be provided in later chapters.
17. Actually, Portuguese missionaries were the first Westerners to see it in 1583, reporting back in Europe that it must have been a far outpost built by the Romans during their empire since no Southeast Asians could have built such an impressive structure. However, Europeans along with a majority of Cambodians had no knowledge of Angkor Wat until the French explorer Henri Mauhot "rediscovered" Angkor Wat in 1859. See Osborne 2008.
18. To be technically correct, of course, the Khmer Rouge "killing fields" were not genocide because the people being killed were of the same race and ethnicity as the majority in Cambodia. It would be more correct to call it patricide, or social class massacre.

Chapter 2

1. Osborne 1995; Taylor 1999; Higham 2002.
2. Taylor 1999; de Casparis and Mabbett 1999; Chandler 1998; Tully 2006.
3. Evans 1998; Evans 1995.
4. Higham 2001.
5. Osborne 2008.
6. Winichakul 1994.
7. Wallerstein 1974; Wallerstein 1980; Wallerstein 1989.

8. Keay 1997.
9. Ibid.
10. Keyes 1989.
11. Turnbull 1999; Myint-U 2006.
12. Ivarsson 2008.
13. Osborne 2008.
14. Ziltener and Kunzler 2011.
15. Handley 2006.
16. Myint-U 2009; Turnbull 1999.
17. All of this is depicted step by step in multimedia film and a large topographical map in the Army Museum in Hanoi. Watching the twenty-minute presentation, one can only shake one's head at the arrogance and stupidity of French generals.
18. Warner 1996; Hamilton-Merritt 1999.
19. Osborne 1994; Kamm 1998.
20. Shawcross 1987.
21. Kamm 1998.
22. Evans 1997; Stuart-Fox 1996.
23. Kamm 1998; Gottesman 2003.
24. For the most detailed account of this period using recently discovered records left by the Vietnamese, see Gottesman 2003.

Chapter 3

1. World Bank 2002.
2. Davis et al. 2006.
3. United Nations Food and Agricultural Organization 2003.
4. World Bank 2008b.
5. World Bank 2006a.
6. Also see Cambodian Development Resource Institute 2006.
7. Ear 2009.
8. Higham 2001.
9. I would like to commend a few NGOs like World Vision and Oxfam because they were some of the few I found doing much in rural Cambodia. Given the large number of Japanese-funded programs I have seen, especially in Cambodia and Laos, the Japanese government should also be commended, along with a few countries in the European Union such as Germany.
10. Remember that this $1 per day figure is based upon how much $1 will buy in the United States. I used the example of a cheap sandwich for $1 in the U.S. Thus, those people living at $1 per day in Cambodia can buy only a cheap sandwich for whatever the equivalent it would cost in Cambodian riel.
11. United Nations 2009.
12. World Bank 2008a.
13. Perhaps one should add here a little note about these figures given by interviewees throughout SE Asia. When beginning this fieldwork, it was rather surprising to hear the quick and precise numbers given in response to questions — exactly 2,500 riel for 0.5 kilo of fish per day, for example. At first one wonders how

do they know that without even thinking to give a reply. After thinking about it more when the same quick replies came again and again in villages across Cambodia, it became understandable. Of course these people living on less than $1 a day know these numbers. A comparatively rich Western foreigner lives in a very different world, a world where people seldom pay that much attention to the grocery tab when leaving the food market.
14. World Bank 2006b; World Bank 2007c.
15. Sedara, Sopal, and Acharya 2002.
16. World Bank 2006b.
17. *Phnom Penh Post*, July 5, 2010.
18. International Food Policy Research Institute 2008.
19. Also see, *Phnom Penh Post*, February 22, 2009.
20. One must keep in mind that these figures for Laos are in some ways better than they seem because some 40 percent of the population, unlike the other countries, are hill tribe people living mostly in remote mountain areas.
21. World Bank 2007c.

Chapter 4

1. The World Bank estimates that about 50 percent of this rural land loss is due to medical bills and the other 50 percent is due to land grabs by the rich. See World Bank 2004a; World Bank 2007c.
2. United Nations World Food Programme 2005.
3. One hectare equals about 10,000 square meters or about two and a half acres.
4. Sopal and Acharya 2002.
5. The Cambodian government should be given a little credit here; in July 2008 it was reported that the rate of dengue fever dropped by around 90 percent in the first half of 2008 compared to the first six months of 2007, with the number of cases in children reduced from 20,836 during the first half of 2007 to only 1811 for the same period in 2008. During that period in 2007 there were 256 deaths compared to only 23 for 2008. The rate of cases, though, was up again by 2010, though not as high as 2007.
6. We saw no American flags stamped on infrastructure projects in Cambodia, though there was a sign for a California branch of Habitat for Humanity in a village of about 4,000 now-homeless slum people forced out of Phnom Penh in the spring of 2008, to be described later. Toward the end of the fieldwork, however, we did find that the USAID and American Bar Association have been funding some human rights organizations who are defending poor Cambodians who are losing their land. In 2010, however, newspapers in the United States and Cambodia reported the United States has pledged

more aid to reduce poverty. The reason given was that the United States is seeking a stronger relation with Cambodia as a counter to more Chinese influence in the region.

7. The countryside around Pailin remains one of the world's most heavily mined areas, with several farm workers and de-mining personnel still killed every year. See Geneva International Center for Humanitarian Demining, www.gichd.org.

8. Tully 2006.

9. United Nations World Food Programme 2005.

10. Ibid.

11. World Bank 2008c.

12. See Kerbo 2006.

13. Taylor 1999; Osborne 1995.

14. Osborne 2000.

15. For example, Kerbo 2008.

Chapter 5

1. For example, see McCarthy and Zald 1977; Kerbo 1982.

2. For example, see McAdam 1982; Jenkins, Craig, Jacobs, and Agnone 2003.

3. As we saw in Table 3-1 in Chapter 3, we only have the World Bank's $1- and $1.25-a-day rate for Malaysia and not a country poverty-line rate. This is again except for the small city-state of Singapore.

4. World Bank 2000; Muscat 1994; Kerbo 2006; Phongpaichit and Baker 1998; Phongpaichit and Baker 1996a; Phongpaichit and Baker 1995.

5. World Bank 2004b.

6. A few years ago I wrote about the capital, Vientiane, as I saw it in 1998: "Laos is a country seemingly stuck in time. Little appears to be happening in the economy (except for the negative impact of the 1997 Asian economic crisis) nor in the government, where communist politburo leaders are almost all over 70 years old."

7. World Bank 2006a; World Bank 2006b.

8. World Bank. 2003; Kerbo 2006.

9. Collier 2007.

10. See especially Part II in Kohli 2004.

11. For a summary of these data, see Kerbo 2006.

12. More than one NGO official in Cambodia, however, told me they doubt this figure is also low because, in their opinion, the homeless urban people were not counted.

13. For the most respected history of Thailand, see Wyatt 1984; Girling 1996; Girling 1981; Baker and Phongpaichit 2005; Slagter and Kerbo 2000.

14. In a book written with a friend a few years ago titled *Who Rules Japan?*, we described a cartoon which appeared in a Japanese newspaper. Two rescue firemen are in front of the Japa-

nese Diet (parliament) building while watching ministers of parliament being carried out to waiting ambulances. One says to the other, "Too bad all those politicians were killed or injured because of that gas leak." The other responds, "Well, at least the actual operation of government won't be harmed."

15. Handley 2006.

16. Muscat 1994.

17. Much of this information is based upon personal interviews with Thai government officials, along with more that 100 personal interviews with Japanese, American, and Thai corporate managers in 24 large corporations in the Bangkok area during 1995 and 1996, as well as over 1,000 questionnaires from Thai employees of these corporations. This research was funded by the World Society Foundation of Zurich, Switzerland. Some of this research has been published in Kerbo and Slagter 2000a; Kerbo and Slagter 2000b; and Slagter and Kerbo 2000.

18. With respect roads and schools in rural Thailand, there is the childhood story of the current president of Silpakorn University in Bangkok. More than 50 years ago his family lived in a little village about 300 miles north of the Malaysian border. His wasn't exactly the story of "I had to walk five miles to school every day when I was a kid." Rather, as he likes to tell people, "I had to walk five miles to the nearest road to take me five miles to the nearest school on that road!" Such a situation is virtually unheard of in Thailand today.

19. Phongpaichit and Baker 2004; McCargo and Pathmanand 2005.

20. In another village a headman laughed when asked if any other programs aiding village people had been changed. For the most part, he said, the new military government of 2006–2007 only changed the names of these programs so they wouldn't sound like former Prime Minister Thaksin's programs. It seems rather clear that Thai governments since 2006 did not want to further alienate people after Thaksin's programs gained him so much support among lower income and rural people in the country.

21. Van Der Cruysse 2002.

22. Gilquin 2005.

23. See *The Nation*, June 14, 2004; *International Herald Tribune* (Thaiday edition in Bangkok), June 15, 2005.

24. *Bangkok Post*, April 1, 2008; BBC News on the web, www.news.bbc.co.uk, July 2004.

25. Odzer 1994; Bishop and Robinson 1998; Seabrook 1996.

26. Lewis 1959; Lewis 1961; Lewis 1966.

27. For example, see the *Phnom Penh Post*, July 20, 2010, and May 16, 2008.

28. Treerat 2005.

29. This explanation is primarily based upon interviews with anthropologists at the University

of Chiang Mai and Hill Tribe Research Institute in Chiang Mai, Thailand. To my knowledge this explanation of Thai prostitution has received little attention by scholars publishing in English. However, see Slagter and Kerbo 2000; Rabibhadana 1996; Muecke 1992; Phillips 1965.

Chapter 6

1. Amnesty International, http://www.amnestyusa.org/all-countries/cambodia/page.do?id=1011128.

2. Cambodian League for the Promotion and Defense of Human Rights, http://www.licadho-cambodia.org/.

3. LICADHO 2009; Amnesty International 2008. "Near landless" is defined as having less than one-half hectare of land.

Chapter 7

1. World Bank Development Report 2008.

2. Jamieson 1995; Kamm 1996; Templer 1998; Evans 1998; Stuart-Fox 1997; Stuart-Fox 1996; Turnbull 1999.

3. We will consider this in more detail in the last two chapters, but see Kerbo 2006, pp 35–38.

4. Vogel 1991; Kohli 2004; Aoki, Kim, and Okuno-Fujiwara 2000.

5. Johnson 1982; Kerbo and McKinstry 1995.

6. Phongpaichit and Baker 1998; Missingham 2003.

7. Jackman 1975.

8. Taylor 1999; Taylor 1983; Reid 1988; Reid 1993.

9. Boothroyd and Nam 2000; Duiker 1995.

10. Kerbo 2006.

11. Glewwe et al. 2004; Trivedi 2004.

12. Iversson 2008; Pholsena and Banomyong 2006; Polsena 2006.

13. In late 2008 investigative reporters found the case was a "sting operation" in which over-zealous FBI agents were trying to persuade Vang Pao to buy these weapons. The charges have since been dropped.

14. Back in 1996 and 1997, this author had a research grant to study Japanese and American corporations in Thailand. In 1996 several Japanese executives said they were considering factories in Vientiane but had trouble working with the Lao government, then the Asian economic crisis of 1997 killed all plans. But by the middle of the next decade, they were slowly moving into Laos.

15. World Bank 2007.

16. Chamberlain 2006.

Chapter 8

1. Easterly 2001; Easterly 2006.

2. Also see International Monetary Fund 2007.

3. Transparency International 2006.

4. Transparency International 2007. With little other means of stopping Cambodian government corruption related to natural resource extractions, the opposition Sam Rainsy Party petitioned the U.S. Congress in August 2010 to have U.S. corporations doing business in Cambodia closely watched by the U.S. Securities and Exchange Commission; see *Phnom Penh Post*, August 21, 2010 (www.phnompenhpost.com).

5. World Bank 2007.

6. Transparency International 2009.

7. An anti-corruption law was passed by the Cambodian parliament in 2009, but informants in government and Western NGOs said they expect no real government action to be taken. Indeed, as noted above, the main opposition party in Cambodia petitioned the U.S. Congress in August 2010 to try to stop corruption forced upon U.S. corporations doing business in Cambodia.

8. During the research for this book, there were interviews with dozens of government officials, academics, and NGO leaders, always asking them about the most serious problems facing Cambodia. As always, these informants were assured everything they said was in strict confidence. Even with this assurance the frank answers were a bit surprising, even from some of the highest Cambodian officials.

9. Also see International Monetary Fund 2007.

10. A few months later, in August 2008, *The Economist* ran a story, "The Battle for Boeung Kak Lake," with almost the exact information given by this NGO informant.

11. BBC News on the web, March 2004.

12. There was a humorous moment during an interview with a Cambodian assistant and a British national who headed up an NGO in Phnom Penh. While on the subject of these bribes to get a job and in response to the example of $20,000 for the customs job, he quickly responded, "That is actually pretty cheap compared to what I have heard." His Cambodian assistant agreed. He suddenly turned serious, asking his Cambodian assistant, "You didn't have to do that here, did you? Please tell me you didn't." She didn't have to pay a bribe to get her current NGO job.

13. *The Economist*, April 23, 2009.

14. See, Kerbo 2006, chapter 7.

15. Chabal and Daloz 1999.

16. See Kerbo 2006, chapter 7.

17. Chandler 1998; Tully 2006

18. More recently there have been doubts

about exactly how much oil is off the Cambodian coast, but there is no doubt millions of dollars will eventually be coming into the country. See, for example, International Monetary Fund 2007.

19. For example, see *International Herald Tribune*, November 5, 2006, and May 3, 2007.

20. Collier 2007.

21. All data about recent scandals involving oil wealth in these countries can be found in several BBC online news articles in 2002 and 2003, as well as the *Los Angeles Times* (January 20, 2003); *International Herald Tribune* (September 19, 2000; June 20, 2002). Other data are from the World Bank 2004c.

22. *Los Angeles Times*, December 18, 2004.

23. *International Herald Tribune* and *New York Times* (February 18, 2004).

24. Collier 2007.

25. The World Bank basically agrees. See World Bank 2007c.

26. *Far Eastern Economic Review*, June 5, 2009.

27. Later there were mass media reports that information about these oil leases and which oil companies are involved has been hidden from the Cambodian people. Discussing it later with a Cambodian academic, his surprised response was "where the hell did you get that information?"

28. World Bank 2007c.

29. Ayres 2000.

30. The IMF also points to these low salaries as one of the most pressing problems in Cambodia. International Monetary Fund 2007.

Chapter 9

1. Chibber 2002; Evans 1995; Weder 1999; Lange and Rueschemeyer 2005. For a review of this research, see Kerbo 2006, chapter 2.

2. Evans and Rauch 1999; Henderson, Hulme, Jalilian, and Phillips 2007.

3. World Bank 2007a.

4. Rusten and Ojendal 2003.

5. This is an issue now hotly debated by Cambodian NGOs as new legislation in 2010 goes through parliament to regulate NGOs in Cambodia. Some Cambodian NGO officials said the coordination of NGO activity is needed, while other fear the legislation will allow the Cambodian government to repress NGOs more critical of the government.

6. "Organic contract farming" is a new idea which means, of course, organic farm production with contracts to major retail distributers, such as the British Tesco-Lotus chain which is now all over Thailand. Organic food is becoming popular in richer countries in Southeast Asian such as Thailand. Poor Cambodian farmers have an advantage; they are too poor to afford any chemicals.

7. Mueller, Kock, Seiler, and Arpagaus 1999; Mueller, Linder, and Ziltener 2002.

8. Kerbo 2006, p. 121. Also see Chanda and Putterman 2005; Ertman 2005.

9. Kerbo 2005; Kerbo 2006.

10. Kerbo and Ziltener. Forthcoming 2011.

11. Chandler 1999; Chandler 1998.

12. Tully 2006.

13. Gottesman 2003.

14. Aoki, Kim, and Okuno-Fujiwara 2000; Kim 1995.

15. Johnson 1982; Kerbo and McKinstry 1995.

16. I do not wish to argue that the dominance of government bureaucracies in rich countries like Japan is the ideal form of government. As John McKinstry and I have argued in *Who Rules Japan?*, part of Japan's economic stagnation in the past 20 years can be blamed on a government too rigid and slow to adjust to changes in the global economy. However, as I have argued elsewhere, especially in my *World Poverty* book, a government with less corrupt, unelected civil servants, who are well trained and experienced, is more likely to promote sustained economic development and poverty reduction in less developed countries today. The trick is to revise that form of government once you become a rich nation, something Japan is trying, but not very successfully.

17. It should be noted again that the political issues from the early 2000s in Thailand have been more complicated by Prime Minister Thaksin and his new "Thais Love Thais Party." Overthrown by the military coup of 2006, Thaksin and his wife were later convicted on several corruption charges. But he has remained highly popular among the rural poor because he was responsible for many new poverty reduction programs that have worked quite well as described in earlier chapters. With some accuracy, many Thai scholars claim Thaksin led a kind of populist government on the lines of Hue P. Long's state government in Louisiana, or that of Chicago's first Mayor Daley, that gave a little to the poor to gain their support for his corrupt government.

18. Ear 2009.

19. Godfrey et al. 2001.

20. Missingham 2003.

21. Chandler 1998.

22. Keyes 1989; Phongpaichit and Baker 1995.

23. Phongpaichit and Baker 1996a.

24. Tully 2006, pp. 62–67.

25. Clarke, Sack, and Goff 1993; Carlson and Rosser-Hogan 1994; Carlson and Rosser-Hogan. 1991.

26. Wrong 2001.

Chapter 10

1. See *The Economist*, October, 2008, BBC News on the web, August 2008.

2. *Phnom Penh Post*, February 8, 2009.

3. A World Bank survey in Cambodia found that most Cambodians rank their courts as the most corrupt institution. World Bank 2007.

4. See "The Battle for Boeung Kak Lake," *The Economist*, October 2008.

5. Ibid.

6. "Disputes Erupt Over Plans to Invest Millions in Rice Farming," *The Economist*, April 23, 2009.

7. Soon after I wrote this the BBC got similar information from human rights activists in Cambodia (BBC News on the web, August 12, 2009). Global Witness, however, reports that it is Hun Sen's close friends who own Pheapimex, and this company owns 7 percent of the land in Cambodia rather than the 10 percent I was told.

8. Amnesty International 2008.

9. Most of this research has been reviewed in Kerbo 2008, chapter 17; Kerbo 2006, chapter 4; Kerbo 2005. Other important research will be noted below.

10. Kerbo 2006, pp. 104–105. Also see Stiglitz 2004, p. 80; Collier 2007.

11. For example, see Bornschier and Chase-Dunn 1985; Bornschier, Chase-Dunn, and Rubinson 1978; Bornschier and Ballmer-Cao; Chase-Dunn 1975; Firebaugh 1996; Firebaugh 1992; Firebaugh and Beck 1994.

12. Remember that Collier's data shows a negative relation between poor countries with extensive natural resources and poverty reduction. Collier 2007.

13. Kentor and Boswell 2003; Kentor 1998.

14. Years later, after reading Kentor and Boswell's research noted above, I realized that during my previously mentioned research on Japanese and American corporations operating in Thailand during the mid–1990s, these Thai bureaucrats seemed to know what they were doing. At the time the Japanese were the most important foreign investors in Thailand, with American corporations further behind. Several times Japanese executives complained to me that the Thai government was being unfair by giving advantages to new American corporations investing in Thailand. In interviews with Thai government officials in the Bureau of Investment (BoI), I was told they were "interested in spreading out investments in Thailand among several countries."

15. World Bank 2000.

16. World Bank 2008.

17. World Bank 2007c; World Bank 2005. Also see Ayres 2000.

18. Ayres 2000.

19. Ahrens and Kemmerer 2002.

20. I have presented much of this in the last chapter of my world poverty book; Kerbo 2006. The best books are by Collier and Easterling, old World Bank guys who know what has been going wrong with world development aid. Collier 2007; Easterly 2006. Other good books are Stiglitz 2002; Stiglitz 2007; Stiglitz and Charlton 2005. While overly optimistic and seemingly biased toward the rich nations, also see Sacks 2005. On the issue of whether or not, and how foreign aid can actually help poor countries, the best work on the subject is Paul Collier's book cited above. However, there is increasing debate on this subject. For example, see Riddell 2007.

Bibliography

Ahrens, Luise, and Frances Kemmerer. 2002. Higher education development. *Cambodia Development Review* 6, no. 1. Phnom Penh: Cambodian Development Resource Institute [www. cdri.org.kh].

Akin Rabibhadana. 1996. *The Organization of Thai Society in the Early Bangkok Period, 1782–1873*. Bangkok, Thailand: Amarin Printing.

Amnesty International. 2008. *Rights Razed: Forced Evictions in Cambodia*, February 2008 [www. amnesty.org].

Anbumozhi, Venkatachalam, and Armin Bauer. 2010. Impact of global recession on sustainable development and poverty linkages. ADBI Working Paper 227. Tokyo: Asian Development. Bank Institute. http://www.adbi.org

Aoki, Masahiko, Hyung-Ki Kim, and Masahiro Okuno-Fujiwara, eds. 2000. *The Role of Government in East Asian Economic Development*. New York: Oxford University Press.

Ayres, David. 2000. *Anatomy of a Crisis: Education, Development, and the State of Cambodia, 1953–1998*. Honolulu: University of Hawaii Press.

Baker, Chris, and Pasuk Phongpaichit. 2005. *A History of Thailand*. Cambridge: Cambridge University Press.

Bishop, Ryan, and Lillian Robinson. 1998. *Night Market: Sexual Cultures and the Thai Economic Miracle*. New York: Routledge.

Boothroyd, Peter, and Pham Xuan Nam, eds. 2000. *Socioeconomic Renovation in Viet Nam: The Origin, Evolution, and Impact of Doi Moi*. Singapore: Institute for Southeast Asian Studies.

Bornschier, Volker, and Christopher Chase-Dunn. 1985. *Transnational Corporations and Underdevelopment*. New York: Praeger.

Bornschier, Volker, Christopher Chase-Dunn, and Richard Rubinson. 1978. Cross-national evidence of the effects of foreign investment and aid on economic growth and inequality: A survey of findings and a reanalysis. *American Journal of Sociology* 84: 651–683.

Bornschier, Volker, and Thank-Huyen Ballmer-Cao. 1979. Income inequality: A cross-national study of the relationships between MNC-penetration, dimensions of the power structure and income distribution. *American Sociological Review* 44: 487–506.

Cambodian Development Resource Institute. 2006. The World Bank's 2006 Cambodian poverty assessment: A CDRI response. *Cambodia Development Review* 10, no. 2. Phnom Penh: Cambodian Development Resource Institute [www.cdri.org.kh].

Carlson, Eve Berstein, and Rhonda Rosser-Hogan. 1991. Trauma experiences, posttraumatic stress, dissociation, and depression in Cambodian refugees. *American Journal of Psychiatry* 148: 1548–1551.

_____. 1994. Cross-cultural response to trauma: A study of traumatic experiences and post-traumatic symptoms in Cambodian refugees. *Journal of Traumatic Stress* 7: 43–58.

Chabal, Patrick, and Gean-Pascal Daloz. 1999. *Africa Works: Disorder as Political Instrument*. Bloomington: Indiana University Press.

Chamberlain, James. 2006. *Participatory Lao Poverty Assessment, 2006.* [Vientiane] : National Statistics Center : Asian Development Bank.

Chanda, Areendam, and Luis Putterman. 2005. State effectiveness, economic growth, and the age of states. In *States and Development: Historical Antecedents of Stagnation and Advance,* ed. Matthew Lange and Dietrich Rueschemeyer. 69–91. New York: Palgrave.

Chandler, David P. 1999. *The Tragedy of Cambodian History: Politics, War, and Revolution Since 1945.* Chiang Mai, Thailand: Silkworm Books.

Chase-Dunn, Christopher. 1975. The effects of international economic dependence on development and inequality: A cross-national study. *American Sociological Review* 40: 720–738.

Chandler, David P. 1998. *A History of Cambodia.* Chiang Mai, Thailand: Silkworm Books.

Chibber, Vivek. 2002. Bureaucratic rationality and the development state. *American Journal of Sociology* 107: 951–989.

Clarke, Greg, William Sack, and Brian Goff. 1993. Three forms of stress in Cambodian adolescent refugees. *Journal of Abnormal Child Psychology* 21: 65–77.

Coates, Karen. 2005. *Cambodia Now: Life in the Wake of War.* London: McFarland.

Collier, Paul. 2007. *The Bottom Billion: Why the Poorest Countries are Failing and What Can Be Done About It.* New York: Oxford University Press.

Davis, James, et al. 2006. *World Distribution of Household Wealth.* United Nations [www.un.org].

de Casparis, J. G., and I. W. Mabbett. 1999. Religion and popular beliefs of Southeast Asia before c. 1500. In *The Cambridge History of Southeast Asia: From Early Times to c. 1500,* vol. 1, part 1, ed. Nicholas Tarling, pp. 276–339. Cambridge: Cambridge University Press.

Dollar, David. 2004. Reform, growth, and poverty. In *Economic Growth, Poverty, and Household Welfare in Vietnam,* ed. Paul Glewwe, Nisha Agrawal, and David Dollar. 29–52. Washington, DC: World Bank.

Duiker, William. 1995. *Vietnam: Revolution in Transition.* Boulder, CO: Westview Press.

Ear, Sophal. The political economy of aid and regime legitimacy in Cambodia. In *Beyond Democracy in Cambodia: Political Reconstruction in a Post-conflict Society,* ed. Joakim Ojendal and Mona Lilja. 151–188. Copenhagen: Nordic Institute of Asian Studies.

Easterly, William. 2006. *The White Man's Burden: Why the West's Efforts to Aid the Rest Have Done So Little Good.* New York: Penguin Press.

_____. 2001. *The Elusive Quest for Growth: Economists' Adventures and Misadventures in the Tropics.* Cambridge, MA: MIT Press; Easterly.

Ertman, Thomas. 2005. Building states — Inherently a long-term process? An argument from comparative history. In *States and Development: Historical Antecedents of Stagnation and Advance,* ed. Matthew Lange and Dietrich Rueschemeyer. 165–182. New York: Palgrave.

Evans, Grant. 1998. *The Politics of Ritual and Remembrance: Laos Since 1975.* Chiang Mai, Thailand: Silkworm Press.

_____. 1995. *Lao Peasants Under Socialism and Post-socialism.* New Haven, CT: Yale University Press.

Evans, Peter. 1995. *Embedded Autonomy: States and Industrial Transformation.* Princeton, NJ: Princeton University Press.

_____, and James E. Rauch. 1999. Bureaucracy and growth: A cross-national analysis of the effects of "Weberian" state structures on economic growth. *American Sociological Review* 64: 748–765.

Firebaugh, Glenn. 1992. Growth effects of foreign and domestic investment. *American Journal of Sociology* 98: 105–130.

_____. 1996. Does foreign capital harm poor nations? New estimates based on Dixon and Boswell's measures of capital penetration. *American Journal of Sociology* 102: 563–578.

_____, and Frank D. Beck. 1994. Does economic growth benefit the masses? Growth, dependence, and welfare in the third world. *American Sociological Review* 59: 631–653.

Gilquin, Michel. 2005. *The Muslims of Thailand.* Chiang Mai, Thailand: Silkworm Books.

Girling, John L. S. 1996. *Interpreting Development: Capitalism, Democracy, and the Middle Class in Thailand.* Ithaca, NY: Cornell Southeast Asia Program Publications.

_____. 1981. *Thailand: Society and Politics.* Ithaca, NY: Cornell University Press.

Glewwe, Paul, Nisha Agrawal, and David Dollar. 2004. Child nutrition, economic growth, and the provision of health care services in Vietnam. In *Economic Growth, Poverty, and Household Welfare in Vietnam*, ed. Paul Glewwe, Nisha Agrawal, and David Dollar. 351–390. New York: World Bank.

Godfrey, Martin, et al. 2001. A study of the Cambodian labor market: Reference to poverty reduction, growth and adjustment to crisis. Working paper 18. Phnom Penh: Cambodian Development Resource Institute [www.cdri.org.kh].

Gottesman, Evan. 2003. *Cambodia After the Khmer Rouge: Inside the Politics of Nation Building*. New Haven, CT: Yale University Press.

Hamilton-Merritt, Jane. 1999. *Tragic Mountains: The Hmong, the Americans, and the Secret Wars for Laos, 1942–1992*. Bloomington: University of Indiana Press.

Handley, Paul M. 2006. *The King Never Smiles: A Biography of Thailand's Bhumibol Adulyadej*. New Haven, CT: Yale University Press.

Henderson, Jeffrey, David Hulme, Hossein Jalilian, and Richard Phillips. 2007. Bureaucratic effects: "Weberian" state agencies and poverty reduction. *Sociology* 41: 515–532.

Higham, Charles. 2002. *Early Cultures of Mainland Southeast Asia*. Bangkok: River Books.

———. 2001. *The Civilization of Angkor*. London: Weidenfeld and Nicolson.

International Food Policy Research Institute. 2008. *Sustainable Solutions for Ending Hunger and Poverty* [www.ifpri.org].

International Monetary Fund. 2007. *Cambodia: Selected Issues and Statistical Appendix*. IMF Country Report, 07/291 [www.imf.org].

Ivarsson, Soren. 2008. *Creating Laos: The Making of a Lao Space Between Indochina and Siam, 1860–1945*. Copenhagen, Denmark: Nordic Institute of Asian Studies Press, 2008.

Jackman, Robert. 1975. *Politics and Social Equality: A Comparative Analysis*. New York: John Wiley and Sons.

Jamieson, Neil. 1995. *Understanding Vietnam*. Berkeley: University of California Press.

Jenkins, J. Craig, David Jacobs, and Jon Agnone. 2003. Political opportunities and African-American protest, 1948–1997. *American Journal of Sociology* 109: 277–303.

Johnson, Chalmers. 1982. *MITI and the Japanese Miracle*. Stanford: Stanford University Press.

Kamm, Henry. 1998. *Cambodia: Report from a Stricken Land*. New York: Arcade Publishing.

———. 1996. *Dragon Ascending: Vietnam and the Vietnamese*. New York: Arcade Publishing.

Keay, John. 1997. *Last Post: The End of Empire in the Far East*. London: John Murray.

Kentor, Jeffrey. 1998. The long term effects of foreign investment dependence on economic growth, 1940–1990. *American Journal of Sociology* 103, no. 4: 1024–1048.

———, and Terry Boswell. 2003. Foreign capital dependence and development: A new direction. *American Sociological Review* 68: 301–313.

Kerbo, Harold. 2008. *Social Stratification and Inequality: Class and Class Conflict in Global, Comparative, and Historical Perspective*. 7th ed. New York: McGraw-Hill.

———. 2006. *World Poverty: Global Inequality and the Modern World System*. New York: McGraw-Hill, 2006.

———. 2005. Foreign investment and disparities in economic development and poverty reduction: A comparative-historical analysis of the Buddhist countries of SE Asia. *International Journal of Comparative Sociology* 46: 425–460.

———. 1982. Movements of "crisis" and movements of "affluence": A critique of deprivation and resource mobilization theories. *Journal of Conflict Resolution* 26: 645–663.

Kerbo, Harold R., and John McKinstry. 1995. *Who Rules Japan? The Inner Circles of Economic and Political Power*. Westport, CT: Greenwood/Praeger.

Kerbo, Harold, and Robert Slagter. 2000a. The Asian economic crisis and the decline of Japanese leadership in Asia. In *The Asian Economic Crisis*, ed. Frank-Jurgen Richter, pp 65–89. New York: Quorum Press.

———. 2000b. Thailand, Japan, and the "East Asian development model": The Asian economic crisis in world system perspective. In *The East Asian Development Model: Economic Growth, Institutional Failure and the Aftermath of the Crisis*, ed. Frank-Jurgen Richter, pp.119–140. London, UK: Macmillan.

Kerbo, Harold, and Patrick Ziltener. Forthcoming 2011. Sustainable development and poverty reduction in the modern world system today: Southeast Asia and the negative case of Cambodia. *Journal of World System Research.*

Keyes, Charles F. 1989. *Thailand: Buddhist Kingdom as Modern Nation-state.* Boulder, CO: Westview Press.

Kim, Young C. (ed.). 1995. *The Southeast Asian Miracle.* New Brunswick, NJ: Transaction Publishers.

Kohli, Atul. 2004. *State-directed Development: Political Power and Industrialization in the Global Periphery.* Cambridge: Cambridge University Press.

Lange, Matthew, and Dietrich Rueschemeyer, eds. 2005. *States and Development: Historical Antecedents of Stagnation and Advance.* New York: Palgrave.

Lewis, Oscar. 1966. *La Vida: A Puerto Rican Family in the Culture of Poverty.* New York: Random House.

_____. 1961. *The Children of Sanchez.* New York: Random House.

_____. 1959. *Five Families: Mexican Case Studies in the Culture of Poverty.* New York: Basic Books.

LICADHO. 2009. *Land Grabbing and Poverty in Cambodia: The Myth of Development* [www. licadho-cambodia.org], May.

McAdam, Doug. 1982. *Political Process and the Development of Black Insurgency, 1930–1970.* Chicago: University of Chicago Press.

McCargo, Duncan, and Ukrist Pathmanand. 2005. *The Taksinization of Thailand.* Copenhagen, Denmark: Nordic Institute of Asian Studies Press, 2005.

McCarthy, John D., and Mayer N. Zald. 1977. Resource mobilization and social movements: A partial theory. *American Journal of Sociology* 82: 1212–1241.

Mills, C. Wright. 1956. *The Power Elite.* New York: Oxford University Press.

Muecke, Marjorie A. 1992. Mother sold food, daughter sells her body: The cultural continuity of prostitution. *Social Science Medicine* 35: 891–901.

Mueller, Hans-Peter, Claudia Kock, Eva Seiler, and Brigitte Arpagaus. 1999. *Atlas vorkolonialer Gesellschaften. Sozialstrukturen und kulturelles Erbe der Staaten Afrikas, Asiens und Melanesiens* [Atlas of pre-colonial societies: Cultural heritage and social structures of African, Asian and Melanesian countries]. Berlin: Reimer.

Mueller, Hans-Peter, Wolf Linder, and Patrick Ziltener. 2002. Culture, democracy, and development: Cultural and political foundations of socio-economic development in Asian and Africa: Empirical answers to a theoretical question. Paper presented at the Conference on Culture and Economic Development. Ascona, Switzerland, October.

Muscat, Robert J. 1994. *The Fifth Tiger: A Study of Thai Development.* Armonk, NY: M. E. Sharpe.

Myint-U, Thant. 2006. *The River of Lost Footsteps: Histories of Burma.* New York: Farrar, Straus, and Giroux.

Odzer, Cleo. 1994. *Patpong Sisters: An American Woman's View of the Bangkok Sex World.* New York: Arcade Publishing.

Osborne, Milton. 2008. *Phnom Penh: A Cultural and Literary History.* Oxford, UK: Signal Books.

_____. 2000. *The Mekong: Turbulent Past, Uncertain Future.* Brisbane: Allen and Unwin.

_____. 1995. *Southeast Asia: An Introductory History.* London: Allen and Unwin.

_____. 1994. *Sihanouk: Prince of Light, Prince of Darkness.* Chiang Mai, Thailand: Silkworm Press.

Phillips, Herbert. 1965. *Thai Peasant Personality: The Patterning of Interpersonal Behavior in the Village of Bang Chan.* Berkeley: University of California Press.

Phongpaichit, Pasuk, and Chris Baker. 2004. *Thaksin: The Business of Politics in Thailand.* Chiang Mai, Thailand: Silkworm Press.

_____. 1998. *Thailand's Boom and Bust.* Chiang Mai, Thailand: Silkworm Books.

_____. 1996. *Thailand's Boom.* Chiang Mai, Thailand: Silkworm Books.

_____. 1995. *Thailand: Economy and Politics.* New York: Oxford University Press.

Polsena, Vatthana. 2006. *Post-war Laos: The Politics of Culture, History and Identity.* Copenhagen, Denmark: Nordic Institute for Asian Studies/Chiang Mai: Silkworm Books, 2006.

Pholsena, Vatthana, and Ruth Banomyong. 2006. *Laos: From Buffer State to Crossroads?* Chiang Mai, Thailand: Mekong Press.

Reid, Anthony. 1998. *Southeast Asia in the Age of Commerce, Vol. 1: The Lands Below the Winds.* New Haven, CT: Yale University Press.

_____. 1993. *Southeast Asia in the Age of Commerce, Vol. 2: Expansion and Crisis.* New Haven, CT: Yale University Press.

Riddell, Roger. 2007. *Does Foreign Aid Really Work?* New York: Oxford University Press.

Rusten, Caroline, and Joakim Ojendal. 2003. Poverty reduction through decentralisation? Lessons from elsewhere and challenges for Cambodia. *Cambodia Development Review* 11, no. 1. Phnom Penh: Cambodian Development Resource Institute [www.cdri.org.kh].

Sacks, Jeffery. 2005. *The End of Poverty: Economic Possibilities for Our Time.* New York: Penguin Press.

Seabrook, Jeremy. 1996. *Travels in the Skin Trade: Tourism and the Sex Industry.* London: Pluto Press.

Sedara, Kim, Chan Sopal, and Sarthi Acharya. 2002. Land, rural livelihoods and food security in Cambodia: A perspective from field reconnaissance. Working Paper 24. Phnom Penh, *Cambodian Development Resource Institute* [www.cdri.org.kh].

Shawcross, William. 1987. *Sideshow: Kissinger, Nixon, and the Destruction of Cambodia* (revised edition). New York: Touchstone.

Slagter, Robert, and Harold Kerbo. 2000. *Modern Thailand.* New York: McGraw-Hill.

Sopal, Chan, and Sarthi Acharya. 2002. *A Perspective from Nine Villages in Cambodia.* Phnom Penh: Cambodian Development Resource Institute.

Stiglitz, Joseph P. 2007. *Making Globalization Work.* New York: Norton.

_____. 2004. Poverty, globalization, and growth: Perspectives on some of the statistical links. In *United Nations Human Development Report, 2003.* 80. New York: Oxford University Press.

_____. 2002. *Globalization and Its Discontents.* New York: Norton.

_____, and Andrew Charlton. 2005. *Fair Trade for All: How Trade Can Promote Development.* New York: Oxford University Press.

Stuart-Fox, Martin. 1997. *A History of Laos.* Cambridge: Cambridge University Press.

_____. 1996. *Buddhist Kingdom, Marxist State: The Making of Modern Laos.* Bangkok: White Lotus Press.

Taylor, Keith W. 1983. *The Birth of Vietnam.* Berkeley: University of California Press.

_____. 1999. The early kingdoms. In *The Cambridge History of Southeast Asia: From Early Times to c. 1500*, vol. 1, part 1, ed. Nicolas Tarling, pp. 137–240. Cambridge: Cambridge University Press.

Taylor, Robert H. 2009. *The State in Myanmar.* Singapore: University of Singapore Press.

Templer, Robert. 1998. *Shadow and Wind: A View of Modern Vietnam.* New York: Penguin Books.

Transparency International. 2009. *Global Corruption Barometer, 2009* [http://www.transparency.org].

_____. 2007. *Global Corruption Report, 2007* [http://www.transparency.org].

_____. 2006. *Corruption Perceptions Index, 2006* [http://www.transparency.org].

Treerat, Nualnoi. 2005. Combating corruption in the transformation of Thailand. In *Corruption and Good Governance in Asia*, ed. Nicholas Tarling, pp. 113–166. New York: Routledge.

Trivedi, Pavin. 2004. Patterns of health care use in Vietnam: Analysis of 1998 Vietnam living standards survey data. In *Economic Growth, Poverty, and Household Welfare in Vietnam*, ed. Paul Glewwe, Nisha Agrawal, and David Dollar. 391–425. New York: World Bank.

Tully, John. 2006. *A Short History of Cambodia: From Empire to Survival.* Sidney: Allen and Unwin.

Tuot, Sokphally, and Hing Vutha. 2007. Is tourism in Siem Reap pro-poor. *Cambodia Development Review* 11, no. 1. Phnom Penh: Cambodian Development Resource Institute [www.cdri.org.kh].

Turnbull, C. M. 1999. Regionalism and nationalism. In *The Cambridge History of Southeast Asia: From World War II to the Present*, vol. 2, part 2. Cambridge: Cambridge University Press.

United Nations. 2009. *Millennium Development Goals report, 2009; Statistical annex* [http://mdgs.un.org/unsd/mdg/Host.aspx?Content=Products/ProgressReports.htm].

United Nations World Food Programme. 2005. *Food Security Atlas of Cambodia, 2005.* New York: United Nations Press.

United Nations Food and Agricultural Organization. 2003. *The State of Food Security in the World, 2003.* Rome: Viale delle Terme di Caracalla.

Van Der Cruysse, Dirk. 2002. *Siam and the West: 1500–1700.* Chiang Mai, Thailand: Silkworm Books.

Vogel, Ezra. 1991. *The Four Little Dragons: The Spread of Industrialization in East Asia.* Cambridge, MA: Harvard University Press.

Wallerstein, Immanual. 1974. *The Modern World-system.* New York: Academic Press.

_____. 1980. *The Modern World-system II: Mercantilism and the Consolidation of the European World Economy, 1600–1750.* New York: Academic Press.

_____. 1989. *The Modern World-system III: The Second Era of Great Expansion of the Capitalist World-economy, 1730–1840s.* New York: Academic Press.

Warner, Roger. 1996. *Shooting at the Moon: The Story of America's Clandestine War in Laos.* South Royalton, VT: Steereforth Press.

Weder, Beatrice. 1999. *Model, Myth, or Miracle? Reassessing the Role of Governments in the East Asian Experience.* United Nations University Press.

Winichakul, Thongchai. 1994. *Siam Mapped: A History of the Geo-body of a Nation.* Chiang Mai, Thailand: Silkworm Press.

World Bank. 2008a. *World Development Report, 2008.* New York: Oxford University Press [http://www.worldbank.org].

_____. 2008b. *World Development Indicators, Poverty Data, a Supplement to World Development Indicators* [www.worldbank.org].

_____. 2007a. *A Decade of Measuring the Quality of Governance* [www.worldbank.org].

_____. 2007b. *Lao PDR: Growing Momentum* [www.worldbank.org].

_____. 2007c. *Cambodia — Sharing Growth: Equity and Development Report, 2007.* Phnom Penh [www.worldbank.org].

_____. 2007d. *Cambodian Poverty Assessment, 2006* [www.worldbank.org].

_____. 2006a. *World Development Report, 2006: Equity and Development in Cambodia* [www.worldbank.org].

_____. 2006b. *Cambodian Poverty Assessment, 2006.* Phnom Penh [www.worldbank.org].

_____. 2005. *Cambodia: Quality Basic Education for All.* [www.worldbank.org].

_____. 2004a. *Cambodia: Halving Poverty by 2015?* [www.worldbank.org].

_____. 2004b. *Poverty: Vietnam Economic Development Report, 2004* [www.worldbank.org].

_____. 2004c. *World Development Report, 2004* [www.worldbank.org].

_____. 2003. *World Development Report, 2003.* New York: Oxford University Press.

_____. 2002. *Global Economic Prospects and the Developing Countries* [http://www.world bank.org].

_____. 2000. *World Development Report, 2000.* New York: Oxford University Press.

Wrong, Michela. 2001. *In the Footsteps of Mr. Kurtz: Living on the Brink of Disaster in Mobutu's Congo.* New York: HarperCollins.

Wyatt, David K. 1984. *Thailand: A Short History.* New Haven, CT: Yale University Press.

Yamagata, Tatsufumi. 2006. The garment industry in Cambodia: Its role in poverty reduction through export-oriented development. Discussion paper 62. Institute of Developing Economies (IDE), Chiba, Japan: Jetro.

Ziltener, Patrick, and Daniel Kunzler. Forthcoming 2011. Measuring the impact of colonialism in Africa and Asia. *Journal of World System Research.*

Index

www.ingramcontent.com/pod-product-compliance
Lightning Source LLC
Chambersburg PA
CBHW031130270326
41929CB00011B/1566

9 780786 464081